# *Delicious Ways*
## *to*
## LOWER CHOLESTEROL

Foreword by
C.E. Butterworth, Jr., M.D.

Professor and Past Chairman
Department of Nutrition Sciences
University of Alabama at Birmingham

Developed by
Nedra P. Wilson, M.S., R.D., and Susan M. Wood, M.A., R.D.,
and the Registered Dietitian Faculty
Department of Nutrition Sciences
Schools of Medicine, Dentistry, and Health Related Professions
University of Alabama at Birmingham

Oxmoor
House®

DELICIOUS WAYS TO LOWER CHOLESTEROL

Library of Congress Catalog Number: 88-64015
ISBN: 0-8487-0777-X

Manufactured in the United States of America
First Printing 1989

Senior Editor: Joan Erskine Denman
Assistant Editor: Laura Massey
Copy Editor: Mary Ann Laurens
Editorial Assistant: Leigh Anne Roberts
Designer: Earl Freedle

Photographer: Jim Bathie
Photo Stylist: Debby Maugans Barton

---

Cover: *A dinner of Delicious Tomato-Topped Fillets
(page 90) complemented by steamed Carrots and Snow
Peas (page 145) and Yummy Oatmeal Yeast Rolls (page
179) offers three delicious ways to lower cholesterol.*

Back cover: *This simply scrumptious Low-Cholesterol
Pound Cake (page 201) is guaranteed to win friends
and influence family.*

Page 1: *Enjoy a casual snack with a Tex-Mex flair by
serving Chili con Queso (page 46) as a dip for Spicy
Corn Chips (page 47), complemented by Dilled Tomato
Juice with celery (page 49).*

Page 2: *Start a beautiful day with nutritious Oatmeal
Pancakes (page 180) topped with Strawberry Sauce
(page 181) and a variety of fresh fruit.*

# Contents

# ACKNOWLEDGMENTS

We are grateful to Carol B. Craig, M.S., R.D., Professor and Director, Division of Human Nutrition and Dietetics, for the opportunity to coordinate the development of *Delicious Ways to Lower Cholesterol*. Her advice and creative thinking were valued throughout the manuscript and recipe development. We want to thank Annie Cornwell, M.S., R.D., for her leadership in the computerized nutritional analysis of the recipes. We give special thanks to Barbara Barnard, R.D., for her culinary skills and dedication to this project. We express appreciation to graduate assistants Lisa Freeman, R.D., for her participation in the development of the manuscript; Margaret Dodson, M.S., R.D., for recipe analysis; and Kay Tumminello, R.D., for recipe testing. To Edith Burke, Research Cook, and Pearl Williamson, Dietetic Technician, thank you for the many hours spent preparing and testing the recipes, and to Kathy Franklin, thanks for continuous secretarial support. We would also like to express our appreciation to our colleagues, friends, and families who so generously provided recipes for modification, participated in taste-testing, and offered valuable suggestions. To Joan Denman and Laura Massey from Oxmoor House, Inc., for their support and guidance in developing this book, very special thanks are given. Lastly, we're indebted to Julius Linn, M.D., for his expert editorial assistance.

Nedra P. Wilson, M.S., R.D.
Assistant Professor
Department of Nutrition Sciences
University of Alabama at Birmingham

Susan M. Wood, M.A., R.D.
Assistant Professor
Department of Nutrition Sciences
University of Alabama at Birmingham

# FOREWORD

In "An Essay on Man" Alexander Pope (1688-1748) wrote: "Know then thyself . . ." This might be paraphrased today to read "know then thy cholesterol." There is ample justification for this advice, since a high level of cholesterol in the blood is a well-recognized risk factor for atherosclerosis, especially for coronary heart disease. Although genetic factors are clearly involved in pre-disposition to heart attacks, the good news is that blood cholesterol can be reduced by dietary modification, and furthermore, that a 1 percent reduction in blood cholesterol results in a 2 percent reduction in your risk of a heart attack. For these reasons the American Heart Association is recommending that individuals learn what their cholesterol level is—either through regular physician visits or various screening programs.

This book has been prepared to put the lessons of clinical medicine and nutrition science to practical use for those who wish to change their own diet and contribute to their own cholesterol-lowering program. This is consistent with the current trend of health-conscious individuals assuming greater responsibility for a share of their own health maintenance. However, past experience has revealed the futility of advising someone to "cut down" on this or that food item. Confusion as to how, how much, and what, has all too often led to frustration and total failure. The present recipes have been developed to alleviate this confusion, using basic knowledge of dietetics, food science, and nutrition. All share the common goal of being useful in programs to lower cholesterol. Most have the added advantage of being lower in total calories and total fat and higher in dietary fiber than their conventional or traditional counterparts. All have been painstakingly tested for accuracy of measurements and for palatability. It is hoped that this volume will find its place on the bookshelf as a supplement to—and in some cases a replacement for—cookbooks that were not designed with health in mind.

C.E. Butterworth, Jr., M.D.
Professor and Past Chairman
Department of Nutrition Sciences
University of Alabama at Birmingham

# INTRODUCTION

In this book, the faculty of the Division of Human Nutrition and Dietetics, Department of Nutrition Sciences, has attempted to provide easily understood answers to some complex questions related to cholesterol and its relationship to heart disease and to the maintenance of a healthy lifestyle.

These answers are presented in a readable and succinct text with key points highlighted for quick reference. The beginning section addresses questions and concerns expressed by our patients and the public who have requested information from our Nutrition Information Service since its inception five years ago.

The creative and energetic leadership of Nedra P. Wilson, M.S., R.D., and Susan M. Wood, M.A., R.D., whose knowledge of nutrition, foods, food science, and consumer dietary habits, as well as their organizational skills and particular interest in educating the public about heart-healthy diets, has been the motivating force behind this project.

The recipes were developed through an extensive process of modifying favorite recipes of individual faculty and staff, as well as selected recipes from other sources. These recipes were prepared and taste-tested in the experimental kitchen of the department and analyzed to meet the criteria established for this book. The criteria conforms with the Dietary Guidelines of the American Heart Association, which are discussed in this book along with suggestions for meeting these guidelines. The recipes are modified in cholesterol, saturated fat, total fat, sodium, and, in most cases, calories. Particular attention has been given to recipes we felt would be widely acceptable for family and special occasion meals and ones which would suggest ways to make your own favorites healthier. In addition to health considerations, these recipes feature food items easily found in the grocery store, use kitchen equipment found in most homes, and utilize easily understood cooking methods. These efforts have culminated in the collection we proudly offer here. We believe that everyone has the right to make informed choices—may this book help you to make healthier choices.

Carol B. Craig, M.S., R.D.
Professor and Director
Division of Human Nutrition and Dietetics
Department of Nutrition Sciences
University of Alabama at Birmingham

# *Eating for a Healthier Life*

We all want to live a long and healthy life. To do that we have to live and eat right. Until recent years we didn't think much about what we were eating in the context of reducing fat and cholesterol. Taste and enjoyment were the primary goals in menu planning. This is understandable because our society revolves around food: we entertain with food, we celebrate with food, we comfort with food, and we alleviate boredom with food. Caught up in these social aspects of food, we sometimes forget its real function—fuel for our bodies.

It is the composition of that fuel that is vital to our health, as evidenced by the *Surgeon General's Report on Nutrition and Health, 1988*. According to the report, convincing research shows that "... our daily diets can bring a substantial measure of better health to all Americans." It is the conclusion of this report that we can improve our chances of avoiding chronic diseases by making changes in our diets. "Of highest priority among these changes is to reduce intake of foods high in fats and to increase intake of foods high in complex carbohydrates and fiber."

**Controllable Risk Factors for Heart Disease**
High blood cholesterol
  levels
Cigarette smoking
High blood pressure
Obesity
Lack of regular
  exercise

One of the chronic diseases under scrutiny in the *Surgeon General's Report* is heart disease. And, although heart disease looms as a major threat to living a long and healthy life, it is encouraging to know that we do have some control in preventing it. Just by taking charge of our lives, we can reduce a number of the factors that put us at risk for this disease. For instance, stopping smoking and increasing physical activity are both positive moves we can make to increase our chances of having a healthy heart.

Other positive moves we can make to reduce our risk of coronary heart disease relate directly to the dietary recommendations in the *Surgeon General's Report*. They are listed:

• Reach and maintain blood cholesterol levels of 200 or below.

• Increase the level of high density lipoproteins (HDLs). (HDLs are components of the blood that act as biological vacuum cleaners by whisking away cholesterol from artery walls.)

• Reach and maintain a desirable body weight.

Lowering your risk of coronary heart disease should be motivation enough to make these positive moves. However, there are other aspects that will probably heighten your resolve and help you take charge. One aspect is the mounting scientific evidence, also mentioned in the *Surgeon General's Report*, that the suggested dietary and lifestyle changes outlined in this book will also enhance your chances of avoiding other chronic diseases, such as cancer and diabetes. Another aspect is the belief that the very act of making changes and taking personal responsibility for your health will have a positive effect on your physical and mental well-being.

While adopting a healthy way of eating that involves reducing fat and cholesterol is beneficial for everyone, such a diet must include enough protein, carbohydrate, fat, vitamins, minerals, and fiber for your body to function properly. In these pages, you'll find the basics of a nutritious diet as well as delicious ways to lower cholesterol and control your weight—all of which will help you feel healthier today, avoid other chronic diseases, and live a long and healthy life.

# Questions about Cholesterol

Because cholesterol and heart disease are so closely linked, you need to understand just what cholesterol is and how it affects your heart.

*What is cholesterol?*

Blood, or serum, cholesterol is a waxy fat-like substance either produced by the liver or consumed. Dietary cholesterol is that found in foods of animal origin, such as meats, eggs, and whole-milk dairy products.

*Why is cholesterol important to me?*

You need a certain amount of cholesterol for the formation of cell walls, the manufacture of hormones and bile acids, and other essential functions. However, you really don't need to consume any cholesterol because your liver produces enough for your body's needs. Problems arise when blood cholesterol levels get too high. A high level of blood cholesterol is a major risk for coronary heart disease.

*What is coronary heart disease, and how common is it?*

Blockages in the arteries that supply blood to the heart muscle are the cause of most cases of coronary heart disease. Excess fat and cholesterol are deposited inside the arteries, narrowing the channel through which blood must travel to reach the heart muscle. When the arteries narrow and harden, the process is called atherosclerosis. When a blood clot forms in the narrowed artery, it blocks the blood and oxygen from reaching the heart muscle, and the result is a heart attack. More than 1.25 million heart attacks occur each year in the U.S., and more than 500,000 people die as a result, making it the leading cause of death in the U.S.

**Sources of Dietary Cholesterol**
Eggs
Organ meats
Whole-milk dairy
  products
Meats
Poultry
Fish
Shellfish

Therefore, it is important that you know your blood cholesterol level. You must also learn how to lower a high level and how to keep it low.

### How do I know if my blood cholesterol level is too high?

Everyone over 20 years old should have his/her blood cholesterol measured. If your cholesterol level is high or borderline high, you should have it rechecked. The following chart will show you where your cholesterol level falls. The cholesterol number is based on the weight of cholesterol in milligrams in a deciliter of blood.

| Cholesterol Number (mg/dl) | Risk Level (blood cholesterol) |
| --- | --- |
| Less than 200 | Desirable |
| 200 to 239 | Borderline high |
| 240 and above | High |

**More than 50 percent of middle-aged Americans have cholesterol levels above 200 milligrams per deciliter, a level at which heart disease risk begins to rise sharply.**

If you find it necessary to have your cholesterol level checked again, ask for a complete lipid profile at the same time. A lipid, or fat, profile will show the ratio of "good" cholesterol to "bad" cholesterol in your blood.

### What is a lipid profile, and what is "good" cholesterol and "bad" cholesterol?

Just as letters must travel through the mail in paper envelopes, cholesterol must travel through the body in protein envelopes. Called lipoproteins or fat-carrying proteins, these envelopes determine where cholesterol will end up in the body. Low-density lipoproteins (LDLs) contain more fat than protein and transport cholesterol to the tissues where excess may accumulate in arteries. High density lipoproteins (HDLs) contain more protein than fat and transport cholesterol away from the arteries back to the liver where it may be recycled or excreted. Simply stated, LDLs are bad because they allow cholesterol to build up in the body, and HDLs are good because they recycle or excrete cholesterol.

A series of blood tests called a lipid profile will show the HDL and LDL levels in your blood. By measuring these lipoproteins, your physician can determine your risk of developing coronary heart disease better than by just measuring total cholesterol levels.

The level of LDLs in your blood will give your doctor a clearer picture of how much cholesterol is being transported to your arteries. The risk levels are noted below.

| LDL Number (mg/dl) | Risk Level |
|---|---|
| less than 130 | Desirable |
| 130 to 159 | Borderline risk |
| 160 and above | High risk |

## What can I do to lower my cholesterol?

The level of cholesterol in the bloodstream reflects how much the liver makes and how much you eat. When you eat animal foods containing cholesterol, the body processes and adds this cholesterol to the supply in the blood. But the dietary factor that is primarily responsible for raising cholesterol levels is saturated fat, which is also found in meats and dairy products. Saturated fat stimulates the liver to produce additional cholesterol. Diets high in saturated fat and cholesterol can significantly increase blood cholesterol. Obesity can also lead to high cholesterol levels. In order to reduce blood cholesterol, you need to maintain ideal body weight, limit your intake of foods high in saturated fat and cholesterol, and observe specific ways to raise HDLs and lower LDLs. To encourage your efforts to change your lifestyle, remember a 1 percent drop in your cholesterol level means a 2 percent drop in your risk for coronary heart disease.

**Saturated fat raises blood cholesterol levels more than anything else in the diet.**

## How do I raise HDLs and lower LDLs?

Although no foods contain HDLs, you can increase the amount in your body by increasing physical activity, losing weight if you're overweight, and quitting smoking.

Actually, lowering your LDLs is more important than lowering your total cholesterol number, because it's the LDLs that carry cholesterol to the artery walls. The recommendations for lowering LDLs include losing weight in addition to eating less fat, especially saturated fat, and increasing the consumption of water-soluble fiber. Water-soluble fiber, found in some fruits and vegetables, oats, barley, and legumes, helps your body excrete cholesterol.

**To Raise HDLs**
Engage in regular
  physical activity
Lose weight
Stop smoking

**To Lower LDLs**
Lose weight
Eat less total fat
Add water-soluble
  fiber to your diet

# *Guidelines for Health*

The American Heart Association is active in educating the American people about overall good health and specific ways to prevent heart disease. One of their tools in this process is their Dietary Guidelines. This cookbook has been designed with these guidelines in mind.

The listing of the guidelines is followed by an explanation about why they are important and how you might adapt them to your own meal planning. In order to achieve permanent lifestyle changes, don't try to make all these changes at once. Instead, incorporate the changes gradually over time, until you form new habits in eating, grocery shopping, cooking, and eating out.

## *Dietary Guidelines*

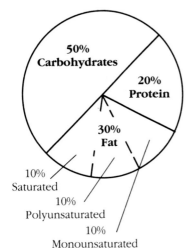

1. Total fat intake should be less than 30 percent of calories.

2. Saturated fat intake should be less than 10 percent of calories.

3. Polyunsaturated fat intake should not exceed 10 percent of total calories.

4. Cholesterol intake should not exceed 300 milligrams a day.

5. Carbohydrate intake should constitute 50 percent or more of daily calories, with emphasis on complex carbohydrates.

6. Protein intake should provide the remainder of the calories.

7. Sodium intake should not exceed 3,000 milligrams a day.

8. Alcohol consumption should not exceed 1 to 2 ounces of ethanol per day (1 ounce of ethanol is contained in 2 ounces of 100 proof whiskey, 8 ounces of wine, or 24 ounces of beer).

9. Total calories should be sufficient to maintain the individual's recommended body weight.

10. A wide variety of foods should be consumed.

# *Limit Fat*

The first three guidelines deal with limiting fat, one of the most important steps in adopting a heart-healthy diet. All fat has the same amount of calories—9 per gram—which is more than twice as many calories as those in a gram of protein or carbohydrate. And eating too much fat will raise blood cholesterol.

By trimming your total fat intake, you will reduce saturated fat as well as reduce your total caloric intake since fat is the richest source of calories. Replace your fat calories with complex carbohydrates, such as those found in fruits, vegetables, and grain products. This change in your eating habits will have a hidden payoff; it will make losing excess weight and maintaining ideal weight easier.

Dietary fat is either saturated or unsaturated. These terms refer to the chemical structure of fat. Saturated fats are solid at room temperature and are found in animal products and whole milk dairy products, the same sources as cholesterol. There are some vegetable products that contain saturated fats; they are coconut, palm kernel and palm oils, cocoa butter found in chocolate, and vegetable oils that have been hardened by hydrogenation. Although these sources probably sound unfamiliar to you, look for them on food labels; they are widely used in commercially baked goods and processed foods, such as commercial desserts and nondairy creamers. Because saturated fat raises blood cholesterol more than any other dietary factor, limit your intake of any food with a high content of this fat.

Unsaturated fats include polyunsaturated fats and monounsaturated fats. They are found in vegetable oils (except coconut, palm, and palm kernel oils) and are liquid at room temperature. Oils high in polyunsaturates are safflower, sunflower, corn, soybean, and cottonseed. Monounsaturated fats are found largely in olive oil, canola oil, and peanut oil. Because research shows that unsaturated fat lowers blood cholesterol, substitute unsaturated fat for saturated fat whenever possible.

However, a note of caution about vegetable oils: hydrogenation of polyunsaturates and monounsaturates essentially converts them into saturated fats. Hydrogenated or partially hydrogenated vegetable oils are found in many stick margarines and are solid or semisolid at room temperature. It is better to avoid hydrogenated vegetable oils and to select liquid vegetable oils and soft tub and

**Sources of Saturated Fat**

Sausage and most
  processed luncheon
  meats
Meat fat
Poultry skin
Butter
Cheese
Whole milk
Cream
Chocolate
Coconut oil
Hydrogenated
  vegetable oil
Lard
Palm kernel oil
Palm oil

**Sources of Polyunsaturated Fat**

Safflower oil
Cottonseed oil
Sunflower oil
Nuts
Corn oil
Seeds
Soybean oil
Fatty fish

**Sources of Monounsaturated Fat**

Olive oil
Peanut oil
Canola oil
  (Rapeseed oil)

squeeze margarines, and to use stick margarines made from an acceptable oil for baking.

## Limit Cholesterol

All animals produce cholesterol for their own body needs, so when you eat animal products, such as beef, pork, chicken, fish, eggs, and whole-milk dairy products, you are consuming cholesterol. It is then processed in the body and added to the supply in your blood. Foods from plants, such as fruits, vegetables, nuts, and grains, contain no cholesterol.

Egg yolks and organ meats are primary sources of cholesterol. Lean meats and skinless poultry contain about the same amount of cholesterol, while fish tend to contain less. Shellfish vary in cholesterol content, but generally they are all low in saturated fat, so they may be included in a low-cholesterol diet occasionally.

However, the fact that foods contain cholesterol does not mean they should be eliminated from your diet. They are also a rich source of protein, calcium, and other nutrients. A practical approach is to eat only small amounts of foods high in cholesterol and choose them less often. The guidelines recommend a limit of 300 milligrams of cholesterol a day, which is a reasonable amount in any menu plan.

## Increase Carbohydrates, Especially Complex Carbohydrates

Carbohydrate nutrients are available to the body in three forms: simple, complex, and refined. Simple carbohydrates occur naturally in fruits, milk, certain vegetables, and honey. Complex carbohydrates, or starches, are found in breads, pasta, rice, cereals, legumes, and certain vegetables. Refined or processed carbohydrates are found in sugars and syrups, as well as products made with these ingredients, such as cookies, cakes, pies, and candies.

Carbohydrates, or starchy foods, have a bad reputation as being high in calories and, therefore, fattening. However, carbohydrates have only 4 calories per gram, which is roughly half as many calories as an equal amount of fat. Having fewer calories per gram while having an abundance of essential nutrients makes most complex carbohydrates nutrient-dense. Another benefit is that these foods

**The U.S. Surgeon General says,** "Reduce consumption of fat (especially saturated fat) and cholesterol. Choose foods relatively low in these substances, such as vegetables, fruits, whole-grain foods, fish, poultry, lean meats, and low-fat dairy products."

tend to give you a feeling of fullness which helps to control weight—all good reasons why it is recommended that 50 to 55 percent of your calories come from carbohydrates, preferably high-fiber, complex carbohydrates.

Complex carbohydrates are abundant in dietary fiber. While both types of dietary fiber, water soluble and water insoluble, are good for you, scientific evidence shows that soluble fiber can help lower the undesirable cholesterol in the blood if eaten on a regular basis. Oat bran is a particularly rich source of soluble fiber. Eating two-thirds of a cup of oat bran every day, as part of a low-saturated-fat, low-cholesterol diet, will be a definite aid in reducing blood cholesterol levels. It takes more oatmeal, but the cholesterol-lowering benefit is still present.

To increase your consumption of water-soluble fiber, eat a variety of fruits and vegetables. In addition, legumes, grains, and oat products should be added to your diet in reasonable amounts. To avoid bloating and abdominal discomfort from these foods, increase the amount of fiber you eat gradually. Also make sure you drink plenty of water throughout the day.

**Sources of Soluble Fiber**
Oat bran
Corn bran
Rice bran
Prunes
Raisins
Apples with skin
Peas
Dried beans
Potato skins
Broccoli
Carrots

## Modify Protein Intake

Only about 15 to 20 percent of your total calories should come from protein. This amounts to about 4 to 6 ounces of meat per day in a healthy diet. Reducing your portion size of meats as a method to lower your intake of saturated fat and cholesterol has an additional benefit—you'll save money.

What are good protein sources? All protein supplies 4 calories per gram, but different sources of protein contain varying amounts of fat. A good way to cut back on fat and still get a sufficient amount of protein is to consume more fish. Fish contains less saturated fat than meat, plus it contains a polyunsaturated fatty acid called omega-3. Research indicates that omega-3 fish oils may reduce the risk of clots forming in the arteries and, in addition, help to lower blood cholesterol and triglyceride levels. Omega-3 is found in the oily, fatty fish, such as herring, mackerel, lake and rainbow trout, salmon, tuna, sardines, smelt, and catfish. You can enjoy numerous health benefits if you increase your consumption of fish to at least three servings a week.

Some people are trying to reap the benefits of the

omega-3 fish oils by taking fish oil supplements. But researchers are warning consumers that ingesting too many fish oil pills can cause bleeding. In addition, scientists are not yet sure about the right dose or possible long-term complications associated with these pills. Therefore, while eating increased amounts of all kinds of fish is a good idea, it is best to avoid fish oil supplements.

## Limit Sodium

Sodium is a chemical element found naturally in many foods, but it is primarily found in table salt, which contains 2,300 milligrams of sodium per teaspoon.  Sodium is also added to commercially prepared food during the many processing procedures and is found in generous amounts in sodium-rich condiments, such as soy sauce, catsup, mustard, and steak sauce.  The best way to reduce sodium in your diet is to gradually reduce your intake of table salt.

Here are some additional ways to reduce sodium.

* Reduce salt used in cooking pasta, rice, noodles, hot cereals, vegetables, and in home-baked products.

* Reduce your use of condiments, or try some of the new products made with less sodium.

* Emphasize fresh vegetables, or choose vegetables which have been frozen or canned without salt.  Recently many vegetables canned without salt have been added to vegetable displays in the market.

* Limit "convenience" and fast foods which often contain a generous amount of sodium.  If you use these products, limit salty foods in your other meals during that day.

## Limit Alcohol

Nutritionally, alcohol contributes nothing to the body except calories.  In fact, a gram of alcohol is equal to 7 calories, almost as much as a gram of fat. Because alcoholic beverages are devoid of bulk, there is a tendency to forget how potent and fattening they are. Try reducing the amount of alcohol you consume by diluting your alcoholic beverage with soda or water, or diluting your wine with seltzer.  When drinking with friends, try alternating a nonalcoholic beverage with an alcoholic beverage.

---

**Sodium Labels**

*Sodium Free* or *Salt Free* — contains 5 milligrams or less of sodium per serving

*Very Low Sodium* — contains 35 milligrams or less of sodium per serving

*Low Sodium* — contains 140 milligrams or less per serving

*Reduced Sodium* — contains 75 percent less sodium than traditional product

*Lower or Less Salt* — contains 25 percent less sodium than traditional product

*Lower your cholesterol deliciously with nutritious oatmeal treats, such as Fruited Oatmeal (page 181) served with your choice of fruit, Oatmeal-Applesauce Bread (page 171) and Trail Mix (page 48).*

## *Maintain a Desirable Weight*

Maintaining your desirable body weight is one of the most important things you can do to lower your blood cholesterol. Studies show that overweight people tend to have higher levels of LDL cholesterol and lower levels of HDL than people of desirable weight. To find your desirable weight, check the Weight Chart on page 213.

No matter what reason you give to explain your being overweight, there is one valid explanation: you take in more calories than your body puts out in energy; therefore, the extra calories are stored as fat. It takes an excess of 3,500 calories to make one pound of fat. To lose one pound of fat a week, you need to reduce your caloric intake by 500 calories per day or increase your physical activity to burn an extra 500 calories per day.

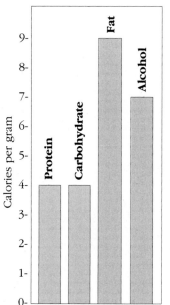

Calories come from four sources: carbohydrate, protein, fat, and alcohol, but their caloric value is not equal as you can see in this graphic; here it is obvious that fat supplies the most calories per gram. So by decreasing the total fat in your diet, you reduce not only saturated fat and cholesterol, but calories as well. Clearly, your main objective should be to trim the fat from your diet. Stay away from obviously high-calorie foods, such as cakes, cookies, pies, regular sodas, and candy. Save these foods for special occasions. While avoiding fats and sweets, continue eating a variety of foods. Use the Recommended Daily Food Guide (page 24) as a guide to select the appropriate number of servings from each food group. Don't skip meals or categories of food because this usually leads to over-eating later. Following this guide will provide a well-balanced diet that is moderate in calories, satisfies hunger, and makes you feel mentally and physically well.

Beware of advertisements for quick and easy weight-loss diets and programs. There are no easy answers to guarantee long-term weight loss. Permanent weight loss

*A Turkey Pita Sandwich (page 115) is the tasty star of this brown bag lunch. A sectioned orange and an Easy Spiced Fruit Square (page 203) complete this power-packed meal.*

doesn't happen overnight. Prepare yourself for slow, steady weight loss. In fact, the latest research supports the theory that weight lost gradually is less likely to be regained than weight lost quickly. You should lose no more than one to two pounds per week. Look at a pound package of meat or bacon and visualize that much loss of body fat as quite an accomplishment. Set clear, short-term goals for yourself. Realize ahead of time that you will encounter setbacks, and determine that you will not let them defeat your long-term goals.

# Exercise Regularly

Regular exercise is the perfect partner with diet control in your efforts to lose weight, lower cholesterol, and live a healthier lifestyle. In the first place, a sedentary lifestyle is one of those risk factors for developing coronary heart disease. By exercising, even moderately, you can reduce several risk factors for heart disease as well as other diseases. For example: regular exercise lowers blood pressure, increases HDL levels, improves diabetic control, and helps break the cigarette habit.

**Exercise Helps Fight:**
Heart disease
High blood pressure
High blood cholesterol
Diabetes
Obesity

As a positive addition to any weight loss program, regular exercise delivers a number of benefits. People who exercise while dieting lose weight faster and tend to maintain their weight loss over a longer period of time than those who only diet to lose weight. Not only will you lose fat, but you'll also tone muscles and add muscle tissue. Muscle tissue requires more energy than fat tissue and, therefore, burns more calories faster. Here are some other benefits of regular exercise:

- Helps control appetite

- Increases energy

- Improves self-image

- Helps counter anxiety and depression

- Helps you to relax and feel less tense

- Improves your ability to fall asleep quickly and to sleep soundly

- Provides an easy way to share an activity with friends or family and an opportunity to meet new friends

Although any kind of exercise is good, only aerobic exercise will improve the conditioning of your heart and lungs. Aerobic exercise is any form of exercise that causes the body to use oxygen to produce energy needed for the activity. It must involve large muscle groups moved constantly and vigorously enough to raise your heart rate to the desired level and keep it there for 15 to 20 minutes. Exercises to be aerobic must have the right intensity, duration, and frequency.

**Intensity:** The exercise should be brisk enough to raise your heart rate to the target level of your age group and keep it there. Find your target zone in the diagram at right. To find your heart rate, place your index and middle fingers over the pulse spot on the inside of your wrist just below the base of your thumb. Count your pulse for 10 seconds, then multiply by 6 to determine the beats per minute.

| Age (years) | Target Zone (beats / minute) |
|---|---|
| 20 | 120-150 |
| 25 | 117-146 |
| 30 | 114-142 |
| 35 | 111-138 |
| 40 | 108-135 |
| 45 | 105-131 |
| 50 | 102-127 |
| 55 | 99-120 |
| 60 | 93-116 |
| 70 | 90-113 |

**Duration:** Each exercise session should last from 25 to 40 minutes and include:

| 5 minutes | **Warmup** (stretching or walking in place) |
|---|---|
| 15-30 minutes | **Exercising** in your target heart rate zone |
| 5 minutes | **Cool down** (Slow down gradually by changing to a less vigorous pace. Abrupt stopping can lead to dizziness.) |

**Frequency:** To achieve aerobic fitness, you should exercise at least three times per week.

## Getting Started

Most people do not need to get their doctor's permission to begin an exercise program. However, if you are older than 40, have any medical problems, take any medication, or have a family member who has had a heart attack before age 50, you should talk to your doctor before starting a new exercise program. Here are some tips to help you select a program that you can continue:

**Examples of Aerobic Exercise**
Brisk walking
Jogging
Running
Jumping rope
Swimming
Aerobic dancing
Cross-country skiing

**People who regularly engage in 30 to 40 minutes of physical activity a day cut their risk of dying from heart disease 30 to 40 percent.**

**If you walk briskly 45 minutes four times a week, you'll burn enough calories to lose 18 pounds in a year.**

- Pick an activity that you enjoy and that conveniently fits into your schedule and stick to it.

- Start at a pace that is comfortable for you. If you have been inactive, start with walking or swimming. When you get in better shape, you can switch to a more vigorous activity.

- Get a partner to exercise with you or join a class.

- Avoid extremes in temperature.

- Drink plenty of water before, during, and after an activity to replace fluids lost in perspiration.

- Wear supportive, comfortable shoes that are appropriate for the activity.

## Eat a Variety of Food

While keeping your fat and cholesterol intake down, it's important to eat a variety of food. In this way you can usually supply your body with all the basic nutrients, including vitamins and minerals. One way to do this is to select foods from each of the food groups shown in the Recommended Daily Food Guide.

| Recommended Daily Food Guide | |
|---|---|
| **Meat, Poultry, and Fish** | up to 6 ounces a day |
| **Dairy Products** (skim or low-fat) | 2 servings a day; 3 servings for women who are pregnant or breastfeeding |
| **Eggs** | no more than 4 egg yolks a week, including those used in cooking |
| **Fats and Oils** (unsaturated) | no more than 6 to 8 teaspoons a day |
| **Breads, Cereals, Pasta, Rice, Dried Legumes and Beans** | 6 or more servings a day |
| **Fruits and Vegetables** | 2 to 4 servings of fruits, 3 to 5 servings of vegetables a day |
| **Sweets and Snacks** | replace with fruit |

# Adopting a Healthier Lifestyle

So far we have discussed all the reasons why excessive cholesterol and fat are health hazards and the changes you can make in your diet to reduce these risks. Where do you need to make changes, and how do you make these changes? An assessment of your present diet is a good first step. To do this, keep a food diary for a week or record what you might eat and drink in a typical day. Record everything, noting the amount and how it was prepared. For an example, refer to the Sample Food Diary (page 216) that includes a breakdown of the important nutrients.

## Evaluating Your Diet

To evaluate your food diary, first complete it like the sample diary by using the Calorie/Nutrient Chart (page 218) to record the nutrient values of the food you have eaten. After calculating the totals for each nutrient, compare those totals with the allowable percentages in the dietary guidelines. To calculate the percentages of the nutrients in your food diary, use the following formula that we have used to calculate the percentage of total fat, except you must use 4 calories for both protein and carbohydrates instead of 9.

To calculate the percent of total fat in your diet, you need two numbers: the total number of calories that you eat in a day and the total number of fat grams that you eat in a day. Use these two numbers in the following steps:

Step 1: Multiply the total grams of fat by 9 to get the number of fat calories.

Step 2: Divide the number you get in step 1 by the total calories you eat each day.

Step 3:  Multiply the number you get in step 2 by 100 to get the percent of calories from fat.  Remember, this number should be below 30 percent for a heart-healthy diet.

Example: A person ate 2000 calories and 66 grams of fat in a day.

Step 1:  66 x 9 = 594 calories from fat

Step 2:  594 ÷ 2000 = .297 rounded off to .30

Step 3:  .30 x 100 = 30 percent calories from fat

A good rule of thumb to use if you are unable to go through all the calculations is to consume no more than 50 to 60 grams of fat per day.

By evaluating your eating habits this way, you can get an idea of where you need to make changes. Start out by making one change at a time. For instance, if you find it difficult to think about drinking 1 percent milk, try first diluting your whole milk with 2 percent milk. Gradually, you can phase out the whole milk. Then you can repeat the process by diluting your 2 percent milk with 1 percent.

## *Steps to Changing Your Eating Habits*

Armed with an understanding of why you need to make changes in your eating habits to reduce fat and lower cholesterol and what changes you need to make, you can now begin to make those changes—one step at a time.  It's helpful to remember that the basic plan of action is to increase the consumption of vegetables, fruits, and grains while reducing fat and cholesterol in the diet.

- Use only small amounts of fats and oils, and choose those that are high in unsaturated fat instead of butter, lard, or shortening.  Good choices would be canola (or rapeseed), safflower, sunflower, corn, soybean, and cottonseed oils and margarines made from these oils.

- Limit consumption of sausage, bacon, and most luncheon meats; they are high in saturated fat.  Choose only processed meat products that are 95% lean or better.

- Choose lean cuts of meats and more poultry and fish.  Trim all visible fat from meats and remove skin from poultry before cooking.  Eat moderate portions.

- Replace meat as a main course with vegetable and grain dishes.  Serve meat as a condiment or side dish.

### Allowable Fat for Varying Calorie Levels

| Calories | Allowable Grams of Fat |
|----------|------------------------|
| 1,500    | 50                     |
| 1,600    | 53                     |
| 1,700    | 57                     |
| 1,800    | 60                     |
| 1,900    | 63                     |
| 2,000    | 67                     |
| 2,500    | 83                     |
| 3,000    | 100                    |

The following Heart-Healthy Substitutions list gives you some low-fat choices (in bold) to replace the high-fat items that you should avoid.

## Heart-Healthy Substitutions

**Choose low-fat products** / Instead of high-fat products

**Skim or 1% milk** / Whole milk or 2% milk

**Low-fat milk, evaporated skim milk** / Nondairy creamers

**Non-fat or low-fat yogurt** / Whole-milk yogurt

**Low-fat yogurt, skim-milk buttermilk or blended low-fat cottage cheese** / Sour cream

**Low-fat cheese made with skim or part-skim milk** / Whole-milk cheeses: Swiss, Cheddar, and Roquefort,

**Low-fat cottage cheese** / Cream cheese

**Non-fat dry milk (directions on package)** / Whipped toppings which contain tropical oils

**Egg white or egg substitutes** / Whole eggs

**Sliced turkey or chicken without skin, tuna fish packed in water, lean ham** / Luncheon meats and weiners, etc.

**Flank, round, or tenderloin steak, ground round, ground turkey, skinless chicken or turkey, fish** / Organ meats, loin and sirloin cuts, ground beef, well-marbled meats

**Canadian bacon or lean ham** / Bacon or sausage

**Fat-free broth thickened with flour or cornstarch** / Gravy

**Bran muffins or bagels, yeast rolls, bread** / Croissants

**Soda or oyster crackers, saltines, melba toast** / Buttery crackers

**Corn oil margarine or other margarine high in polyunsaturated fat** / Butter or meat drippings

**Liquid oils or stick margarine high in polyunsaturated fat, non-stick vegetable spray** / Shortening

**Lemon, vinegar, or fat-free salad dressings** / Salad dressings with oil

**Non-fat yogurt, lemon, herbs or spices** / Cream and butter sauces

**Fresh fruit, desserts made using unsaturated fat in low-cholesterol recipes** / Pies or cakes, commercial desserts or mixes

**Sherbet, ice milk, frozen low-fat yogurt, sorbet** / Ice cream

**Powdered cocoa** / Baking chocolate

**Bits of dried fruit** / Coconut

## *Making Wise Choices at the Market*

One of the first questions a person on a low-saturated-fat, low-cholesterol diet will ask is "What can I eat?" The truth is, you can eat anything, as long as you do so in moderation. Just because you are trying to limit high-fat foods doesn't mean you can never eat another piece of fried chicken. Your everyday eating pattern matters more than an occasional splurge. The best way to abide by the dietary guidelines on a daily basis is to make wise choices at the grocery store. Apply the basic principles of a low-saturated-fat, low-cholesterol diet to the foods that you buy. Fortunately, food producers and grocery stores are now making available a wide variety of foods that are low in fat and cholesterol.

### *Reading Labels*

You may have noticed some products with labels that read *cholesterol-free, low-cholesterol, cholesterol-reduced,* or *low-fat.* Sometimes these products are found in the special diet section of the grocery store. But, be careful. Some of these products may not be the wisest choice. You can judge for yourself whether or not a product is a heart-healthy choice by reading the whole label. Many products now offer nutrition information, and most products have an ingredient list on the label similar to the one below. Make it a habit to check product labels.

Each ingredient is listed in order of its predominance in a product. The first ingredient is the one present in the greatest quantity. For example, the ingredients listed on a mayonnaise label might look like this:

---

**Mayonnaise**

**Ingredients:** Vegetable salad oil, whole eggs, vinegar, water, egg yolks, salt, lemon juice, and natural flavors. Calcium disodium EDTA added to protect flavor

---

As you can see, this mayonnaise contains more vegetable oil than any other ingredient since it is listed first. Whole eggs are the second most plentiful ingredient, and so on. Reading the ingredient list can help you determine if a food is truly low in fat and cholesterol. For instance, you've probably seen vegetable shortening that is labeled *no cholesterol.* When you look at the ingredient list, however, you'll see it has been hydrogenated, which makes the shortening very saturated, thus not a good choice.

Be sure to check the ingredient list for the following fats: palm oil, palm kernel, meat fat, coconut oil, and hydrogenated vegetable oils. If one or more of these fats is listed in the first five ingredients, you should look for another product. Remember, eating saturated fat causes the body to produce cholesterol.

**Saturated and hydrogenated fats tend to be solid at room temperature. Polyunsaturated or monounsaturated fats tend to be liquid at room temperature.**

## Nutrition Information

The nutrition information panel on a product label is where you can find a wealth of information about a food, including the number of fat grams in a serving. This panel often includes the calories, the grams of fat, polyunsaturated fat, saturated fat, and the milligrams of cholesterol per serving. Look closely at the serving size, because the amount that you eat may be considerably different from the serving size listed.

The nutrition information panel on mayonnaise may look like this:

---

**Mayonnaise**

**Nutrition Information Per Serving**

| | |
|---|---|
| Serving size | 1 Tablespoon (14 grams) |
| Servings per container | 64 |
| Calories | 100 |
| Protein | 0 grams |
| Carbohydrate | 0 grams |
| Fat | 11 grams |
| Polyunsaturated | 5 grams |
| Saturated | 2 grams |
| Cholesterol (50 mg/100gms) | 10 milligrams |

Percentage of U. S. Recommended Daily Allowances (U.S. RDA). Contains less than 2 percent of the U. S. RDA of protein, vitamin A, vitamin C, thiamin, riboflavin, calcium, iron.

---

At present, monounsaturated fat is not included on the label. However, you can figure out how much monounsaturated fat is in the food if polyunsaturated and saturated fat are listed. Simply add the grams of polyunsaturated and saturated fat together, then subtract the result from the total fat. This will tell you the amount of monounsaturated fat.

By reading this information panel you can see that the mayonnaise contains 11 grams of fat per serving. Five grams are polyunsaturated and two grams are saturated. That means, four grams must be monounsaturated. Notice that the cholesterol is listed in two ways —as "milligrams (mg) of cholesterol per serving" and as "milligrams per 100 grams of food." (One hundred grams is about 3½ ounces or about ½ cup.)

Not all foods have a nutrition label. For instance, when was the last time you saw one on a pear? Fresh fruits, vegetables, meats, and bakery breads usually do not have a nutrition label. In order to determine their nutritional value, you may need to look up some foods in the Calorie/Nutrient Chart (page 218), or follow the guidelines in the book for selecting foods without labels.

**Don't be fooled by the *No Cholesterol* label on vegetable oils or products. No vegetable products ever contain cholesterol. Cholesterol is found only in products of animal origin. However, these products often contain saturated fat.**

People who are following a low-saturated-fat, low-cholesterol diet often ask, "Will I have to buy special foods that are more expensive?" Everyone is concerned with saving money, and one way is to cut costs at the grocery store. Surprisingly, the foods high in cholesterol and saturated fat make up the biggest portion of your food bill. Think about it. Most convenience and snack foods, processed meats, such as hot dogs, bologna, and luncheon meats, are expensive and very high in fat. When you cut your purchases of snack chips, cookies, dessert cakes, and fatty cuts of meat, you'll save money. You don't have to go out and buy special diet foods that are usually expensive and unnecessary. For example, you don't have to buy a vegetable oil that claims *no cholesterol* on the label. Remember, cholesterol only comes from animal sources, so none of the vegetable oils will contain cholesterol. When in doubt about a food, read the label.

## *Eating Out*

Eating out in a restaurant or in someone else's home is no reason to give up healthy eating. You can still stick to a low-saturated-fat, low-cholesterol diet if you are selective in your food choices. When choosing from a restaurant menu follow these basic guidelines:

• Choose broiled or baked chicken and fish entrées rather than other meats.

• Select sliced turkey breast, London broil, lean roast beef or veal if they are not prepared or served with added fats.

- Avoid extras, like butter sauce, cream sauce, cheese sauce, or gravy.  Ask to have these served on the side.

- Ask the server to leave off the baked potato toppings, such as sour cream, butter, bacon bits, and cheese.

- Try vegetable salads which are excellent fillers because they are high in bulk and can be low in calories.  Use salad dressings, cheese, boiled eggs, bacon bits, and fatty meats sparingly, and add generous amounts of vegetables, such as tomatoes, mushrooms, broccoli, or cauliflower.  Try topping your salad with vinegar, lemon juice, or reduced-calorie salad dressing.

- Choose vegetable plates without fried foods or added sauces.

- Ask the server what the dish contains if you are unsure about the ingredients.

**A typical ladle at a salad bar holds about 4 tablespoons of dressing.  Add that much French, blue cheese, or thousand island dressing, and you'll be adding about 300 calories, most of which come from fat.**

Sometimes you will find yourself in situations where you have little choice in food selection, especially when eating at someone else's home.  Here are some things you can do: if you're served a meat that has been fried, you can eliminate some of the fat by removing the skin or breaded coating; trim the visible fat from the edge of meat; eat around the gravies and sauces.

Remember, if you are unable to stick to your diet at one particular meal, don't use this as an excuse to give up.  After your splurge, get back on track immediately.  One meal will not make that much difference, unless you allow it to become an excuse for overdoing it the rest of the week.

## Healthy Ways to Cook

Once you buy healthy foods at the grocery store, you want to select a healthy way of preparing the food.  A few small changes in food preparation can make a big difference in the amount of fat and cholesterol you take in.

Here are some hints for preparing foods the low-fat, low-cholesterol way:

### Meats

- When broiling or roasting meat and poultry, place on a rack and allow fat to drain away.

- When browning lean ground beef, begin in a cold skillet without added fat. After browning, place ground beef in a colander to allow the fat to drip away. More fat can be blotted away with paper towels.

- Chicken and fish can be oven fried without adding fat.

- Homemade soups and stews should be cooked ahead of time and chilled. After chilling, the fat can be skimmed from the surface.

- Dried peas and beans not seasoned with pork fat can be used as a meat substitute for main dishes. This will decrease fat and increase fiber. An added bonus is their low cost.

## Vegetables

- Steam or cook vegetables with a small amount of water. The less time they cook, the more fiber they will retain. Cook vegetables in the microwave without added fat and rediscover their natural flavor and texture.

**The U.S. Surgeon General says,** "Use food preparation methods that add little or no fat."

- Avoid adding cream sauce, cheese sauce, or other sauces that are usually high in cholesterol and saturated fat. Enjoy the flavor of the vegetable itself.

- Homemade broth (after the fat has been skimmed from the top), bouillon cubes, or bouillon granules make excellent seasoning for vegetables. (Bouillon is high in sodium—so homemade broth is better.)

- Try an oil-free salad dressing, such as lemon or vinegar.

## Grains and Cereals

- Rice, pasta, grains, and most sliced breads contain little fat and no cholesterol.  So, serve these often.

- Serve breads, rolls, pancakes, and grains with no added butter or margarine.

- English muffins and bagels are better choices than doughnuts and croissants, which are high in fat.

## Snacks and Desserts

- Use nuts sparingly in cooking and baking because they are high in fat and calories.  Chop them coarsely, and sprinkle only a few on the top for flavor.

- Coconut is high in saturated fat and can easily be omitted from many recipes.

- Prepare fruit, sherbet, fruit ice, or angel food cake for dessert instead of ice cream or pie.

## Modify Favorite Recipes

There's no reason for you to throw out your favorite recipes. You can still enjoy the dishes you have made for years. However, you may need to modify them. Use these tips to cut the fat and cholesterol from your recipes:

- Omit those fats of animal origin, such as butter, lard, bacon grease, saturated vegetable fats from coconut and palm oils, and hydrogenated shortenings. Substitute with unsaturated fats (see list of sources on page 15).

- Try cutting the total fat by one-third in baked goods. This also includes the acceptable oils and margarines.

- Use nonstick vegetable spray instead of oil for stir-fry cooking or browning meats.

- Simmer vegetables for a casserole in a little water or broth instead of sautéing them in margarine or oil.

- Two egg whites can be substituted for one whole egg in many recipes. This will cut down on the cholesterol and fat from the yolk.

- Reduce the amount of cheese in casseroles and pizzas or use small amounts of low-fat cheese, which is readily available in grocery stores. By grating the cheese, you'll probably use less.

- Use a low-fat version of a crumb crust or a single crust made with oil instead of double-pastry pie shells when baking pies.

- Substitute Neufchâtel or a "light" cream cheese when a recipe calls for cream cheese.

- Make your own sour cream by mixing low-fat ricotta cheese with low-fat yogurt, non-fat yogurt, or skim buttermilk. Reduced-fat sour cream is also readily available. (Don't allow dairy products to boil after adding them to your recipes.)

- Use three tablespoons of cocoa plus one tablespoon of acceptable margarine or oil when a recipe calls for a 1-ounce square of chocolate.

## *Make Use of Herbs and Spices*

Add zest to a low-fat, reduced-sodium diet by using more herbs and spices. The Herb and Spice Chart (page 214) will be helpful in choosing seasonings.

Herbs and spices differ in strength, so no rule of thumb tells you the correct amount to use. If you don't have a recipe to go by, start out by adding one-fourth teaspoon of spice for every pound of meat or for every pint of sauce. Increase the amount according to taste. Be more careful with strong flavors like red pepper or garlic powder— start off with one-eighth teaspoon.

You can purchase whole or ground spices. Store them in a cool, dry place in airtight containers to extend their life. People have a tendency to store spices next to the oven or stove, but the heat will diminish the intensity of their flavor over time. That's why ground spices should not be added to food until the final 15 minutes of cooking. Whole spices, on the other hand, are best used in slow cooking dishes. Add them at the beginning of the cooking period, and allow them to simmer. You'll be surprised by the new life you can give to an old recipe by spicing it up.

# Recipes
## for a
# Healthier Life

In developing a recipe to include as a *delicious way to lower cholesterol*, three important factors were considered: 1) the cooking method, 2) the ingredients, and 3) the taste. The first two factors involved reducing the saturated fat and cholesterol while still maintaining a delicious product. Changing cooking techniques played a vital role. Nonstick skillets were used for stove-top cooking, and vegetable cooking spray for sautéing, browning, and coating baking dishes. Stir-frying, baking, and broiling were favored cooking methods, and defatting soups, stews, and gravies was standard procedure. Regarding high-fat and high-cholesterol ingredients, some were reduced, some eliminated completely, and some replaced with a more acceptable ingredient. For instance, recipes that called for lard, shortening, bacon drippings, and coconut or palm oil were modified to use acceptable margarines and oils. Evaporated skim milk was used in place of cream, reduced-fat cheese for regular cheese or a lesser amount of regular cheese, and skim milk for whole milk. Egg substitutes or fewer egg yolks were used in place of whole eggs, cornstarch was favored for thickening, smaller portions of meat were used in entrées, and recipes with legumes were selected for their cholesterol-lowering effect. Finally, the recipes were tested and re-tested to insure good taste for your pleasure.

35

# Explanation of Analysis

To be included in this book, each recipe had to meet the nutritional guidelines for a heart-healthy diet by falling within the following parameters: sodium—no more than 500 milligrams for an entrée, no more than 800 milligrams per one-dish meal; fat—less than 10 grams saturated fat per recipe, no more than 25 to 30 grams total fat per recipe; cholesterol—less than 120 milligrams per recipe, with no more than 300 milligrams cholesterol per day.

To assist you in planning meals to reduce fat and cholesterol, the nutritional analysis for a single serving of each recipe has been included and is located in a grid next to the recipe. The breakdown includes calories plus carbohydrate, protein, fat, saturated fat, and polyunsaturated fat listed in grams with cholesterol and sodium listed in milligrams.

Nutrient values are generally listed in whole numbers. If a nutrient is analyzed to have a value of 0.5 or more, it is rounded up to a whole number. If it is found to be less than 0.5, then a trace amount of the nutrient is available and will be indicated by the abbreviation "tr." If a nutrient has no value in a recipe, "0" will be listed. Cholesterol is not a nutrient; it is included in the analysis of each recipe to aid in the management of dietary cholesterol. Although monounsaturated fat is not listed in the grid, the amount of it in the recipe can be determined by adding the grams of saturated fat and polyunsaturated fat and subtracting that total from the total fat content.

# *Appetizers, Snacks, and Beverages*

Make good choices and these three categories of foods can be a boon to your low-fat, low-cholesterol diet. For instance, an appetizer or a snack or even a beverage can take the edge off of a hearty appetite while providing good nutrition at the same time. Children, in particular, like finger foods, and young folks like foods they can eat on the run. Fruit and vegetable dips, crackers, chips and spreads, and cereal mixes enable you to provide them with healthy food painlessly. They'll never know that those Spicy Corn Chips (page 47) are made with high-fiber cornmeal and non-fat buttermilk or that Chili con Queso (page 46) is made with corn oil margarine, skim milk, and reduced-fat cheese or that broccoli and cauliflower pieces dipped into Party Vegetable Spread (page 43) are full of vitamins and minerals. But party guests will know, and they'll appreciate your delicious tasting, low-fat, low-cholesterol, and low-calorie party foods.

# Baked Chicken Fingers

1   pound boneless chicken breast halves
½   cup ready-to-serve chicken broth
¼   cup low-sodium soy sauce
3   tablespoons vinegar
2   tablespoons sugar
2   tablespoons brown sugar
1   teaspoon ground ginger
¼   teaspoon garlic powder
¼   teaspoon pepper

**Approximate analysis per serving:**
Calories  60
Protein  9 g
Carbohydrate   4 g
Fat   1 g
Saturated Fat   tr.
Polyunsaturated Fat   tr.
Sodium   145 mg
Cholesterol   22 mg

Cut chicken into 16 (1-inch) strips, and place in a 12- x 8- x 2-inch baking dish. Combine broth and next 6 ingredients, stirring until well blended.

Pour broth mixture over chicken strips in dish, and sprinkle evenly with pepper. Cover and marinate in refrigerator 2 hours, turning frequently. Bake chicken strips in marinade, uncovered, at 325° for 10 to 12 minutes or until chicken is done, basting with marinade after 5 minutes. Serve hot. **Yield:** 16 appetizer servings. **Serving size:** 1 chicken finger.

# Salmon Canapés

1   (7¾-ounce) can boned and skinned pink salmon,
      drained and flaked
¼   cup reduced-calorie mayonnaise
3   tablespoons catsup
¼   teaspoon salt
2   drops hot sauce
¼   cup minced green pepper
20  pieces melba toast

**Approximate analysis per serving:**
Calories   44
Protein   3 g
Carbohydrate   5 g
Fat   2 g
Saturated Fat   tr.
Polyunsaturated Fat   tr.
Sodium   174 mg
Cholesterol   6 mg

Combine first 5 ingredients in a small bowl, stirring until well blended. Stir in green pepper. Cover and refrigerate until thoroughly chilled. Spread 1 tablespoon salmon mixture on each piece of melba toast. **Yield:** 20 appetizer servings. **Serving size:** 1 canapé.

# Crab-Stuffed Celery

15 stalks celery
½ pound fresh crabmeat, drained and flaked
1 cup peeled, chopped tomato
2 tablespoons minced fresh parsley
2 tablespoons minced celery
1 tablespoon minced green pepper
¼ cup low-calorie Catalina dressing
1 tablespoon lemon juice
⅛ teaspoon salt
⅛ teaspoon pepper
Fresh parsley sprigs (optional)

**Approximate analysis per serving:**
Calories 7
Protein 1 g
Carbohydrate 1 g
Fat tr.
Saturated Fat tr.
Polyunsaturated Fat tr.
Sodium 28 mg
Cholesterol 4 mg

Cut each celery stalk into 4 pieces (about 2 inches long). Set aside.

Combine crabmeat and next 8 ingredients; toss lightly to mix. Spoon 2 teaspoons crabmeat mixture into each celery piece. Garnish each piece with a parsley sprig, if desired. **Yield:** 60 appetizer servings. **Serving size:** 1 piece stuffed celery.

# Antipasto

2 cups cauliflower flowerets
1 cup diagonally sliced carrot
1 (14-ounce) can artichoke hearts, drained and quartered
1 (8-ounce) can whole mushrooms, drained
1 (8-ounce) bottle commercial oil-free Italian dressing
2 cups cherry tomatoes, halved

**Approximate analysis per serving:**
Calories 18
Protein 1 g
Carbohydrate 4 g
Fat tr.
Saturated Fat tr.
Polyunsaturated Fat tr.
Sodium 61 mg
Cholesterol 0

Combine first 4 ingredients in a large bowl; add dressing, and toss gently to coat well. Cover and marinate in refrigerator at least 2 hours, stirring occasionally.

When ready to serve, stir in cherry tomatoes, and drain off excess dressing. Arrange on a lettuce-lined serving platter, and serve with wooden picks. **Yield:** 18 appetizer servings. **Serving size:** ⅓ cup.

# Baked Bananas

3   small, firm bananas, peeled
½   teaspoon grated orange rind
1   tablespoon brown sugar
1   tablespoon lemon juice
⅛   teaspoon salt
⅛   teaspoon ground cinnamon
⅛   teaspoon ground nutmeg
1   tablespoon corn oil margarine, melted

**Approximate analysis
per serving:**
Calories   41
Protein   tr.
Carbohydrate   9 g
Fat   1 g
Saturated Fat   tr.
Polyunsaturated Fat   tr.
Sodium   34 mg
Cholesterol   0

Cut each banana crosswise into 8 slices. Arrange banana slices in an 8-inch square baking dish. Sprinkle evenly with orange rind, sugar, juice, salt, and spices; drizzle with margarine.

Bake, uncovered, at 350° for 45 minutes, basting after 15 minutes with liquid in dish. Serve banana slices hot on wooden picks. **Yield:** 12 appetizer servings. **Serving size:** 2 banana slices

# Marinated Mushrooms and Artichoke Hearts

¾   pound small fresh mushrooms
1   (14-ounce) can artichoke hearts, drained and
      quartered
2   tablespoons vegetable oil
2   tablespoons lemon juice
2   tablespoons red wine vinegar
1   bay leaf
1   clove garlic, halved
½   teaspoon grated lemon rind
¼   teaspoon salt
¼   teaspoon dry mustard
¼   teaspoon pepper
¼   teaspoon dried whole oregano
⅛   teaspoon dried whole thyme

**Approximate analysis
per serving:**
Calories   49
Protein   2 g
Carbohydrate   4 g
Fat   3 g
Saturated Fat   tr.
Polyunsaturated Fat   2 g
Sodium   68 mg
Cholesterol   0

Wash mushrooms. Combine mushrooms and remaining ingredients in a large skillet, stirring well to mix. Cover and cook over low heat, stirring frequently, 15 minutes or until mixture is thoroughly heated. Remove from heat, and pour into a shallow serving dish. Cover and marinate in refrigerator at least 8 hours, stirring occasionally. Remove bay leaf and garlic before serving. Serve mushrooms and artichoke hearts in marinade on wooden picks. **Yield:** 9 appetizer servings. **Serving size:** ⅓ cup.

# Cracker Bread  *(photograph on page 192)*

1   package dry yeast
1   teaspoon sugar
½   teaspoon salt
1   cup warm water (105° to 115°)
¼   cup olive oil
2   tablespoons sesame seeds, toasted
1¾  cups all-purpose flour, divided
1   cup whole wheat flour
Vegetable cooking spray

**Approximate analysis per serving:**
Calories  81
Protein  2 g
Carbohydrate  12 g
Fat  3 g
Saturated Fat  tr.
Polyunsaturated Fat  tr.
Sodium  45 mg
Cholesterol  tr.

Dissolve yeast, sugar, and salt in warm water in a large bowl; let stand 5 minutes. Stir in olive oil and sesame seeds. Gradually add 1½ cups all-purpose flour and whole wheat flour, stirring until smooth. Turn dough out onto a surface sprinkled with remaining ¼ cup all-purpose flour, and knead 8 to 10 minutes or until dough is smooth and elastic. Place dough in a large bowl coated with cooking spray, turning to coat top. Cover and let rise in a warm place (85°), free from drafts, 30 minutes or until doubled in bulk.

Punch dough down, and divide into 4 equal portions. Place each portion of dough on a large baking sheet coated with cooking spray; roll to ⅛-inch thickness (about a 14- x 10-inch rectangle). Cut dough into 2-inch squares, using a pizza cutter or sharp knife. Bake at 350° for 12 to 15 minutes or until golden brown. **Yield:** 110 squares. **Serving size:** 5 squares.

# Yogurt Cheese Spread  *(photograph on page 192)*

1½ cups plain low-fat yogurt
½   cup firm tofu
1    tablespoon chopped fresh parsley
1    tablespoon chopped green pepper
1    tablespoon chopped green onions
1    teaspoon dried whole dillweed
½   teaspoon lemon-pepper seasoning
1    large radish, shredded
Pumpernickel or rye bread slices (optional)

**Approximate analysis
per serving:**
Calories   51
Protein   5 g
Carbohydrate   4 g
Fat   2 g
Saturated Fat   1 g
Polyunsaturated Fat   1 g
Sodium   33 mg
Cholesterol   3 mg

Spoon yogurt into a cheesecloth-lined sieve; place over a small bowl. Cover with plastic wrap, and refrigerate at least 8 hours or until all liquid drains off yogurt.

Transfer drained yogurt to container of an electric blender; add tofu and next 5 ingredients. Cover and process on high until smooth. Transfer yogurt mixture to a small bowl; add shredded radish, and stir until well combined. Cover and chill at least 6 hours to blend flavors. Serve spread on pumpernickel or rye bread, if desired. **Yield:** 1 cup. **Serving size:** 2 tablespoons.

**Note:**  Yogurt Cheese Spread may be served on Cracker Bread (see recipe with analysis on page 41).

# Apricot-Yogurt Spread  *(photograph on page 191)*

2   cups plain nonfat yogurt
½  cup finely chopped dried apricots

**Approximate analysis
per serving:**
Calories   10
Protein   tr.
Carbohydrate   2 g
Fat   tr.
Saturated Fat   tr.
Polyunsaturated Fat   tr.
Sodium   5 mg
Cholesterol   tr.

Spoon yogurt into a cheesecloth-lined sieve; place over a small bowl. Cover with plastic wrap, and refrigerate at least 8 hours or until all liquid drains off yogurt.

Transfer drained yogurt to a serving bowl; add apricots, and stir until well combined. Use immediately, or cover and chill thoroughly. Spread may be served on gingersnaps or crackers. **Yield:** 1½ cups. **Serving size:** 1 teaspoon.

# Party Vegetable Spread

1    (8-ounce) package Neufchâtel cheese, softened
½    teaspoon salt
⅛    teaspoon white pepper
⅔    cup finely grated carrot
¼    cup minced onion
¼    cup finely chopped celery
¼    cup finely chopped green pepper
¼    cup finely chopped cucumber
2    teaspoons lemon juice

**Approximate analysis per serving:**
Calories   50
Protein   2 g
Carbohydrate   2 g
Fat   4 g
Saturated Fat   2 g
Polyunsaturated Fat   tr.
Sodium   139 mg
Cholesterol   14 mg

Combine cheese, salt, and pepper in a medium bowl; beat at medium speed of an electric mixer until mixture is light and fluffy. Stir in carrot and remaining ingredients. Cover and chill at least 4 hours. Spread may be served on crackers or firm bread rounds. **Yield:** 1¾ cups. **Serving size:** 2 tablespoons.

# Artichoke Spread

2    (14-ounce) cans artichoke hearts, drained and
         chopped
½    cup grated Parmesan cheese
½    cup reduced-calorie mayonnaise
¼    teaspoon garlic powder
Vegetable cooking spray

**Approximate analysis per serving:**
Calories   69
Protein   3 g
Carbohydrate   5 g
Fat   5 g
Saturated Fat   1 g
Polyunsaturated Fat   tr.
Sodium   186 mg
Cholesterol   7 mg

Combine first 4 ingredients in a medium bowl, stirring well to mix. Spoon mixture into an 8-inch square baking dish coated with cooking spray. Bake at 350° for 20 minutes or until mixture bubbles. Spread may be served warm on crackers or firm bread rounds. **Yield:** 2½ cups. **Serving size:** ¼ cup.

# Bean Dip

½    cup chopped onion
1    clove garlic, minced
1    teaspoon corn oil margarine, melted
1    (15-ounce) can New Orleans-style red kidney beans,
       undrained and mashed
1    (4-ounce) can chopped green chiles, undrained
¼    cup (1 ounce) shredded reduced-fat Cheddar
       cheese, divided

**Approximate analysis
per serving:**
Calories    23
Protein    1 g
Carbohydrate    3 g
Fat    1 g
Saturated Fat    tr.
Polyunsaturated Fat    tr.
Sodium    75 mg
Cholesterol    1 mg

Sauté onion and garlic in margarine in a medium skillet 1 minute or until tender. Add beans, and cook over medium heat, stirring constantly, 10 minutes or until mixture thickens. Add chiles and 2 tablespoons cheese; stir until cheese melts. Transfer mixture to container of an electric blender. Cover and process 1 minute or until smooth.

Spoon mixture into a serving dish. Sprinkle remaining 2 tablespoons cheese on top. Serve with pita bread triangles or assorted chips. **Yield:** 3 cups. **Serving size:** 2 tablespoons.

# Creamy Fruit Dip    *(photograph on page 192)*

1    cup fresh strawberries, hulled
1    cup low-fat cottage cheese
1    large ripe banana, cut into large pieces
2    tablespoons powdered sugar

**Approximate analysis
per serving:**
Calories    24
Protein    2 g
Carbohydrate    4 g
Fat    tr.
Saturated Fat    tr.
Polyunsaturated Fat    tr.
Sodium    46 mg
Cholesterol    1 mg

Place strawberries in container of an electric blender. Cover and process on high speed until pureed. Add cottage cheese, banana, and powdered sugar; cover and continue to process until well blended. Transfer to a serving container; cover and chill thoroughly. Serve as a dip or  dressing with assorted fresh fruit. **Yield:** 2½ cups. **Serving size:** 2 tablespoons.

# Lemony Salmon Dip

1    (7¾-ounce) can boned and skinned pink salmon,
      drained and flaked
½    cup minced celery
¼    cup finely chopped green onions
¼    cup low-fat sour cream
1    teaspoon dried parsley flakes
½    teaspoon grated lemon rind
1    teaspoon lemon juice
¼    teaspoon seasoned salt
⅛    teaspoon paprika

**Approximate analysis
per serving:**
Calories   22
Protein   3 g
Carbohydrate   1 g
Fat   1 g
Saturated Fat   tr.
Polyunsaturated Fat   tr.
Sodium   80 mg
Cholesterol   6 mg

Combine all ingredients except paprika in a small bowl, stirring well to mix. Sprinkle paprika evenly on top. Cover and refrigerate until dip is thoroughly chilled. Serve with assorted raw vegetables. **Yield:** 2 cups. **Serving size:** 2 tablespoons.

# Oriental Dip

1    cup low-fat sour cream
1    (8-ounce) package Neufchâtel cheese, softened
2    tablespoons reduced-calorie mayonnaise
1    teaspoon soy sauce
½    teaspoon ground coriander
⅛    teaspoon ground ginger
½    cup minced green onions
¼    cup chopped fresh parsley
1    tablespoon minced water chestnuts

**Approximate analysis
per serving:**
Calories   55
Protein   1 g
Carbohydrate   2 g
Fat   5 g
Saturated Fat   3 g
Polyunsaturated Fat   tr.
Sodium   64 mg
Cholesterol   7 mg

Combine first 6 ingredients in a small bowl; beat at medium speed of an electric mixer until well blended. Stir in green onions, parsley, and water chestnuts. Cover and refrigerate until mixture is thoroughly chilled. Serve Oriental Dip with assorted raw vegetables. **Yield:** 2 cups. **Serving size:** 2 tablespoons.

# Cucumber Dip

1   large cucumber, shredded
1   cup plain low-fat yogurt
1   tablespoon minced green onions
1   teaspoon dried whole dillweed
¼   teaspoon garlic powder
⅛   teaspoon salt
⅛   teaspoon pepper

Combine all ingredients in a small bowl, stirring well to mix. Cover mixture, and refrigerate 2 hours. Serve dip with assorted raw vegetables. **Yield:** 2 cups. **Serving size:** 2 tablespoons.

**Approximate analysis per serving:**
Calories   11
Protein   1 g
Carbohydrate   2 g
Fat   tr.
Saturated Fat   tr.
Polyunsaturated Fat   tr.
Sodium   26 mg
Cholesterol   tr.

# Chili con Queso   *(photograph on page 1)*

1   tablespoon corn oil margarine
2   tablespoons all-purpose flour
1   cup evaporated skim milk
1   (16-ounce) can Italian-style tomatoes, drained and chopped
½   teaspoon finely chopped garlic
½   teaspoon salt
1   (4-ounce) can chopped green chiles, drained
1   cup (4 ounces) shredded Monterey Jack cheese
½   cup (2 ounces) shredded reduced-fat Cheddar cheese

Melt margarine in a heavy saucepan over low heat; add flour, stirring with a wire whisk until smooth. Cook 1 minute, stirring constantly. Gradually add milk; cook over medium heat, stirring constantly, until mixture is thickened and smooth. Remove from heat, and set aside.

Combine tomatoes, garlic, and salt in a large heavy skillet. Cook, uncovered, over medium heat until mixture is heated thoroughly. Reduce heat to low, and stir in white sauce and chiles. Gradually add cheeses, ¼ cup at a time, stirring well after each addition. Continue to cook over low heat, stirring constantly, until cheeses melt and mixture is heated. Serve hot with crackers or chips. **Yield:** 10 appetizer servings. **Serving size:** ¼ cup.

**Approximate analysis per serving:**
Calories   105
Protein   7 g
Carbohydrate   7 g
Fat   6 g
Saturated Fat   2 g
Polyunsaturated Fat   1 g
Sodium   358 mg
Cholesterol   11 mg

# Spicy Corn Chips   *(photograph on page 1)*

1   cup yellow cornmeal
½   cup all-purpose flour
1   teaspoon salt
½   teaspoon baking soda
½   teaspoon chili powder
¼   teaspoon ground cumin
½   cup nonfat buttermilk
3   tablespoons vegetable oil
Vegetable cooking spray
⅛   teaspoon paprika

**Approximate analysis per serving:**
Calories   58
Protein   1 g
Carbohydrate   8 g
Fat   3 g
Saturated Fat   tr.
Polyunsaturated Fat   1 g
Sodium   126 mg
Cholesterol   0

Combine first 6 ingredients in a small bowl, stirring well. Add buttermilk and oil; knead until smooth and well combined. Divide dough in half, and roll each half to ⅛-inch thickness on a baking sheet coated with cooking spray, forming a 12- x 8-inch rectangle on each sheet. Sprinkle dough evenly with paprika.

Prick dough with a fork; cut into 1¼-inch squares. Bake at 350° for 15 minutes or until crisp. Separate chips, and let cool on wire racks. Store in an airtight container. **Yield:** 140 chips. **Serving size:** 7 chips.

# Parmesan-Pita Triangles

1   (6-inch) whole wheat pita bread round
2   teaspoons corn oil margarine, melted
¼   teaspoon garlic powder
¼   teaspoon onion powder
2   tablespoons grated fresh Parmesan cheese

**Approximate analysis per serving:**
Calories   56
Protein   2 g
Carbohydrate   5 g
Fat   3 g
Saturated Fat   1 g
Polyunsaturated Fat   1 g
Sodium   124 mg
Cholesterol   2 mg

Separate pita bread into 2 rounds, and place rough side up on an ungreased baking sheet. Set aside.

Combine melted margarine, garlic and onion powder. Spread half of margarine mixture over each pita round. Cut each round into 8 wedges. Leave triangles in place on baking sheet, and sprinkle evenly with cheese. Bake at 375° for 8 minutes or until crisp. Serve hot, or let cool, and store in an airtight container. **Yield:** 16 triangles. **Serving size:** 4 triangles.

# Cereal Snack Mix

3    tablespoons corn oil margarine
½    teaspoon garlic salt
¼    teaspoon onion salt
1    tablespoon Worcestershire sauce
2    teaspoons lemon juice
2    cups toasted whole grain oat cereal
2    cups crispy corn cereal squares
2    cups crispy rice cereal squares
2    cups thin pretzel sticks

**Approximate analysis per serving:**
Calories   87
Protein   2 g
Carbohydrate   14 g
Fat   3 g
Saturated Fat   tr.
Polyunsaturated Fat   1 g
Sodium   230 mg
Cholesterol   0

Melt margarine in a 15- x 10- x 1-inch jellyroll pan in a 250° oven. Remove pan from oven, and stir in garlic salt, onion salt, Worcestershire sauce, and lemon juice. Add cereal and pretzels, stirring until well coated. Bake at 250° for 45 minutes, stirring every 15 minutes. Drain on paper towels. Store in an airtight container. **Yield:** 8 cups. **Serving size:** ½ cup.

# Trail Mix *(photograph on page 19)*

1    cup uncooked regular oats
¼    cup wheat germ
¼    cup sliced almonds
¼    cup unsalted peanuts
⅓    cup honey
1    tablespoon vegetable oil
1    cup coarsely chopped dried apricots
½    cup raisins

**Approximate analysis per serving:**
Calories   231
Protein   6 g
Carbohydrate   39 g
Fat   7 g
Saturated Fat   1 g
Polyunsaturated Fat   2 g
Sodium   57 mg
Cholesterol   0

Combine oats, wheat germ, almonds, and peanuts in a large bowl, stirring to mix. Combine honey and oil, stirring until well blended; add to cereal mixture, stirring well to coat.

Spread mixture evenly in a 13- x 9- x 2-inch baking pan. Bake at 275° for 1 hour, stirring after 30 minutes. Remove from oven, and transfer to another pan to cool (do not stir). Break into pieces. Stir in chopped apricots and raisins, and store in an airtight container. **Yield:** 4 cups. **Serving size:** ½ cup.

# Hot Spiced Cider *(photograph on page 137)*

2 quarts apple juice
1 small orange, thinly sliced
2 tablespoons brown sugar
2 tablespoons lemon juice
2 (2½-inch) sticks cinnamon
1 teaspoon whole cloves
3 whole allspice
Additional cinnamon sticks (optional)
Lemon slices (optional)

**Approximate analysis per serving:**
Calories  66
Protein  tr.
Carbohydrate  17 g
Fat  tr.
Saturated Fat  tr.
Polyunsaturated Fat  tr.
Sodium  4 mg
Cholesterol  0

Combine first 7 ingredients in a Dutch oven, stirring well to mix. Cover and bring to a boil. Reduce heat, and simmer 20 minutes.

Strain cider, and serve hot. If desired, garnish each serving with a cinnamon stick and lemon slice. **Yield:** 2 quarts. **Serving size:** ½ cup.

# Dilled Tomato Juice *(photograph on page 1)*

2 cups no-salt-added tomato juice
1 tablespoon lime juice
½ teaspoon lemon-pepper seasoning
¼ teaspoon dried whole dillweed
¼ teaspoon celery seeds
⅛ teaspoon pepper
¼ teaspoon prepared horseradish
½ teaspoon low-sodium Worcestershire sauce
Celery sticks (optional)

**Approximate analysis per serving:**
Calories  49
Protein  2 g
Carbohydrate  12 g
Fat  tr.
Saturated Fat  tr.
Polyunsaturated Fat  tr.
Sodium  50 mg
Cholesterol  0

Combine first 8 ingredients, stirring until well blended. Cover and chill at least 6 hours before serving over ice. Garnish each serving with a celery stick, if desired. **Yield:** 2 cups. **Serving size:** 1 cup.

# Cranberry Punch *(photograph on page 50)*

1   quart cranberry juice cocktail
1   quart apple juice
1   quart lemon-lime carbonated beverage, chilled

Combine cranberry juice cocktail and apple juice in a large container, stirring well to blend; cover and chill thoroughly. Stir in lemon-lime beverage just before serving. Serve chilled. **Yield:** 3 quarts. **Serving size:** ½ cup.

**Approximate analysis per serving:**
Calories   58
Protein   tr.
Carbohydrate   14 g
Fat   tr.
Saturated Fat   tr.
Polyunsaturated Fat   tr.
Sodium   7 mg
Cholesterol   0

# Banana Milkshake

1   medium-size ripe banana
1   cup skim milk
1   tablespoon sugar
¼   teaspoon vanilla extract

Remove peel from banana. Wrap banana in heavy-duty plastic wrap, and freeze until firm.

Remove banana from freezer, and cut into large chunks. Place banana in container of an electric blender; Add milk, sugar, and vanilla. Cover and process on high speed 2 minutes or until smooth. Pour into chilled glasses to serve. **Yield:** 1½ cups. **Serving size:** ¾ cup.

**Approximate analysis per serving:**
Calories   119
Protein   5 g
Carbohydrate   25 g
Fat   1 g
Saturated Fat   tr.
Polyunsaturated Fat   tr.
Sodium   64 mg
Cholesterol   2 mg

# Orange-Pineapple Slush

1   cup orange juice
½   cup pineapple juice
1   teaspoon honey

Combine all ingredients, stirring well to blend. Pour mixture into a freezer tray or an 8-inch square baking pan, and freeze until almost firm.

Remove frozen mixture from freezer. Break mixture into large pieces, and place in container of an electric blender. Cover and process several seconds or until slushy. Serve immediately. **Yield:** 1½ cups. **Serving size:** ½ cup.

**Approximate analysis per serving:**
Calories   63
Protein   1 g
Carbohydrate   15 g
Fat   tr.
Saturated Fat   tr.
Polyunsaturated Fat   tr.
Sodium   2 mg
Cholesterol   0

# Soups
## and
## Stews

In preparing soups and stews to lower cholesterol, get rid of the meat fat by chilling the stock and then skimming the fat off the top before using or heating the stock. Don't despair if you feel that skimming off the meat fat will diminish flavor. Soups and stews are menu items that lend themselves to creative seasoning with herbs and spices, such as bay leaves, basil, parsley, thyme, and even celery leaves. The Unsalted Chicken Stock recipe (page 56) features a Bouquet Garni which is a cheesecloth bag filled with herbs. After the herbs have flavored the stock, the bag of herbs can be discarded. A nutritious plus for soups and stews is that the liquid base contains vitamins and minerals that are ordinarily thrown away when vegetables are drained.

# Garden Vegetable Soup

3    medium carrots, scraped and sliced
2    medium stalks celery, chopped
1    medium onion, chopped
1    (28-ounce) can whole tomatoes, undrained
2    medium potatoes, peeled and cubed
½    cup uncooked rice
7    cups water
5    beef-flavored bouillon cubes
½    teaspoon dried whole sage
½    teaspoon dried whole rosemary
⅛    teaspoon dried whole basil
1    cup shredded cabbage

**Approximate analysis per serving:**
Calories   45
Protein   1 g
Carbohydrate   10 g
Fat   0
Saturated Fat   tr.
Polyunsaturated Fat   tr.
Sodium   378 mg
Cholesterol   0

Combine all ingredients except cabbage in a large saucepan, stirring well. Cover and bring to a boil; reduce heat, and simmer 20 minutes or until vegetables are crisp-tender. Add cabbage, and simmer an additional 7 minutes. **Yield:** 5 quarts. **Serving size:** 1 cup.

# Gazpacho   *(photograph on page 52)*

1    large tomato, peeled
1    large sweet red pepper, seeded
1    large cucumber, peeled and seeded
¼    cup minced red onion
2    tablespoons chopped fresh parsley
2½    cups tomato juice, divided
1    tablespoon red wine vinegar
1    tablespoon Worcestershire sauce
¼    teaspoon hot sauce
¼    teaspoon salt

**Approximate analysis per serving:**
Calories   31
Protein   1 g
Carbohydrate   7 g
Fat   tr.
Saturated Fat   tr.
Polyunsaturated Fat   tr.
Sodium   363 mg
Cholesterol   0

Mince ¼ cup each of first 3 ingredients; combine with minced red onion, stirring well. Cover and refrigerate to use as garnish.

Coarsely chop remaining tomato, sweet red pepper, and cucumber. Combine coarsely chopped vegetables, parsley, and ¾ cup tomato juice in container of an electric blender. Process until vegetables are finely chopped, but not pureed. Stir in remaining 1¾ cups tomato juice, vinegar,

Worcestershire sauce, hot sauce, and salt. Cover and refrigerate at least 1 hour or until thoroughly chilled. Garnish soup with reserved minced vegetables. **Yield:** 6 cups. **Serving size:** ¾ cup soup with 2 tablespoons minced vegetables.

# Hearty Vegetable and Bean Soup

¾  cup dried Great Northern beans
1½ quarts water
1    teaspoon salt
½   cup chopped onion
¼   cup chopped fresh parsley
2    tablespoons chopped fresh celery leaves
1    tablespoon olive oil
1    (14½-ounce) can ready-to-serve beef broth
1    (14½-ounce) can whole tomatoes, undrained and
       chopped
1    cup water
1    cup peeled, diced potato
1    cup diced celery
¾   cup diced carrot
½   teaspoon dried whole thyme
2    cups shredded cabbage
1    teaspoon dried whole basil
2    cups chopped zucchini

**Approximate analysis per serving:**
Calories  88
Protein  4 g
Carbohydrate   15 g
Fat  2 g
Saturated Fat   tr.
Polyunsaturated Fat   tr.
Sodium  362 mg
Cholesterol  0

Sort and rinse beans; place in a large Dutch oven. Cover with water 2 inches above beans; bring to a boil. Remove from heat, and let stand 1 hour. Drain off water, reserving beans in Dutch oven. Add 1½ quarts water and salt to beans. Cover and  simmer 3½ hours or until beans are tender. Transfer beans and liquid to container of an electric blender. Cover and process until smooth. Set aside.

Sauté onion, parsley, and celery leaves in olive oil in Dutch oven until onion is tender. Add pureed bean mixture, beef broth, tomatoes, 1 cup water, potato, celery, carrot, and thyme; stir until well combined. Cover and cook over low heat 15 minutes. Stir in cabbage and basil; cover and cook 15 minutes. Add zucchini; cover  and cook 5 minutes. **Yield:** 3 quarts. **Serving size:** 1 cup.

# Potato-Celery Chowder

1    (14½-ounce) can ready-to-serve chicken broth
4    cups peeled, cubed potato
1    cup sliced celery
½    cup chopped onion
¼    teaspoon salt
2½  cups skim milk
2    teaspoons corn oil margarine
2    teaspoons chopped fresh parsley

**Approximate analysis per serving:**
Calories   178
Protein   7 g
Carbohydrate   35 g
Fat   2 g
Saturated Fat   tr.
Polyunsaturated Fat   1 g
Sodium   479 mg
Cholesterol   2 mg

Combine broth, potato, celery, onion, and salt in a large saucepan. Cook over medium heat 15 minutes or until vegetables are tender.

Add milk and margarine to vegetables in saucepan; cook over low heat until margarine melts, stirring constantly. Remove from heat. Transfer mixture to container of an electric blender; process about 1½ minutes or until smooth. Return chowder to saucepan, and cook over low heat until thoroughly heated. Sprinkle with parsley, and serve. **Yield:** 6 cups. **Serving size:** 1 cup.

# Potato-Cheese Soup

4    cups ready-to-serve chicken broth
4    cups peeled, cubed potatoes
2    cups thinly sliced carrots
2    cups minced onion
2    tablespoons chopped fresh parsley
¼    teaspoon salt
¼    teaspoon pepper
1    tablespoon dried whole dillweed
¾    cup (3 ounces) shredded reduced-fat Cheddar
       cheese

**Approximate analysis per serving:**
Calories   141
Protein   8 g
Carbohydrate   20 g
Fat   3 g
Saturated Fat   2 g
Polyunsaturated Fat   tr.
Sodium   549 mg
Cholesterol   8 mg

Combine first 7 ingredients in a Dutch oven. Cover and bring to a boil. Reduce heat, and simmer 25 to 30 minutes or until vegetables are tender. Stir in dillweed. Remove mixture from heat, and let stand at room temperature 5 minutes to cool slightly.

Transfer mixture in batches to food processor bowl fitted with a steel knife blade. Cover and process until mixture is smooth. Combine pureed mixture and shredded cheese in Dutch oven, stirring well; cook over low heat until cheese melts and soup is thoroughly heated. Serve immediately. **Yield:** 2 quarts. **Serving size:** 1 cup.

# Creamy Chicken and Rice Soup

½   cup uncooked brown rice
1½ cups water
4   cups ready-to-serve chicken broth
½   cup diced green pepper
½   cup diced celery
¼   cup diced onion
¼   cup shredded carrot
2   tablespoons chopped fresh mushrooms
½   teaspoon minced garlic
2   tablespoons corn oil margarine, melted
½   cup all-purpose flour
1½ cups diced cooked chicken
2   tablespoons chopped fresh parsley
1   tablespoon diced pimiento
¼   teaspoon salt
¼   teaspoon white pepper
1   cup evaporated skim milk

**Approximate analysis per serving:**
Calories   193
Protein   14 g
Carbohydrate   20 g
Fat   6 g
Saturated Fat   1 g
Polyunsaturated Fat   2 g
Sodium   552 mg
Cholesterol   23 mg

Combine rice and water in a large saucepan. Cover and bring to a boil; reduce heat, and simmer 15 minutes. Drain. Add chicken broth to rice in saucepan; cover and simmer 30 minutes. Remove from heat, and set aside.

Sauté green pepper, celery, onion, carrot, mushrooms, and garlic in margarine in a large skillet until tender. Stir in flour, and cook over medium heat 1 to 2 minutes.

Add chicken, parsley, pimiento, salt, pepper, and rice mixture to mixture in skillet. Stir in evaporated skim milk. Cook over medium heat, stirring frequently, until mixture is thoroughly heated (do not boil). **Yield:** 2 quarts. **Serving size:** 1 cup.

# Unsalted Chicken Stock

1   (2½- to 3-pound) broiler-fryer
2½ quarts water
1   large carrot, scraped and cut into 2-inch pieces
1   large stalk celery with top, cut into 2-inch pieces
1   large onion, quartered
Bouquet Garni (recipe follows)

**Approximate analysis
per serving:**
Calories   14
Protein   tr.
Carbohydrate   1 g
Fat   1 g
Saturated Fat   tr.
Polyunsaturated Fat   tr.
Sodium   5 mg
Cholesterol   0

Rinse chicken thoroughly with cold water; pat dry. Place in a large Dutch oven.

Add water, carrot, celery, and onion.  Bring to a boil, and skim off residue and foam that rise to the surface, using a metal spoon. Add Bouquet Garni to Dutch oven; reduce heat. Cover and simmer 3 hours.

Line a large strainer with a triple thickness of dampened cheesecloth. Strain stock into a large bowl, and cool to room temperature. Cover and refrigerate overnight. Remove congealed fat from top of stock. **Yield:** 6½ cups. **Serving size:** 1 cup.

**Note:** Refrigerate Unsalted Chicken Stock in a covered container up to 3 days, or freeze in 1-quart freezer bags or containers. Stock can be kept frozen up to 6 months. To reduce sodium levels, Unsalted Chicken Stock may be substituted in recipes calling for chicken stock or broth. If a concentrated chicken stock is desired, simmer Unsalted Chicken Stock, uncovered, until reduced by half.

**Bouquet Garni:**

3   sprigs fresh parsley
1   bay leaf
6   whole black peppercorns
½   teaspoon dried whole thyme

Combine all ingredients in a double layer of cheesecloth, and tie securely with string or twine. **Yield**: 1 Bouquet Garni.

# Unsalted Beef Stock

1   (2-pound) lean chuck roast, with bone
2   medium onions, cut into wedges
2   medium carrots, scraped and coarsely chopped
2   medium stalks celery, coarsely chopped
3   cloves garlic, halved
3   quarts water
4   sprigs fresh parsley
4   whole cloves
1   bay leaf
¾   teaspoon dried whole thyme

**Approximate analysis per serving:**
Calories   14
Protein   tr.
Carbohydrate   1 g
Fat   1 g
Saturated Fat   tr.
Polyunsaturated Fat   tr.
Sodium   5 mg
Cholesterol   0

Cut roast into large pieces, and crack bone. Place roast and bones in a roasting pan, and bake at 400° for 30 minutes. Arrange onion, carrot, celery, and garlic around roast in pan; continue to bake 30 minutes.

Transfer browned meat, bones, and vegetables to a large Dutch oven. Add 3 quarts water, and bring to a boil; skim off residue and foam that rise to the surface, using a metal spoon.

Combine parsley, cloves, bay leaf, and thyme in a double layer of cheesecloth; tie securely with string or twine.  Add spice bag to Dutch oven; reduce heat, cover, and simmer 5 hours.

Line a large strainer with a triple thickness of dampened cheesecloth. Strain stock into a large bowl, and cool to room temperature. Cover and refrigerate overnight. Remove congealed fat from top of stock. **Yield:** 6 cups. **Serving size:** 1 cup.

**Note:**  Refrigerate Unsalted Beef Stock in a covered container up to 3 days, or freeze in 1-quart freezer bags or containers. Stock can be kept frozen up to 6 months. To reduce sodium levels, Unsalted Beef Stock may be substituted in recipes calling for beef stock or broth. If a concentrated beef stock is desired, simmer Unsalted Beef Stock, uncovered, until reduced by half.

# Beef and Barley Soup

½   pound lean boneless round steak
2   quarts plus 1 cup water, divided
2   (14½-ounce) cans whole tomatoes, undrained and chopped
1   (10½-ounce) can beef consommé, undiluted
½   cup chopped onion
1   clove garlic, minced
½   teaspoon dried whole basil
¼   teaspoon salt
2   bay leaves
½   cup barley
1   (10-ounce) package frozen peas and carrots

**Approximate analysis per serving:**
Calories   116
Protein   10 g
Carbohydrate   16 g
Fat   5 g
Saturated Fat   1 g
Polyunsaturated Fat   tr.
Sodium   531 mg
Cholesterol   23 mg

Trim fat from steak, and cut steak into 1-inch cubes. Combine 2 quarts water, meat, tomatoes, beef consommé, onion, garlic, basil, salt, and bay leaves in a 4-quart Dutch oven, stirring well. Cover and bring to a boil; reduce heat, and simmer 1 hour.

Place barley in a strainer, and rinse with cold water. Gradually add barley and remaining 1 cup water to Dutch oven; stir well. Cover and simmer 1 hour. Skim off visible fat from surface of soup, using a metal spoon. Stir in frozen vegetables; cover and simmer 30 to 45 minutes or until meat and vegetables are tender. Remove bay leaves before serving. **Yield:** 2½ quarts. **Serving size:** 1 cup.

---

*Although barley was an important food for the ancient Hebrews, Greeks, and Romans and remains so for the Asian peoples of Japan and China, it has been grown in this country primarily as a feed for animals or as a fermenting agent in making beer. However, barley is beginning to regain favor because it is high in protein, B vitamins, and dietary fiber while it contains very little fat and almost no sodium. Preliminary research also shows that barley may contain a cholesterol-lowering enzyme for animals as well as people.*

---

# Beef Stew

1½ pounds lean boneless round steak
Vegetable cooking spray
1   (16-ounce) can tomatoes, undrained
1   cup sliced onion
1   clove garlic, minced
1   teaspoon salt
¼   teaspoon pepper
1   bay leaf
1   tablespoon lemon juice
1   teaspoon Worcestershire sauce
6   carrots, scraped and sliced
4   medium potatoes, peeled and quartered
½   cup sliced celery
½   cup water
¼   cup all-purpose flour

**Approximate analysis per serving:**
Calories   243
Protein   26 g
Carbohydrate   23 g
Fat   2 g
Saturated Fat   2 g
Polyunsaturated Fat   tr.
Sodium   434 mg
Cholesterol   67 mg

Trim fat from steak, and cut steak into 1-inch cubes. Brown meat in a Dutch oven coated with cooking spray over low heat.

Drain tomatoes, reserving liquid. Chop tomatoes, and set aside. Add water to reserved liquid to equal 4 cups. Add liquid mixture, onion, and next 6 ingredients to Dutch oven. Cover and simmer 2 hours, stirring occasionally.

Add carrot, potato, and celery, and continue to cook, covered, 20 minutes. Stir in tomatoes, and cook 15 minutes or until meat and vegetables are tender. Combine ½ cup water and flour, stirring until well blended. Add to stew, and simmer, stirring frequently, 5 minutes or until mixture thickens. Remove bay leaf before serving. **Yield:** 2 quarts. **Serving size:** 1 cup.

*Carrots are a favored ingredient in vegetable soups and stews, not only for their sweet flavor but also for their crunchy texture even after being cooked. But carrots offer even more in nutrients. They are a valuable source of vitamin A — one carrot supplying more than the recommended daily amount — and they are very rich in beta-carotene, a cancer-preventing substance found in dark green and deep yellow fruits and vegetables.*

# Chili con Carne

¾   pound lean ground round
1    large onion, chopped
1    medium-size green pepper, chopped
2    (16-ounce) cans pinto beans
1    (16-ounce) can whole tomatoes, undrained and
      chopped
1    (8-ounce) can tomato sauce
1    tablespoon plus 1½ teaspoons chili powder
1    teaspoon salt
1    teaspoon ground cumin
⅛   teaspoon paprika
⅛   teaspoon red pepper
1    bay leaf

**Approximate analysis
per serving:**
Calories   174
Protein   16 g
Carbohydrate   22 g
Fat   3 g
Saturated Fat   1 g
Polyunsaturated Fat   tr.
Sodium   779 mg
Cholesterol   27 mg

Combine meat, onion, and green pepper in a Dutch oven. Cook over medium heat, stirring constantly, until meat is browned and vegetables are tender. Stir in beans and remaining ingredients. Cover and bring to a boil; reduce heat, and simmer 1½ hours. Remove bay leaf before serving. **Yield:** 2 quarts plus 1 cup. **Serving size:** 1 cup.

*Legumes, a class of vegetables which includes pinto beans and other dried peas and beans, deserve an honored place in your pantry and on your table. Legumes are richer in protein than any other plant food, and they are completely devoid of saturated fat and cholesterol. An additional benefit is that they are generously endowed with both soluble and insoluble fiber.*

# Casseroles and One-Dish Meals

Casseroles and one-dish meals are old favorites that will move into the 21st century with ease. They are usually easy to prepare and are certainly easy to serve, needing only a green salad and perhaps a bread to complete the meal. Most casseroles and one-dish meals can be prepared ahead of time and frozen, to be served any time you want. They are economical, and because they so often include foods in the complex-carbohydrate and high-fiber groups, they fit well into a low-fat, low-cholesterol diet. Some adjustments are usually necessary, however, such as making the binding sauce low-fat. To do this use undiluted evaporated skim milk. Also, fresh ground turkey, which is one of the leanest meats you can buy, makes a good substitute for ground beef. Read the turkey label to be sure that the skin has been removed. Also, breadcrumbs and croutons for casseroles can be made low-fat by cutting up slices of whole-grain bread and then browning the bread pieces in a skillet prepared with non-stick vegetable spray and your favorite herb mixture.

# Zucchini Lasagna

6    uncooked lasagna noodles
1    cup sliced fresh mushrooms
½    cup chopped onion
1    clove garlic, minced
1    teaspoon olive oil
2    (8-ounce) cans tomato sauce
1    teaspoon dried whole basil
½    teaspoon sugar
½    teaspoon dried whole oregano
⅛    teaspoon pepper
Vegetable cooking spray
3    cups thinly sliced zucchini
2    cups low-fat cottage cheese
½    cup grated fresh Parmesan cheese
1    tablespoon all-purpose flour
1    cup (4 ounces) shredded mozzarella cheese

**Approximate analysis per serving:**
Calories   312
Protein   21 g
Carbohydrate   30 g
Fat   12 g
Saturated Fat   7 g
Polyunsaturated Fat   tr.
Sodium   744 mg
Cholesterol   39 mg

Cook noodles according to package directions, omitting salt and fat. Drain well, and set aside.

Sauté mushrooms, onion, and garlic in olive oil in a medium skillet until tender. Stir in tomato sauce, basil, sugar, oregano, and pepper. Cook over medium heat 20 minutes, stirring occasionally. Remove tomato sauce mixture from heat, and set aside.

Coat a 9-inch square baking dish with cooking spray. Layer half each of noodles and zucchini in bottom of dish; top with half of tomato sauce mixture. Combine cottage cheese, Parmesan cheese, and flour in container of an electric blender, and process until smooth. Spread half of cheese mixture over layers in dish, using a spatula. Repeat layers with remaining noodles, zucchini, tomato sauce mixture, and cheese mixture. Sprinkle with mozzarella, and bake, uncovered, at 350° for 45 minutes. Let stand 15 minutes before cutting into 6 equal portions to serve. **Yield:** 6 servings. **Serving size:** 1 portion.

# Cheesy Vegetables with Pasta

1   cup uncooked medium-size shell macaroni
½   pound fresh broccoli
1½ cups cauliflower flowerets
2   medium carrots, scraped and shredded
1   cup sliced fresh mushrooms
1   cup (4 ounces) shredded mozzarella cheese
1   teaspoon dried parsley flakes
½   teaspoon garlic powder
½   teaspoon ground marjoram
½   teaspoon dried whole oregano
½   teaspoon dried whole basil
¼   teaspoon salt

**Approximate analysis per serving:**
Calories   108
Protein   7 g
Carbohydrate   15 g
Fat   3 g
Saturated Fat   1 g
Polyunsaturated Fat   tr.
Sodium   139 mg
Cholesterol   8 mg

Cook macaroni according to package directions, omitting salt and fat. Drain well, and set aside.

Trim off large leaves of broccoli, and remove tough ends of lower stalks. Wash broccoli thoroughly. Cut tops into flowerets, and cut stalks into ¼-inch slices. Set aside ¾ cup each of broccoli flowerets and slices. Reserve remaining broccoli for use in other recipes.

Cook broccoli flowerets and slices, cauliflower, carrots, and mushrooms in batches in a steaming rack over boiling water 6 to 8 minutes or until crisp-tender. Combine macaroni, steamed vegetables, cheese, and remaining ingredients; toss lightly to mix. Spoon mixture into a 2-quart casserole, and bake at 350° for 10 minutes or until cheese melts. **Yield:** 8 servings. **Serving size:** 1 cup.

# Deep-Dish Vegetarian Pizza

1   package dry yeast
1   teaspoon sugar
1   cup warm water (105° to 115°)
2¾ cups all-purpose flour, divided
2   tablespoons vegetable oil
¼   teaspoon salt
Vegetable cooking spray
2   tablespoons cornmeal
Herbed Pizza Sauce (recipe follows)
1   cup sliced fresh mushrooms
½   cup chopped green pepper
1   (14-ounce) can artichoke hearts, drained and
       quartered
¼   cup chopped onion
½   cup (2 ounces) shredded mozzarella cheese
⅓   cup grated Parmesan cheese

**Approximate analysis
per serving:**
Calories   267
Protein   10 g
Carbohydrate   43 g
Fat   7 g
Saturated Fat   2 g
Polyunsaturated Fat   2 g
Sodium   233 mg
Cholesterol   6 mg

Dissolve yeast and sugar in warm water. Let stand 5 minutes.

Combine yeast mixture, 2½ cups flour, oil, and salt in a medium bowl. Stir about 20 times, using firm beating stokes to make a soft dough.

Turn dough out onto a lightly floured surface and knead 5 minutes or until smooth and elastic, working in remaining ¼ cup flour. Shape dough into a smooth ball.

Coat a 13- x 9- x 2-inch baking pan lightly coated with cooking spray, and sprinkle with cornmeal. Place dough in pan, and let rest 5 minutes. Pat dough evenly over bottom and up sides of pan. Spread Herbed Pizza Sauce evenly over crust, and top with vegetables and cheeses. Bake at 425° for 25 minutes on lower rack of oven. Cut into 8 equal portions, and serve immediately. **Yield:** 8 servings. **Serving size:** 1 portion.

**Herbed Pizza Sauce:**

1    cup undrained canned Italian-style tomatoes
½    cup water
1    (6-ounce) can tomato paste
1    small onion, sliced
2    tablespoons minced fresh parsley
1    clove garlic, minced
1    bay leaf
½    teaspoon sugar
¼    teaspoon dried whole oregano
¼    teaspoon dried whole basil
⅛    teaspoon pepper

Combine all ingredients in a 2-quart saucepan, and simmer, uncovered, 45 minutes, stirring frequently. Remove bay leaf before serving. **Yield:** 2 cups.

*Commercial pizza can be extremely high in fat, especially when the topping includes Italian sausage, pepperoni, or other fatty meats. Because the topping of our Deep-Dish Vegetarian Pizza is made up of low-fat vegetables and the crust is made with vegetable oil, the total fat content is only 7 grams a serving. One of the ingredients that makes this pizza so appealing is the artichoke hearts, which lend an unusual taste to this traditional favorite.*

# Vegetable Quiche *(photograph on page 69)*

Potato Crust (recipe follows)
1    cup fresh broccoli flowerets
1    cup sliced fresh mushrooms
¼    cup chopped sweet red pepper
¼    cup chopped onion
2    tablespoons chopped green chiles
1    cup low-fat cottage cheese
¼    cup plus 2 tablespoons egg substitute
¼    cup uncooked, unprocessed oat bran
¼    teaspoon salt
¼    teaspoon dry mustard
¼    teaspoon paprika
½    cup (2 ounces) shredded Swiss cheese
1    egg white
¼    teaspoon cream of tartar
Fresh Tomato Topping (recipe follows)

**Approximate analysis per serving:**
Calories   202
Protein   12 g
Carbohydrate   21 g
Fat   8 g
Saturated Fat   3 g
Polyunsaturated Fat   1 g
Sodium   514 mg
Cholesterol   10 mg

Prepare Potato Crust, and set aside.

Place broccoli and next 4 ingredients in a vegetable steamer over boiling water. Cover and steam 5 minutes or until crisp-tender. Set aside.

Place cottage cheese in container of an electric blender; add egg substitute, oat bran, salt, dry mustard, and paprika. Cover and process until mixture is smooth. Pour mixture over cooked vegetables, and add shredded Swiss cheese. Stir well to combine.

Beat egg white (at room temperature) and cream of tartar at high speed of an electric mixer until stiff peaks form. Fold egg white into vegetable-cheese mixture, and spoon evenly into Potato Crust. Bake at 325° for 45 minutes or until top is golden and filling is set. Let stand 10 minutes before cutting into wedges to serve. Top each wedge with 2 tablespoons Fresh Tomato Topping. **Yield:** 6 servings. **Serving size:** 1 wedge.

**Potato Crust:**

½  pound potatoes, unpeeled and quartered
½  cup water
1  tablespoon plus 1½ teaspoons corn oil margarine,
      melted
1  tablespoon all-purpose flour
¼  teaspoon salt
⅛  teaspoon pepper
½  cup uncooked quick-cooking oats
Vegetable cooking spray

   Combine potatoes and water in a small saucepan. Cover and bring to a boil. Reduce heat, and simmer 15 minutes or until potatoes are tender. Drain. Transfer potatoes to a large bowl, and add margarine, flour, salt, and pepper. Mix well with a potato masher. Add oats, stirring well to combine.
   Compress mixture with hands, and place in a 9-inch pieplate coated with cooking spray. Press mixture in bottom and up sides of pieplate. Bake at 375° for 12 minutes. **Yield:** one 9-inch crust.

**Fresh Tomato Topping:**

1  small tomato, finely chopped
1½ teaspoons minced green onions
1½ teaspoons olive oil
⅛  teaspoon ground coriander or cumin
⅛  teaspoon pepper

   Combine all ingredients in a small bowl, stirring gently to combine. Cover and chill at least 30 minutes before serving. **Yield:** ¾ cup.

# Tuna-Noodle Casserole

1    tablespoon corn oil margarine
2    tablespoons all-purpose flour
2    cups skim milk
¼    cup (1 ounce) shredded reduced-fat Cheddar
       cheese
¼    teaspoon salt
3    cups cooked egg noodles (cooked without salt
       or fat)
1    (10-ounce) package frozen English peas
1    (6½-ounce) can white tuna in water, drained and
       flaked
1    (4-ounce) can sliced mushrooms, drained
¼    cup chopped green pepper
⅛    teaspoon pepper
¼    teaspoon hot sauce
Vegetable cooking spray
½    cup fine, dry breadcrumbs

**Approximate analysis
per serving:**
Calories   263
Protein   16 g
Carbohydrate   34 g
Fat   6 g
Saturated Fat   2 g
Polyunsaturated Fat   1 g
Sodium   486 mg
Cholesterol   28 mg

   Melt margarine in a large skillet over low heat; add flour, stirring until smooth. Cook 1 minute, stirring constantly. Gradually add milk; cook over medium heat, stirring constantly, until mixture is thickened and bubbly. Stir in cheese and salt; cook over low heat, stirring constantly, until cheese melts. Remove from heat.
   Combine cheese sauce, noodles, and next 6 ingredients. Spoon mixture into a 2-quart casserole coated with cooking spray. Sprinkle evenly with breadcrumbs. Bake at 375° for 35 minutes or until casserole is bubbly and top is browned. **Yield:** 6 servings. **Serving size:** 1¼ cups.

*The most delectable way to enjoy your complex carbo-hydrates and fiber – Vegetable Quiche (page 66) with a hearty Potato Crust and a Fresh Tomato Topping complemented by Fruited Carrot Salad (page 163).*

# Scalloped Salmon and Potatoes

3   medium potatoes, unpeeled
½   cup chopped onion
⅓   cup chopped green pepper
2   tablespoons corn oil margarine, melted
3   tablespoons all-purpose flour
¼   teaspoon dried whole basil
¼   teaspoon pepper
1½ cups skim milk
1   (15½-ounce) can salmon, drained and flaked
3   cups saltine cracker crumbs

**Approximate analysis per serving:**
Calories   183
Protein   14 g
Carbohydrate   17 g
Fat   7 g
Saturated Fat   2 g
Polyunsaturated Fat   2 g
Sodium   507 mg
Cholesterol   26 mg

Combine potatoes and water to cover in a large saucepan; cover and bring to a boil. Reduce heat, and simmer 15 minutes or until potatoes are tender. Drain and let cool. Cut into thin slices, and set aside.

Sauté onion and green pepper in margarine in a large skillet until tender. Blend in flour, basil, and pepper; cook over medium heat 1 minute, stirring constantly. Gradually add milk; cook over medium heat, stirring constantly, until mixture is thickened and bubbly. Remove from heat, and add potato slices. Stir gently to coat well.

Layer half each of coated potato slices and salmon in a 1½-quart casserole. Repeat layers, and sprinkle cracker crumbs over top. Bake at 350° for 30 minutes or until thoroughly heated. **Yield:** 6 servings. **Serving size:** 1 cup.

*Savor the variety of flavors and textures in this low-calorie luncheon of Gazpacho (page 52), Chicken and Pasta Salad (page 74) and Low-Cholesterol Corn Sticks (page 176).*

# Chicken Pot Pie

3    celery stalks with leaves
6¼ cups water, divided
1½ pounds chicken breast halves, skinned
1    bay leaf
1½ teaspoons salt, divided
¼    teaspoon pepper
1½ cups cubed potato
¾    cup sliced carrot
½    cup diced celery
¼    cup minced onion
¼    teaspoon ground thyme
¼    teaspoon pepper
3    tablespoons cornstarch
1    cup all-purpose flour
⅓    cup skim milk
3    tablespoons vegetable oil
1¼ teaspoons baking powder
⅛    teaspoon paprika

**Approximate analysis
per serving:**
Calories   186
Protein   20 g
Carbohydrate   15 g
Fat   3 g
Saturated Fat   2 g
Polyunsaturated Fat   3 g
Sodium   257 mg
Cholesterol   50 mg

Cut celery tops with leaves from stalks; reserve stalks for use in other recipes. Combine celery tops, 6 cups water, chicken, bay leaf, 1 teaspoon salt, and ¼ teaspoon pepper in a Dutch oven. Cover and bring to a boil. Reduce heat; simmer 1½ hours or until chicken is done. Remove chicken from broth, reserving 3 cups broth. Chill reserved broth. Bone chicken, and cut into bite-size pieces; set aside.

Skim congealed fat from surface of chilled broth. Combine broth, potatoes, and next 5 ingredients; cook over medium heat until vegetables are tender. Dissolve cornstarch in remaining ¼ cup water. Stir into vegetable mixture, and continue to cook until mixture thickens. Stir in chicken. Remove from heat, and spoon mixture into a 3-quart casserole.

Combine flour, milk, oil, baking powder, and remaining ½ teaspoon salt; stir well to mix. Spoon mixture into 8 equal mounds over top of chicken mixture; sprinkle with paprika. Bake at 450° for 15 minutes or until top is browned. **Yield:** 8 servings. **Serving size:** ¾ cup chicken mixture plus 1 biscuit.

# Chicken Tetrazzini

1   (2½-pound) broiler-fryer, cut up and skinned
3   cups water
1   stalk celery with leaves
1   small onion, peeled
1   bay leaf
1   (8-ounce) package spaghetti
Vegetable cooking spray
½   cup diced celery
⅓   cup chopped onion
2   (4-ounce) cans mushroom stems and pieces,
      drained
2   tablespoons plus 1 teaspoon dried parsley flakes,
      divided
½   teaspoon salt
2   tablespoons corn oil margarine
3   tablespoons plus 1½ teaspoons all-purpose flour
1   cup skim milk
¼   teaspoon pepper
2   tablespoons grated Parmesan cheese

**Approximate analysis
per serving:**
Calories   241
Protein   21 g
Carbohydrate   20 g
Fat   8 g
Saturated Fat   2 g
Polyunsaturated Fat   2 g
Sodium   219 mg
Cholesterol   52 mg

Combine first 5 ingredients in a Dutch oven. Cover and bring to a boil. Reduce heat; simmer 1½ hours. Remove chicken, reserving 1½ cups broth. Chill reserved broth. Bone chicken, and cut into bite-size pieces; set aside.

Break spaghetti in half, and cook according to package directions, omitting salt and fat. Drain well, and set aside.

Coat a large skillet with cooking spray. Place over medium heat until hot. Add diced celery, chopped onion, and mushrooms. Cook, stirring constantly, until vegetables are tender. Remove from heat, and stir in chicken, 1 teaspoon parsley flakes, and salt. Set aside.

Melt margarine over low heat; add flour, stirring until smooth. Cook 1 minute, stirring constantly. Skim fat from reserved broth. Combine broth, milk, and pepper; gradually add to flour mixture. Cook over medium heat, stirring constantly, until mixture is thickened and bubbly.

Combine spaghetti, chicken mixture, and white sauce; stir until well mixed. Spoon mixture into a 3-quart casserole; sprinkle evenly with remaining 2 tablespoons parsley flakes and cheese. Bake at 350° for 20 to 25 minutes or until hot and bubbly. **Yield:** 10 servings. **Serving size:** 1 cup.

# Chicken and Pasta Salad   *(photograph on page 70)*

1½ cups diced cooked chicken breast (skinned before
    cooking and cooked without salt)
1   cup commercial oil-free Italian dressing
4   ounces uncooked corkscrew macaroni
1   cup small broccoli flowerets
1   cup coarsely chopped sweet red pepper
½   cup cherry tomato halves
¼   cup chopped green onions
¼   cup chopped celery
1   tablespoon chopped fresh parsley
1   clove garlic, minced
½   teaspoon salt
¼   teaspoon dried whole basil
⅛   teaspoon pepper

**Approximate analysis per serving:**
Calories   116
Protein   11 g
Carbohydrate   14 g
Fat   1 g
Saturated Fat   tr.
Polyunsaturated Fat   tr.
Sodium   569 mg
Cholesterol   25 mg

Combine chicken and dressing in a large bowl. Cover and marinate in refrigerator 30 minutes.

Cook macaroni according to package directions, omitting salt and fat. Drain well. Add macaroni and remaining ingredients to chicken mixture in bowl. Toss gently to coat well. Cover and refrigerate at least 2 hours before serving. **Yield:** 8 servings. **Serving size:** 1 cup.

*To prepare cooked chicken to use as an ingredient in a recipe, first determine how much chicken you need to cook. Count on ½ cup of chopped chicken per chicken breast half. Remove the skin if you have not already done so. Place the chicken in a Dutch oven, and cover with water. Bring to a boil. Cover, reduce heat, and simmer for 30 minutes or until chicken is tender. Drain chicken, and let cool to touch. Chicken can then be boned and cut up according to the recipe directions.*

# Creamy Chicken-Rice Casserole

1½ pounds chicken breast halves, skinned
6   cups water
1   (6-ounce) package long-grain and wild rice mix
1   (4-ounce) can sliced mushrooms, undrained
½   cup chopped onion
1   tablespoon corn oil margarine, melted
¼   cup all-purpose flour
1½ cups evaporated skim milk
¼   cup diced pimiento
2   tablespoons minced fresh parsley
¼   teaspoon salt
¼   teaspoon pepper

**Approximate analysis per serving:**
Calories   230
Protein   24 g
Carbohydrate   23 g
Fat   4 g
Saturated Fat   1 g
Polyunsaturated Fat   1 g
Sodium   485 mg
Cholesterol   52 mg

Place chicken and water in a Dutch oven; cover and bring to a boil. Reduce heat, and simmer 25 minutes or until chicken is done. Remove chicken from broth; reserving 1 cup broth. Chill reserved broth. Bone chicken, and cut into bite-size pieces; set aside.

Prepare rice mix according to package directions. Set cooked rice aside.

Drain mushrooms, reserving liquid. Set mushrooms and liquid aside.

Sauté onion in margarine in a 2-quart saucepan until tender. Stir in flour, and cook 1 minute, stirring constantly. Skim congealed fat from surface of chilled broth. Add broth, mushroom liquid, and milk to flour mixture. Cook over medium heat, stirring constantly, until mixture is thickened and bubbly. Stir in chicken, rice, mushrooms, pimiento, parsley, salt, and pepper. Spoon mixture into a 2-quart casserole, and bake at 350° for 25 to 30 minutes or until thoroughly heated. **Yield:** 8 servings. **Serving size:** 1 cup.

# Turkey Tacos   *(photograph on page 137)*

Vegetable cooking spray
1   pound ground fresh turkey
¼   cup chopped onion
1   (1.25-ounce) package taco seasoning mix
8   commercial taco shells
½   medium head lettuce, shredded (about 6 cups)
2   medium tomatoes, chopped
¼   cup (1 ounce) shredded reduced-fat Cheddar
    cheese
¾   cup commercial taco sauce

**Approximate analysis per serving:**
Calories   144
Protein   8 g
Carbohydrate   14 g
Fat   7 g
Saturated Fat   1 g
Polyunsaturated Fat   1 g
Sodium   441 mg
Cholesterol   21 mg

Coat a large skillet with cooking spray; place over medium heat until hot. Add turkey and onion, and cook, stirring constantly, until turkey is browned. Stir in taco seasoning mix and water according to package directions; simmer 4 minutes. Remove from heat, and keep warm.

Warm taco shells according to package directions. Fill shells evenly with turkey mixture, lettuce, tomatoes, and cheese. Serve with taco sauce. **Yield:** 8 servings. **Serving size:** 1 filled taco shell with 1 tablespoon plus 1½ teaspoons taco sauce.

# Brown Rice and Turkey Salad

2   cups cubed cooked turkey breast (skinned before
    cooking and cooked without salt)
2   cups cooked brown rice
1   cup frozen English peas
½   cup sliced seedless green grapes
¼   cup reduced-calorie mayonnaise
½   teaspoon curry powder
⅛   teaspoon white pepper
Lettuce leaves (optional)

**Approximate analysis per serving:**
Calories   221
Protein   20 g
Carbohydrate   25 g
Fat   4 g
Saturated Fat   tr.
Polyunsaturated Fat   tr.
Sodium   292 mg
Cholesterol   47 mg

Combine turkey, rice, peas, and grapes in a medium bowl. Combine mayonnaise, curry powder, and pepper, stirring well to blend; pour over turkey mixture, and toss lightly to combine. Cover and chill several hours. Serve salad on individual lettuce-lined serving plates, if desired. **Yield:** 5 servings. **Serving size:** 1 cup.

# Turkey Chili-Mac  *(photograph on page 87)*

1   (8-ounce) package elbow macaroni
1   pound ground fresh turkey
½   cup chopped onion
¼   cup chopped green pepper
1   clove garlic, minced
1   (12-ounce) can tomato juice
1   (8-ounce) can tomato sauce
1   teaspoon chili powder
1   teaspoon ground cumin
½   teaspoon salt
1   (15-ounce) can red kidney beans

**Approximate analysis
per serving:**
Calories   235
Protein   19 g
Carbohydrate   34 g
Fat   2 g
Saturated Fat   1 g
Polyunsaturated Fat   1 g
Sodium   662 mg
Cholesterol   36 mg

Cook macaroni according to package directions, omitting salt and fat. Drain well, and set aside.

Place ground turkey in a Dutch oven. Cook over medium heat 15 minutes or until turkey is browned, stirring to crumble. Add onion, green pepper, and garlic. Cook 5 minutes or until vegetables are tender, stirring constantly. Stir in tomato juice and next 4 ingredients. Cover and simmer 20 minutes, stirring occasionally. Add kidney beans and macaroni; simmer an additional 15 minutes, stirring occasionally. Serve hot. **Yield:** 8 servings. **Serving size:** 1 cup.

*Fresh ground turkey, a reasonably new product on the market, is fast becoming a staple. It's not surprising considering that turkey is naturally low in fat, even lower than chicken. But when buying ground turkey, you must make sure that it was ground without the skin. A 3½-ounce serving of turkey with the skin, for example, has 8 grams of fat, but the same amount of white meat without skin has only 1 gram of fat. That's a good reason to buy fresh ground turkey without skin.*

# Baked Pork Chop Dinner

4    (¼-pound) lean pork chops, trimmed
Vegetable cooking spray
4    medium potatoes, peeled and sliced
4    medium carrots, cut into ½-inch diagonal slices
2    medium onions, sliced
½    teaspoon salt
¼    teaspoon pepper
1    cup ready-to-serve chicken broth
⅓    cup Chablis or other dry white wine

**Approximate analysis
per serving:**
Calories   356
Protein   27 g
Carbohydrate   39 g
Fat   9 g
Saturated Fat   3 g
Polyunsaturated Fat   1 g
Sodium   512 mg
Cholesterol   68 mg

Place pork chops in a large nonstick skillet; brown on both sides over medium heat. Transfer pork chops to a 13- x 9- x 2-inch baking dish coated with cooking spray. Layer potatoes, carrots, and onions over pork chops. Sprinkle evenly with salt and pepper. Pour broth and wine over top. Cover and bake at 375° for 1½ hours or until chops are tender. **Yield:** 4 servings. **Serving size:** 1 pork chop with ¼ of vegetable mixture.

# Stir-Fried Pork and Vegetables

1    pound lean pork tenderloin, trimmed
1¼ cups water, divided
1    tablespoon low-sodium soy sauce
2    teaspoons cornstarch
1    teaspoon ground ginger
1    teaspoon chicken-flavored bouillon granules
2    teaspoons corn oil margarine
¼    teaspoon salt
1    cup thinly sliced carrot
4    green onions, thinly sliced
1    clove garlic, minced
1½ cups thinly sliced celery
2    cups hot cooked spaghetti (cooked without salt or
       fat)

**Approximate analysis
per serving:**
Calories   269
Protein   17 g
Carbohydrate   28 g
Fat   9 g
Saturated Fat   3 g
Polyunsaturated Fat   2 g
Sodium   602 mg
Cholesterol   43 mg

Partially freeze pork; slice diagonally across grain into ¼-inch strips. Set aside.

Combine 1 cup water, soy sauce, cornstarch, ginger, and bouillon granules. Stir until mixture is well blended, and set aside.

Melt margarine in a large skillet over medium heat; add pork and salt. Cook, stirring constantly, until pork is browned. Stir in carrot, onions, and garlic, and continue to cook 4 to 5 minutes.

Add remaining ¼ cup water to skillet; cover and cook over medium heat 4 minutes. Add celery, and cook 3 minutes, stirring constantly. Stir in cornstarch mixture; cook until clear and slightly thickened. Serve pork mixture over spaghetti. **Yield:** 4 servings. **Serving size:** 1 cup pork mixture with ½ cup spaghetti.

# Oriental Beef Casserole

1 pound ground round
1 cup chopped onion
½ cup chopped celery
1 (8-ounce) can whole water chestnuts, undrained
1 (4-ounce) can whole mushrooms, undrained
⅔ cup uncooked brown rice
⅓ cup low-sodium soy sauce
½ teaspoon pepper
¼ teaspoon salt

**Approximate analysis per serving:**
Calories  204
Protein  24 g
Carbohydrate  16 g
Fat  4 g
Saturated Fat  2 g
Polyunsaturated Fat  tr.
Sodium  473 mg
Cholesterol  61 mg

Combine ground round, onion, and celery in a large skillet. Cook over medium heat, stirring constantly, until meat is browned and vegetables are tender. Drain mixture on paper towels. Transfer to a large bowl, and set aside.

Drain water chestnuts and mushrooms, reserving liquid. Add water to drained liquid to yield 2 cups. Chop water chestnuts and mushrooms. Add liquid mixture, water chestnuts, and mushrooms to meat mixture in bowl. Stir in rice and remaining ingredients. Spoon into a 2-quart casserole. Cover and bake at 350° for 1 hour or until all liquid is absorbed. **Yield:** 6 servings. **Serving size:** 1 cup.

# Hearty Macaroni and Beef

Vegetable cooking spray
1    pound ground round
1    cup chopped onion
¼    teaspoon garlic powder
⅛    teaspoon pepper
1    (14½-ounce) can whole tomatoes, undrained and
       chopped
2    (8-ounce) cans tomato sauce
1    (4-ounce) can sliced mushrooms, undrained
½    teaspoon salt
2    cups uncooked elbow macaroni
1    cup water

**Approximate analysis
per serving:**
Calories   176
Protein   19 g
Carbohydrate   17 g
Fat   4 g
Saturated Fat   1 g
Polyunsaturated Fat   tr.
Sodium   652 mg
Cholesterol   46 mg

Coat a large skillet with cooking spray; place over medium heat until hot. Add ground round, onion, garlic powder, and pepper. Cook, stirring constantly, until meat is browned and onion is transparent.

Add remaining ingredients, stirring well. Cover and cook over medium heat 20 minutes, stirring occasionally to prevent sticking; add more water, if needed. **Yield:** 8 servings. **Serving size:** 1 cup.

# Stir-Fried Beef and Broccoli

1    (1-pound) lean boneless round steak
1    cup water
⅓    cup low-sodium soy sauce
2    tablespoons cornstarch
1    teaspoon ground ginger
1    tablespoon brown sugar
3    tablespoons white cooking wine
1    beef-flavored bouillon cube
1    clove garlic, minced
1    large bunch fresh broccoli
2    tablespoons vegetable oil
2    cups sliced onion
4    cups hot cooked rice (cooked without salt or fat)

**Approximate analysis
per serving:**
Calories   299
Protein   19 g
Carbohydrate   31 g
Fat   7 g
Saturated Fat   2 g
Polyunsaturated Fat   3 g
Sodium   476 mg
Cholesterol   43 mg

Trim fat from steak. Partially freeze steak; slice diagonally across grain into ¼-inch strips. Place in a shallow dish. Combine water and next 7 ingredients, stirring well to mix; pour over meat. Cover and marinate in refrigerator 15 to 20 minutes.

Trim broccoli, and wash thoroughly. Cut tops into flowerets, and cut stalks into ¼-inch slices. Set aside 2 cups each of flowerets and slices. Reserve remaining broccoli for use in other recipes.

Place oil in a Dutch oven; heat over medium heat until hot. Drain meat, reserving marinade. Add meat in batches; cook only until lightly browned. Remove meat from Dutch oven, and drain on paper towels. Set aside.

Add onion to Dutch oven, and cook over medium heat 1 minute, stirring constantly. Stir in broccoli flowerets and slices and ½ cup marinade. Cover and cook an additional 2 to 3 minutes or until broccoli is crisp-tender. Add meat and remaining marinade to Dutch oven; continue to cook until slightly thickened. Serve meat mixture over rice. **Yield:** 8 servings. **Serving size:** 1 cup meat mixture with ½ cup rice.

# Easy Salmagundi

¾  pound ground round
1  cup chopped onion
½  cup chopped green pepper
2  (8-ounce) cans tomato sauce
2  cups water
¾  cup uncooked brown rice
2  teaspoons chili powder
½  teaspoon salt
¼  teaspoon pepper
1  (12-ounce) can whole kernel corn, undrained

**Approximate analysis per serving:**
Calories  232
Protein  19 g
Carbohydrate  30 g
Fat  4 g
Saturated Fat  1 g
Polyunsaturated Fat  tr.
Sodium  793 mg
Cholesterol  46 mg

Place ground round in a Dutch oven; cook over medium heat, stirring constantly, until lightly browned. Add onion and green pepper, and continue to cook until vegetables are tender, stirring occasionally.

Add tomato sauce and water to Dutch oven, and bring to a boil. Stir in brown rice, chili powder, salt, and pepper. Reduce heat, cover, and simmer 50 minutes. Stir in corn and additional water, if needed. Cover and cook an additional 10 minutes or until rice is done. **Yield:** 6 servings. **Serving size:** 1 cup.

# Eggplant Spaghetti with Meatballs

1    (16-ounce) package spaghetti
⅓    cup chopped onion
1    clove garlic, crushed
2    tablespoons vegetable oil
1    (16-ounce) can whole tomatoes, undrained and
        chopped
1    (6-ounce) can tomato paste
½    cup ready-to-serve beef broth
½    teaspoon dried whole oregano
1    teaspoon sugar
¼    teaspoon salt
Meatballs (recipe follows)
2    cups peeled, cubed eggplant (about 1½ pounds)
2    tablespoons chopped fresh parsley
2    tablespoons grated Parmesan cheese

**Approximate analysis per serving:**
Calories    356
Protein    18 g
Carbohydrate    56 g
Fat    7 g
Saturated Fat    2 g
Polyunsaturated Fat    2 g
Sodium    581 mg
Cholesterol    24 mg

Cook spaghetti according to package directions, omitting salt and fat. Drain well, and set aside.

Sauté onion and garlic in oil in a large Dutch oven 5 minutes or until onion is transparent. Stir in tomatoes, tomato paste, broth, oregano, sugar, and salt; bring to a boil. Add meatballs, eggplant, and parsley. Reduce heat, cover, and simmer 45 minutes, stirring occasionally. Serve meatball mixture over spaghetti; sprinkle evenly with cheese. **Yield:** 8 servings. **Serving size**: 3 meatballs and ¾ cup sauce with ½ cup spaghetti.

**Meatballs:**

2    slices sandwich bread, torn into large pieces
¼    cup skim milk
½    pound ground round
½    cup chopped green pepper
¼    cup chopped onion
1    tablespoon chopped fresh parsley
1    clove garlic, crushed
½    teaspoon salt
⅛    teaspoon pepper
Vegetable cooking spray

Combine bread pieces and milk in a medium bowl, stirring well to mix. Let stand 5 minutes.

Add ground round and next 6 ingredients; stir until well combined. Shape mixture into 24 meatballs. Place meatballs in a Dutch oven coated with cooking spray; cook over medium heat, turning gently, until evenly browned. Remove from Dutch oven. **Yield:** 2 dozen.

# Lima Bean-Meatball Casserole

1   cup dried lima beans
1   pound ground round
1   cup evaporated skim milk
¾   cup uncooked regular oats
2   tablespoons instant minced onion
½   teaspoon salt
½   teaspoon pepper
1   cup catsup
½   cup water
2   tablespoons vinegar
1   teaspoon sugar

**Approximate analysis per serving:**
Calories   483
Protein   43 g
Carbohydrate   62 g
Fat   7 g
Saturated Fat   2 g
Polyunsaturated Fat   tr.
Sodium   817 mg
Cholesterol  75 mg

Cook lima beans according to package directions, omitting salt. Drain well, and place in a 3-quart casserole. Set aside.

Combine ground round, milk, oats, onion, salt, and pepper, stirring until well combined. Shape mixture into 10 meatballs. Arrange meatballs over lima beans in casserole.

Combine catsup and remaining ingredients, stirring until well blended; pour sauce over meatballs. Cover and bake at 350° for 1 hour. Uncover and bake an additional 30 to 45 minutes or until meatballs are browned and thoroughly heated. **Yield:** 5 servings. **Serving size:** 2 meatballs with ¾ cup bean mixture.

# Eggplant-Beef Casserole

1    pound ground round
Vegetable cooking spray
1    medium eggplant, unpeeled
⅓    cup all-purpose flour
1    tablespoon olive oil
2    (8-ounce) cans tomato sauce
½    teaspoon dried whole oregano
2    tablespoons grated Parmesan cheese
½    cup (2 ounces) shredded reduced-fat Cheddar
      cheese

**Approximate analysis per serving:**
Calories   188
Protein   20 g
Carbohydrate   10 g
Fat   8 g
Saturated Fat   3 g
Polyunsaturated Fat   tr.
Sodium   434 mg
Cholesterol   54 mg

Shape ground round into 8 patties. Coat a large skillet with cooking spray; place over medium heat until hot. Add patties, and brown evenly on both sides. Remove from skillet, and set aside.

Cut eggplant into 8 thick slices, and coat evenly with flour. Place olive oil in skillet; heat over medium heat until hot. Add eggplant slices, and brown evenly on both sides. Transfer eggplant slices to a 13- x 9- x 2-inch baking dish, and top each slice with a browned beef patty.

Combine tomato sauce and oregano, stirring well; pour over patties. Sprinkle evenly with Parmesan cheese, and bake at 300° for 30 minutes. Sprinkle Cheddar cheese over top, and bake an additional 5 minutes. **Yield:** 8 servings. **Serving size:** 1 patty with 1 eggplant slice and tomato sauce.

# Meatballs with Stir-Fried Vegetables

1    pound ground round
¼    teaspoon salt
3½   cups water, divided
1    large onion, peeled and cut into wedges
1    clove garlic, minced
Vegetable cooking spray
2    small carrots, scraped and cut into julienne strips
1    cup sliced fresh mushrooms
3    cups broccoli flowerets
1    tablespoon cornstarch
1    tablespoon chicken-flavored bouillon granules
1    tablespoon low-sodium soy sauce
4    cups hot cooked noodles (cooked without salt
     or fat)

**Approximate analysis
per serving:**
Calories   219
Protein   21 g
Carbohydrate   24 g
Fat   4 g
Saturated Fat   2 g
Polyunsaturated Fat   tr.
Sodium   552 mg
Cholesterol   46 mg

Combine ground round and salt, stirring to mix well. Shape mixture into 32 meatballs. Place 2 cups water in a large saucepan, and bring to a boil. Gently drop meatballs into water. Reduce heat, cover, and simmer 10 to 15 minutes or until meatballs are done. Remove meatballs from liquid, and drain in a colander. Set aside.

Sauté onion and garlic in a large skillet coated with cooking spray until onion is transparent. Add carrots and mushrooms; continue to cook, stirring constantly, 2 minutes. Add ½ cup water. Cover and bring to a boil. Add broccoli. Reduce heat, and simmer 3 minutes.

Combine remaining 1 cup water, cornstarch, bouillon granules, and soy sauce, stirring until well blended. Add to vegetables, and cook over medium heat, stirring until sauce is thickened and clear. Add meatballs to skillet, and cook an additional 2 minutes or until thoroughly heated, stirring gently. Serve meatballs and vegetable mixture over noodles. **Yield:** 8 servings. **Serving size:** 4 meatballs and ⅛ cup of vegetable mixture with ½ cup noodles.

# Meatball Cassoulet

1¼ cups dried navy beans
7   cups water, divided
½   pound ground round
2   tablespoons Worcestershire sauce, divided
1   teaspoon salt, divided
½   cup chopped onion
½   cup chopped celery
1   clove garlic, minced
½   teaspoon dried whole basil
½   teaspoon dried whole oregano
½   teaspoon paprika
1   (14½-ounce) can whole tomatoes, undrained and
      chopped
1   (8-ounce) can tomato sauce
1   (4-ounce) can chopped green chiles, undrained
1   medium carrot, scraped and grated
3   cups hot cooked rice (cooked without salt or fat)

**Approximate analysis per serving:**
Calories   210
Protein   15 g
Carbohydrate   32 g
Fat   3 g
Saturated Fat   1 g
Polyunsaturated Fat   tr.
Sodium   759 mg
Cholesterol   30 mg

Sort and wash beans; place in a large Dutch oven. Add 4 cups water; let soak 8 hours. Drain off water, reserving beans in Dutch oven.

Combine ground round, 1 tablespoon Worcestershire sauce, and ¼ teaspoon salt, stirring well to mix. Shape mixture into 18 meatballs. Place meatballs in a large nonstick skillet; cook over medium heat, turning gently, until evenly browned. Remove from heat.

Add meatballs, onion, celery, garlic, remaining ¾ teaspoon salt, remaining 1 tablespoon Worcestershire sauce, basil, oregano, and paprika to beans in Dutch oven. Stir in remaining 3 cups water. Cover and bring to a boil. Reduce heat, and simmer 1½ hours or until beans are tender. Stir in tomatoes, tomato sauce, chiles, and carrot. Cover and simmer an additional 10 minutes. Ladle into individual serving bowls, and top each serving with ½ cup rice. **Yield:** 6 servings. **Serving size:** 1½ cups meatball mixture with ½ cup rice.

*Energize an active family with this easy-to-fix supper featuring Turkey Chili-Mac (page 77), Fresh Vegetable Salad (page 159), and Creole Muffins (page 176).*

# Fish
# and
# Shellfish

Fish, as a source of animal protein, is highly recommended by nutritionists. It is generally low in fat, and the fatty species contain omega-3 fatty acids, which help to lower cholesterol and prevent heart disease. Fish also fits well into an active lifestyle, because it is the ultimate in fast food. Pick up your fish or shellfish an hour before dinnertime, and it can be on the table in less than thirty minutes. Grilling, broiling, and baking are favored cooking methods for fish, but poaching is also simple and fat-free. Place your fish fillet or fish steak in any simmering liquid (water, wine, or fat-free broth), and cook gently until the fish flakes easily with a fork. Flaking easily with a fork is the approved test for doneness of fish. Another general rule is to bake or broil ten minutes for every inch of fish thickness. Even though shellfish contain more cholesterol per ounce than fish, they are low in saturated fat and calories. The dietary recommendation is to limit servings to once a week.

*Regardless of where you do your outdoor cooking, Grilled Grouper Kabobs (page 96) skewered with vegetables and served with corn in husks and hard rolls will make a memorable meal.*

# Zesty Orange Roughy Amandine

1    tablespoon plus 1 teaspoon sliced almonds
2    teaspoons corn oil margarine
2    tablespoons minced fresh parsley
1    tablespoon grated lemon rind
3    tablespoons lemon juice
¼    teaspoon salt
4    (¼-pound) orange roughy fillets

**Approximate analysis per serving:**
Calories   175
Protein   17 g
Carbohydrate   2 g
Fat   11 g
Saturated Fat   2 g
Polyunsaturated Fat   1 g
Sodium   241 mg
Cholesterol   23 mg

Brown almonds in a small nonstick skillet over low heat until lightly toasted. Set almonds aside.

Melt margarine in skillet over low heat; add parsley, lemon rind, lemon juice, and salt, stirring well. Remove from heat, and set aside.

Cover a broiler pan with aluminum foil. Place in oven 6 inches from heating element; preheat 3 minutes.

Arrange fish in preheated pan, and baste evenly with margarine mixture. Broil 6 inches from heat 8 minutes or until fish flakes easily when tested with a fork. Sprinkle toasted almonds over fish before serving. **Yield:** 4 servings. **Serving size:** 1 (3-ounce) fillet

# Delicious Tomato-Topped Fillets *(photograph on cover)*

3    green onions, chopped
1    clove garlic, minced
1    teaspoon olive oil
2    tablespoons chopped fresh parsley
1    teaspoon dried whole basil
½    teaspoon salt
⅛    teaspoon pepper
1    large tomato, peeled and coarsely chopped
4    (¼-pound) orange roughy fillets
Fresh basil sprigs (optional)

**Approximate analysis per serving:**
Calories   165
Protein   17 g
Carbohydrate   3 g
Fat   9 g
Saturated Fat   2 g
Polyunsaturated Fat   tr.
Sodium   367 mg
Cholesterol   23 mg

Sauté green onions and garlic in olive oil in a medium skillet until tender. Add parsley, dried whole basil, salt, and pepper, and cook over low heat until thoroughly heated. Remove from heat; stir in tomato, and set aside.

Cover a broiler pan with aluminum foil. Place in oven 6 inches from heating element; preheat 3 minutes. Arrange fish in preheated pan. Broil 6 inches from heat 5 minutes; top each fillet with ¼ cup tomato mixture, and continue to broil 3 minutes or until fish flakes easily when tested with a fork. Garnish each serving with fresh basil, if desired. **Yield:** 4 servings. **Serving size:** 1 (3-ounce) fillet with ¼ cup tomato mixture

# Lemon Baked Fillets with Red Potatoes

Vegetable cooking spray
¼  cup water
3   tablespoons lemon juice
2   tablespoons Chablis or other dry white wine
½   teaspoon chicken-flavored bouillon granules
4   medium-size red potatoes, cut into ¼-inch slices
2   green onions, chopped
4   (¼-pound) orange roughy fillets
¼   teaspoon salt
⅛   teaspoon pepper

**Approximate analysis per serving:**
Calories   263
Protein   20 g
Carbohydrate   27 g
Fat   8 g
Saturated Fat   2 g
Polyunsaturated Fat   2 g
Sodium   332 mg
Cholesterol   23 mg

Coat a 9-inch square baking dish with cooking spray. Add water, lemon juice, wine, and bouillon granules; stir until granules dissolve. Line bottom of dish with potato slices. Cover with heavy-duty plastic wrap, and microwave at HIGH 8 to 10 minutes, rotating dish once. Add green onions; cover and microwave at HIGH 1 minute.

Sprinkle fish with salt and pepper. Add to baking dish, and baste with liquid in dish. Cover and microwave at HIGH 4 minutes. Rotate dish, and microwave at HIGH an additional 4 to 5 minutes or until fish flakes easily when tested with a fork. Let stand, covered, 2 minutes. Serve immediately. **Yield:** 4 servings. **Serving size:** 1 (3-ounce) fillet with ¼ of sliced potatoes.

# Mustard-Baked Salmon

6    (6-ounce) salmon steaks
½    cup Rhine or other dry white wine
2    tablespoons Dijon mustard
2    tablespoons corn oil margarine, melted
2    tablespoons lemon juice
½    teaspoon salt
⅛    teaspoon pepper

Place salmon in a 13- x 9- x 2-inch baking dish. Pour wine into dish. Combine mustard, margarine, lemon juice, salt, and pepper. Brush evenly over salmon steaks. Bake, uncovered, at 400° for 20 to 25 minutes or until fish flakes easily when tested with a fork. Broil 6 inches from heat 2 minutes or until lightly browned. **Yield:** 6 servings. **Serving size:** 1 salmon steak.

**Approximate analysis per serving:**
Calories   273
Protein   32 g
Carbohydrate   1 g
Fat   13 g
Saturated Fat   3 g
Polyunsaturated Fat   1 g
Sodium   349 mg
Cholesterol   56 mg

# Poached Mackerel in Chicken Stock

3½   cups ready-to-serve chicken broth
½    cup chopped celery with leaves
½    cup sliced carrot
¼    cup sliced onion
2    tablespoons chopped fresh parsley
1    bay leaf
⅛    teaspoon pepper
4    (¼-pound) Spanish mackerel fillets
Modified Tartar Sauce (recipe follows)
Lemon wedges (optional)

Combine first 7 ingredients in a large skillet, stirring well. Cover and bring to a boil. Reduce heat, and simmer 15 to 18 minutes or until vegetables are tender.

Add fish; cover and simmer gently 20 minutes. Carefully remove fish from liquid with a slotted spatula, and serve each fillet immediately with 2 tablespoons Modified Tartar Sauce and, if desired, lemon wedges. **Yield:** 4 servings. **Serving size:** 1 (3-ounce) fillet with 2 tablespoons Modified Tartar Sauce.

**Approximate analysis per serving:**
Calories   272
Protein   23 g
Carbohydrate   5 g
Fat   21 g
Saturated Fat   4 g
Polyunsaturated Fat   4 g
Sodium   286 mg
Cholesterol   76 mg

**Note:** Cooking liquid may be reserved for use in fish soup or chowder.

**Modified Tartar Sauce:**

⅓  cup reduced-calorie mayonnaise
1   tablespoon chopped onion
1   tablespoon sweet pickle relish
1½ teaspoons lemon juice

Combine mayonnaise, onion, pickle relish, and lemon juice, stirring well to mix. Cover and refrigerate until thoroughly chilled. **Yield:** ½ cup.

# Flounder Fillets with Oat Bran

2   tablespoons minced fresh parsley
2   tablespoons lemon juice
2   teaspoons corn oil margarine, melted
¼   teaspoon salt
⅛   teaspoon pepper
6   (¼-pound) flounder fillets (1-inch thick)
2   tablespoons uncooked, unprocessed oat bran

**Approximate analysis per serving:**
Calories  193
Protein  26 g
Carbohydrate  2 g
Fat  8 g
Saturated Fat  2 g
Polyunsaturated Fat  1 g
Sodium  299 mg
Cholesterol  77 mg

Combine first 5 ingredients, stirring until well combined. Brush mixture evenly over fish.

Cover a broiler pan with aluminum foil. Place in oven 6 inches from heating element; preheat 3 minutes. Arrange fish in preheated pan, and sprinkle evenly with oat bran. Broil 6 inches from heat 10 minutes or until fish flakes easily when tested with a fork. **Yield:** 6 servings. **Serving size:** 1 (3-ounce) fillet.

# Herbed Fish in White Wine

---

¼   cup chopped green onions
2   tablespoons minced fresh parsley
3   tablespoons Chablis or other dry white wine
2   teaspoons corn oil margarine, melted
1   clove garlic, minced
½   teaspoon salt
⅛   teaspoon pepper
4   (¼-pound) lean white fish fillets (flounder, turbot, or orange roughy)

**Approximate analysis per serving:**
Calories   202
Protein   26 g
Carbohydrate   1 g
Fat   9 g
Saturated Fat   2 g
Polyunsaturated Fat   1 g
Sodium   470 mg
Cholesterol   77 mg

Combine onions, parsley, wine, margarine, garlic, salt, and pepper, stirring until well combined. Set aside.

Cover a broiler pan with aluminum foil. Place in oven 6 inches from heating element; preheat 3 minutes. Arrange fish in preheated broiler pan, and pour wine sauce over top. Broil 6 inches from heat 8 minutes or until fish flakes easily when tested with a fork. Serve each fillet with ¼ of wine sauce. **Yield:** 4 servings. **Serving size:** 1 (3-ounce) fillet with ¼ of sauce.

# Baked Fish with Lime

---

4   (¼-pound) lean white fish fillets (flounder, turbot, or orange roughy)
Vegetable cooking spray
¼   cup lime juice
2   tablespoons corn oil margarine
½   teaspoon dried parsley flakes
¼   teaspoon salt
⅛   teaspoon garlic powder
⅛   teaspoon pepper
Lime slices (optional)

**Approximate analysis per serving:**
Calories   230
Protein   26 g
Carbohydrate   2 g
Fat   13 g
Saturated Fat   3 g
Polyunsaturated Fat   2 g
Sodium   395 mg
Cholesterol   77 mg

Arrange fish in a 13- x 9- x 2-inch baking pan coated with cooking spray. Combine lime juice, margarine, parsley, salt, garlic powder, and pepper in a small saucepan. Cook over medium heat until margarine melts and mixture is well blended, stirring frequently.

Pour lime juice mixture evenly over fish. Bake at 375° for 15 minutes or until fish flakes easily when tested with a fork. Transfer fish to a serving platter, and garnish with lime slices, if desired. **Yield:** 4 servings. **Serving size:** 1 (3-ounce) fillet.

# Baked Fish with Crab Sauce

1  pound lean white fish fillets, cut into 8 pieces
   (flounder, turbot, or orange roughy)
½  cup Chablis or other dry white wine
¼  teaspoon white pepper, divided
½  cup chopped fresh mushrooms
¼  cup minced onion
1  tablespoon plus ½ teaspoon corn oil margarine, divided
2  tablespoons all-purpose flour
1  cup evaporated skim milk
¼  teaspoon salt
½  pound fresh crabmeat, drained and flaked
¼  cup (1 ounce) shredded low-fat Monterey Jack cheese

**Approximate analysis per serving:**
Calories   155
Protein   17 g
Carbohydrate   6 g
Fat   6 g
Saturated Fat   2 g
Polyunsaturated Fat   1 g
Sodium   239 mg
Cholesterol   58 mg

Arrange fish in a shallow baking pan, and pour wine over top. Sprinkle fish evenly with ⅛ teaspoon white pepper. Bake at 350° for 20 minutes or until fish flakes easily when tested with a fork.

Sauté mushrooms and onion in 2 teaspoons margarine until tender. Remove from heat, and set aside.

Melt remaining 1½ teaspoons margarine in a heavy saucepan over low heat; add flour, stirring until smooth. Cook 1 minute, stirring constantly. Gradually add milk; cook over medium heat, stirring constantly, until mixture is thickened and bubbly. Add mushroom mixture, salt, and remaining ⅛ teaspoon white pepper, stirring until well combined. Remove sauce from heat, and set aside.

Remove fish from wine with a slotted spatula, and place 1 piece into each of 8 individual ramekins. Sprinkle crabmeat evenly over top of each serving. Top each with 2 tablespoons sauce and 1½ teaspoons cheese. Bake at 350° for 5 minutes or until hot and bubbly and cheese melts. **Yield:** 8 servings. **Serving size:** 1 ramekin.

# Grilled Grouper Kabobs   *(photograph on page 88)*

¼   cup vegetable oil
3   tablespoons finely chopped onion
2   tablespoons minced fresh parsley
2   tablespoons lemon juice
2   tablespoons water
2   cloves garlic, minced
½   teaspoon dried whole thyme
⅛   teaspoon hot sauce
⅛   teaspoon pepper
1   pound grouper fillets, cut into 32 (1-inch) pieces
2   medium-size yellow squash, cut into 16 (¼-inch) slices
1   large green pepper, cut into 16 (1-inch) pieces
16   pearl onions, peeled
16   cherry tomatoes
Vegetable cooking spray

**Approximate analysis per serving:**
Calories   269
Protein   23 g
Carbohydrate   12 g
Fat   16 g
Saturated Fat   2 g
Polyunsaturated Fat   9 g
Sodium   55 mg
Cholesterol   39 mg

Combine oil, onion, parsley, lemon juice, water, garlic, thyme, hot sauce, and ⅛ teaspoon pepper in a zip-top heavy-duty plastic bag. Place fish in bag; and secure tightly, turning bag to coat fish thoroughly with marinade. Marinate in refrigerator 2 hours. Remove fish from marinade, reserving marinade.

Alternate fish, squash, green pepper, pearl onions, and tomatoes on eight 10-inch skewers. Lightly coat cold grill rack with cooking spray. Grill kabobs over medium coals 8 to 12 minutes or until fish flakes easily when tested with a fork. Turn kabobs after 4 minutes, and baste frequently with marinade. **Yield:** 4 servings. **Serving size:** 2 kabobs.

# Salmon Salad

1   (15½-ounce) can red salmon, drained
½   cup chopped green pepper
½   cup diced celery
¼   cup chopped dill pickle
¼   cup reduced-calorie mayonnaise
2   tablespoons lemon juice
Lettuce leaves (optional)
Lemon twist (optional)

**Approximate analysis per serving:**
Calories  183
Protein  16 g
Carbohydrate  3 g
Fat  12 g
Saturated Fat  2 g
Polyunsaturated Fat  tr.
Sodium  345 mg
Cholesterol  30 mg

Remove and discard skin and bones from salmon; flake salmon with a fork. Combine salmon, green pepper, celery, and pickle in a medium bowl; add mayonnaise and lemon juice, stirring well to mix. Cover and chill 2 hours. If desired, transfer salad to a lettuce-lined serving platter, and garnish with a lemon twist. **Yield:** 5 servings. **Serving size:** ½ cup.

# Tuna Salad

1   hard-cooked egg
1   medium-size unpeeled Red Delicious apple
1   (6½-ounce) can white tuna in water, drained and flaked
¼   cup reduced-calorie mayonnaise
2   tablespoons diced celery
1   tablespoon sweet pickle relish
½   teaspoon lemon juice

**Approximate analysis per serving:**
Calories  100
Protein  8 g
Carbohydrate  8 g
Fat  5 g
Saturated Fat  tr.
Polyunsaturated Fat  tr.
Sodium  153 mg
Cholesterol  5 mg

Remove yolk from hard-cooked egg, and discard. Finely chop egg white, and set aside.

Remove core and seeds from apple. Chop half of apple. Set remaining half aside.

Combine egg white, chopped apple, tuna, mayonnaise, celery, pickle relish, and lemon juice; stir until well combined. Cover and chill 2 hours. Cut reserved apple into 8 slices, and use to garnish top of salad. **Yield:** 4 servings. **Serving size:** ½ cup salad with 2 apple slices.

# Salmon Burgers

1   (15½-ounce) can red salmon, undrained and
      flaked
½   cup chopped onion
1   tablespoon corn oil margarine, melted
2   egg whites, slightly beaten
1   cup uncooked, unprocessed oat bran
1   teaspoon prepared mustard
¼   teaspoon salt
¼   cup fine, dry breadcrumbs
1   tablespoon vegetable oil
6   hamburger buns

**Approximate analysis
per serving:**
Calories   354
Protein   24 g
Carbohydrate   34 g
Fat   14 g
Saturated Fat   2 g
Polyunsaturated Fat   3 g
Sodium   576 mg
Cholesterol   33 mg

Place undrained salmon in a medium bowl; mash with a fork to blend. Sauté onion in margarine until transparent. Add onion, egg whites, oat bran, mustard, and salt to salmon, stirring until well combined. Shape into 6 patties. Coat patties evenly with breadcrumbs. Heat oil in a large skillet over medium heat until hot. Add patties to skillet, and cook 5 minutes on each side or until evenly browned. Drain patties on paper towels, and serve on warm hamburger buns. **Yield:** 6 servings. **Serving size:** 1 burger.

# Broiled Tuna-Tomato Sandwiches

1   (7-ounce) can white tuna in water, drained and
      flaked
¼   cup reduced-calorie mayonnaise
2   tablespoons chopped green chiles
2   teaspoons grated onion
1½ teaspoons prepared mustard
¼   teaspoon Worcestershire sauce
3   English muffins, split
6   tomato slices
¼   cup (1 ounce) shredded reduced-fat Cheddar
      cheese

**Approximate analysis
per serving:**
Calories   143
Protein   9 g
Carbohydrate   17 g
Fat   5 g
Saturated Fat   1 g
Polyunsaturated Fat   tr.
Sodium   225 mg
Cholesterol   8 mg

Combine first 6 ingredients, stirring until well combined. Spoon evenly onto cut side of each English muffin half. Top each with a tomato slice, and sprinkle evenly with cheese. Transfer open-face sandwiches to a baking sheet. Broil 4 inches from heat until cheese melts. **Yield:** 6 servings. **Serving size:** 1 open-face sandwich.

# Alabama Catfish Stew

½  cup chopped onion
2  teaspoons corn oil margarine, melted
1  (14½-ounce) can tomatoes, undrained and diced
1  cup diced potato
½  cup catsup
¼  cup water
2  tablespoons Worcestershire sauce
¼  teaspoon pepper
1  bay leaf
1  pound catfish fillets, cut into 1-inch pieces

**Approximate analysis per serving:**
Calories  154
Protein  15 g
Carbohydrate  15 g
Fat  4 g
Saturated Fat  1 g
Polyunsaturated Fat  1 g
Sodium  607 mg
Cholesterol  41 mg

Sauté onion in margarine in a large saucepan until transparent. Add tomatoes and next 6 ingredients to saucepan. Cover and bring to a boil. Reduce heat, and simmer 30 minutes, stirring occasionally.

Gently stir in fish; continue to simmer 20 minutes or until fish flakes easily when tested with a fork. Remove bay leaf before serving. **Yield:** 6 cups. **Serving size:** 1 cup.

# Shrimp Creole

1   tablespoon corn oil margarine
1   tablespoon all-purpose flour
¾   cup chopped green onions
½   cup chopped onion
⅓   cup chopped green pepper
¼   cup chopped celery
1   clove garlic, minced
1   (14-ounce) can Italian-style tomatoes, undrained
1   (8-ounce) can tomato sauce
2   tablespoons chopped fresh parsley
2   tablespoons Worcestershire sauce
1   teaspoon sugar
1   teaspoon salt
¼   teaspoon dried whole basil
¼   teaspoon dried whole thyme
⅛   teaspoon hot sauce
1   (10-ounce) package frozen sliced okra
½   pound peeled and deveined medium-size fresh
      shrimp
4   cups hot cooked rice (cooked without salt or fat)

**Approximate analysis per serving:**
Calories   177
Protein   10 g
Carbohydrate   29 g
Fat   2 g
Saturated Fat   tr.
Polyunsaturated Fat   1 g
Sodium   468 mg
Cholesterol   41 mg

Melt margarine in a large Dutch oven over medium heat; add flour, and cook, stirring constantly, until roux is golden brown. Add chopped onions, green pepper, celery, and garlic to roux; cook, stirring frequently, until vegetables are tender. Stir in tomatoes and next 8 ingredients. Cover and bring to a boil. Reduce heat, and simmer 30 minutes, stirring occasionally.

Add okra to Dutch oven, and cook according to package directions. Stir in shrimp, and cook an additional 5 minutes or until shrimp turn pink. Serve shrimp mixture over rice. **Yield:** 8 servings. **Serving size:** 1 cup shrimp mixture with ½ cup rice.

**Note:** To successfully make a roux, you must use a heavy Dutch oven or skillet which does not have a non-stick surface.

# Shrimp Fettuccine

2   (4-ounce) cans sliced mushrooms, drained
5   green onions, chopped
2   cloves garlic, minced
2   tablespoons corn oil margarine, melted
1   pound peeled and deveined medium-size fresh
    shrimp
1   (8-ounce) package fettuccine
¾   cup grated Romano cheese
¾   cup grated Parmesan cheese
¾   cup skim milk
½   teaspoon salt
¼   cup chopped fresh parsley

**Approximate analysis
per serving:**
Calories   272
Protein   21 g
Carbohydrate   25 g
Fat   9 g
Saturated Fat   4 g
Polyunsaturated Fat   1 g
Sodium   636 mg
Cholesterol   101 mg

Sauté mushrooms, onions, and garlic in margarine in a large skillet 10 minutes. Add shrimp, and sauté 5 minutes or until shrimp turn pink. Remove from heat; cover and keep warm.

Cook fettuccine in a large saucepan according to package directions, omitting salt and fat. Drain off liquid, reserving fettuccine in saucepan.

Add cheeses, milk, and salt to fettuccine, stirring well to mix. Add shrimp mixture and parsley. Toss gently, and serve immediately. **Yield:** 8 servings. **Serving size:** 1 cup.

*Although shellfish had been on the high-cholesterol list, recent research has proved otherwise except for shrimp. Even at 90 milligrams of cholesterol in 3 ounces, a serving of shrimp still contains one third less cholesterol than the yolk of an egg. An additional benefit of all shellfish is that it is low in fat and, consequently, low in calories.*

# Party Seafood Casserole

¾  cup uncooked brown rice
½  cup uncooked wild rice
2  cups sliced fresh mushrooms
1  cup chopped green pepper
½  cup chopped onion
½  cup chopped celery
1  tablespoon corn oil margarine, melted
½  pound peeled and deveined medium-size fresh
   shrimp
½  cup fresh crabmeat, drained and flaked
1  cup ready-to-serve chicken broth
1  cup evaporated skim milk
¼  cup all-purpose flour
2  teaspoons lemon juice
4  drops hot sauce
¼  teaspoon dried parsley flakes
¼  teaspoon salt
⅛  teaspoon pepper
¼  cup fine, dry breadcrumbs

**Approximate analysis
per serving:**
Calories   225
Protein   21 g
Carbohydrate   27 g
Fat   3 g
Saturated Fat   tr.
Polyunsaturated Fat   1 g
Sodium   626 mg
Cholesterol   90 mg

Cook rice according to package directions, omitting salt and fat. Set aside. Sauté mushrooms, green pepper, onion, and celery in margarine in a large skillet until tender. Add shrimp and crabmeat, and cook, stirring frequently, 5 minutes or until shrimp turn pink. Remove from heat, and set aside.

Combine broth and milk in a large saucepan, stirring well. Gradually add flour, beating with a wire whisk until smooth. Cook over medium heat, stirring constantly with whisk, until sauce thickens.

Add shrimp mixture, rice, lemon juice, hot sauce, parsley, salt, and pepper to broth mixture, stirring well to combine. Spoon mixture into a 2-quart casserole. Sprinkle breadcrumbs over top. Bake at 400° for 30 minutes or until hot and bubbly. **Yield:** 8 servings. **Serving size:** 1 cup.

# *Poultry*

Poultry is a good protein choice. It is high in body-building nutrients, low in fat, and easy on the pocketbook. And its versatility makes it appropriate for almost any occasion. The first rule in preparing chicken or turkey for a low-fat, low-cholesterol diet is to remove the skin. The skin and clumps of yellow fat underneath is where most of the fat in poultry accumulates. Then you can prepare it in one of several different ways. If you feel that giving up crispy fried chicken is too much of a hardship, try baking your chicken in the oven with a crispy coating. Brush the chicken pieces all over with reduced-calorie mayonnaise and then lightly roll the pieces in fat-free breadcrumbs before baking or broiling. When broiling or grilling poultry of any kind, place the pieces on a rack or broiling pan so that the fat that remains after you have removed the skin drains off. Also, if you enjoy stir-fry dishes, the quick-cook quality and mild flavor of poultry will make a delicious addition to your stir-fry.

# Chicken Cacciatore

2    tablespoons olive oil
1    (2½- to 3-pound) broiler-fryer, skinned and cut up
1½ cups sliced onion
2    (14½-ounce) cans whole tomatoes, undrained and
        chopped
1    clove garlic, halved
1    teaspoon salt
¼    teaspoon white pepper
3    cups hot cooked spaghetti (cooked without salt or
        fat)

**Approximate analysis
per serving:**
Calories   367
Protein   33 g
Carbohydrate   30 g
Fat   12 g
Saturated Fat   3 g
Polyunsaturated Fat   2 g
Sodium   602 mg
Cholesterol   84 mg

Heat olive oil in a large Dutch oven over medium heat;
add chicken, and cook until lightly browned, turning frequently to brown pieces evenly. Add onion to Dutch oven,
and cook until tender. Stir in tomatoes, garlic, salt, and
pepper. Cover and bring to a boil. Reduce heat, and
simmer 40 to 45 minutes or until chicken is done.

Remove chicken from Dutch oven, and keep warm.
Increase heat to high, and cook until volume of sauce is
reduced and thickened. Remove garlic, and serve chicken
and sauce over spaghetti. **Yield:** 6 servings. **Serving size:**
⅙ of chicken and sauce with ½ cup spaghetti.

# Chicken Chow Mein

1½ pounds chicken breast halves, skinned
6    cups water
1    Bouquet Garni (see page 56)
2    tablespoons corn oil margarine
1    small green pepper, seeded and cut into thin strips
½    cup sliced onion
½    cup diced celery
¼    cup sliced fresh mushrooms
1    tablespoon low-sodium soy sauce
2    tablespoons cornstarch
1    tablespoon cold water
1    (16-ounce) can bean sprouts, drained
3    cups hot cooked rice (cooked without salt or fat)

**Approximate analysis
per serving:**
Calories   294
Protein   28 g
Carbohydrate   27 g
Fat   7 g
Saturated Fat   2 g
Polyunsaturated Fat   2 g
Sodium   338 mg
Cholesterol   67 mg

Place chicken in a Dutch oven; add water and Bouquet Garni. Cover and bring to a boil. Reduce heat, and simmer 25 minutes or until chicken is done.

Remove chicken and Bouquet Garni from broth, reserving 2 cups broth. Discard Bouquet Garni. Chill reserved broth, and skim congealed fat from surface. Bone chicken, and cut chicken into bite-size pieces; set aside.

Melt margarine in a large skillet over medium heat; add green pepper and next 3 ingredients, and cook until tender and slightly browned. Add broth and soy sauce to vegetable mixture, stirring until well combined. Dissolve cornstarch in cold water. Add to liquid in skillet; bring to a boil. Boil 1 minute or until mixture thickens, stirring constantly. Stir in chicken and bean sprouts; cook over low heat until heated. Serve chicken mixture over rice. **Yield:** 6 servings. **Serving size:** 1 cup chicken mixture with ½ cup rice.

# Barbecued Chicken Breasts

1    cup tomato juice
½    cup catsup
¼    cup sugar
2    tablespoons vinegar
2    tablespoons lemon juice
2    tablespoons Worcestershire sauce
2    tablespoons prepared mustard
¼    teaspoon salt
¾    teaspoon pepper
4    (¼-pound) chicken breast halves, skinned

**Approximate analysis per serving:**
Calories   156
Protein   24 g
Carbohydrate   6 g
Fat   3 g
Saturated Fat   1 g
Polyunsaturated Fat   1 g
Sodium   327 mg
Cholesterol   67 mg

Combine first 9 ingredients in a large saucepan, stirring to blend. Bring to a boil. Boil until sugar dissolves and mixture is well blended, stirring constantly. Remove barbecue sauce from heat, and let cool.

Pour 1½ cups sauce over chicken in shallow dish. Set remaining ½ cup sauce aside. Cover and marinate chicken in refrigerator 2 to 4 hours. Discard marinade.

Place chicken on grill over medium coals. Grill 50 to 55 minutes or until chicken is done, turning and basting with reserved barbecue sauce every 10 minutes. **Yield:** 4 servings. **Serving size**: 1 chicken breast half with 2 tablespoons sauce.

# Chicken Divan Casserole

1½ pounds chicken breast halves, skinned
6   cups water
1   Bouquet Garni (see page 56)
2   (10-ounce) packages frozen broccoli spears
2   tablespoons corn oil margarine
¼   cup plus 1 tablespoon all-purpose flour
½   cup evaporated skim milk
3   tablespoons cooking sherry
½   teaspoon salt
⅛   teaspoon white pepper
¼   cup grated Parmesan cheese, divided

**Approximate analysis per serving:**
Calories   241
Protein   29 g
Carbohydrate   12 g
Fat   8 g
Saturated Fat   2 g
Polyunsaturated Fat   2 g
Sodium   362 mg
Cholesterol   64 mg

Place chicken in a Dutch oven; add water and Bouquet Garni. Cover and bring to a boil. Reduce heat, and simmer 25 minutes or until chicken is done. Remove chicken and Bouquet Garni from broth, reserving 2 cups broth. Discard Bouquet Garni. Chill reserved broth, and skim congealed fat from surface. Bone and slice chicken; set aside.

Cook broccoli according to package directions. Drain well. Arrange broccoli spears crosswise in a 13- x 9- x 2-inch baking dish. Set aside. Melt margarine in a large skillet over low heat; add flour, stirring until smooth. Cook 1 minute, stirring constantly. Gradually add reserved broth; cook over medium heat, stirring constantly, until mixture is thickened and bubbly. Remove from heat, and stir in milk, sherry, salt, and pepper.

Pour half of sauce over broccoli, and top with chicken slices. Add 2 tablespoons cheese to remaining sauce in skillet; stir until well blended, and pour over chicken. Sprinkle with remaining 2 tablespoons cheese, and bake at 350° for 20 minutes or until casserole is thoroughly heated and top is golden brown. **Yield:** 6 servings. **Serving size:** ⅙ of casserole.

# Chicken à la King

1 pound chicken breast halves, skinned
5 cups water
1 Bouquet Garni (see page 56)
2 tablespoons corn oil margarine
3 tablespoons all-purpose flour
1 cup skim milk
¼ cup chopped pimiento
½ teaspoon salt
½ teaspoon paprika
¼ teaspoon pepper
2 cups hot cooked rice (cooked without salt or fat)

**Approximate analysis per serving:**
Calories  331
Protein  29 g
Carbohydrate  30 g
Fat  9 g
Saturated Fat  2 g
Polyunsaturated Fat  3 g
Sodium  406 mg
Cholesterol  68 mg

Place chicken in a Dutch oven; add water and Bouquet Garni. Cover and bring to a boil. Reduce heat, and simmer 25 minutes or until chicken is done. Remove chicken and Bouquet Garni from broth, reserving 1 cup broth. Discard Bouquet Garni. Chill reserved broth, and skim congealed fat from surface. Bone chicken, and cut chicken into bite-size pieces; set aside.

Melt margarine in a 2-quart saucepan over low heat; add flour, stirring until smooth. Cook 1 minute, stirring constantly. Gradually add reserved broth and milk; cook over medium heat, stirring constantly, until mixture is thickened and bubbly. Add pimiento, salt, paprika, and pepper, stirring to mix. Stir in chicken, and continue to cook until thoroughly heated. Serve chicken mixture over rice. **Yield:**  4 servings. **Serving size:** 1 cup chicken mixture with ½ cup rice.

# Crispy Baked Chicken Breasts

4   (¼-pound) boneless and skinless chicken breast
     halves
3   tablespoons reduced-calorie mayonnaise
½   cup Italian-seasoned breadcrumbs
Vegetable cooking spray

**Approximate analysis
per serving:**
Calories   246
Protein   34 g
Carbohydrate   10 g
Fat   7 g
Saturated Fat   1 g
Polyunsaturated Fat   1 g
Sodium   245 mg
Cholesterol   90 mg

Brush chicken breast halves with mayonnaise. Dredge chicken in breadcrumbs, and place on rack of a broiler pan coated with cooking spray. Bake at 425° for 15 to 20 minutes or until chicken is done and coating is crispy. **Yield:** 4 servings. **Serving size:** 1 chicken breast half.

# Baked Chicken and Vegetables

Vegetable cooking spray
2   medium onions, sliced
4   (¼-pound) boneless and skinless chicken breast
     halves
1   tablespoon plus 1 teaspoon Dijon mustard
¼   teaspoon salt
⅛   teaspoon pepper
4   cups sliced yellow squash
1   cup sliced fresh mushrooms
8   cherry tomatoes, halved
1   teaspoon dried whole basil
1   clove garlic, minced
1   tablespoon plus 1 teaspoon corn oil margarine

**Approximate analysis
per serving:**
Calories   272
Protein   35 g
Carbohydrate   15 g
Fat   8 g
Saturated Fat   2 g
Polyunsaturated Fat   2 g
Sodium   246 mg
Cholesterol   84 mg

Cut 4 (18- x 12-inch) sheets heavy-duty aluminum foil, and coat each sheet with cooking spray. Arrange one-fourth of sliced onion evenly in center of each sheet of foil; top each with a chicken breast half. Spread 1 teaspoon mustard over each breast half, and sprinkle evenly with salt and pepper. Top each with one-fourth of squash, mushrooms, and tomatoes; sprinkle evenly with basil and garlic. Dot each with 1 teaspoon margarine.

Fold edges of foil over, and wrap securely. Place packets on an ungreased baking sheet. Bake at 400° for 25 to 30 minutes. Serve in foil packets. **Yield:** 4 servings. **Serving size:** 1 packet.

# Gingered Chicken

4  (¼-pound) boneless and skinless chicken breast halves
½  cup commercial oil-free Italian dressing
¼  cup low-sugar orange marmalade
1  teaspoon ground ginger
⅛  teaspoon pepper

Place chicken in a 9-inch square baking dish. Pour Italian dressing over chicken, turning to coat evenly. Cover and marinate in refrigerator at least 3 hours, turning occasionally. Drain and discard marinade, reserving chicken in dish.

Combine orange marmalade, ginger, and pepper, stirring to blend; brush marmalade mixture evenly over chicken breast halves. Bake, uncovered, at 350° for 40 to 50 minutes or until chicken is done. **Yield:** 4 servings. **Serving size:** 1 chicken breast half.

**Approximate analysis per serving:**
Calories  221
Protein  35 g
Carbohydrate  9 g
Fat  4 g
Saturated Fat  1 g
Polyunsaturated Fat  1 g
Sodium  504 mg
Cholesterol  95 mg

# Party Chicken

¾  cup Chablis or other dry white wine
¼  cup lemon juice
1  tablespoon dried whole salad herbs
¼  teaspoon pepper
4  (¼-pound) boneless and skinless chicken breast halves
1  (14-ounce) can artichoke hearts, drained and quartered
1  cup sliced fresh mushrooms
2  cups hot cooked rice (cooked without salt or fat)

Combine wine, lemon juice, and seasonings in a large skillet, stirring until well combined. Add chicken. Cover and bring to a boil. Reduce heat, and simmer 45 minutes or until chicken is done. Add artichoke hearts and mushrooms; continue to simmer, stirring frequently, until thoroughly heated. Serve chicken and vegetable mixture over rice. **Yield:** 4 servings. **Serving size:** 1 chicken breast half and ¼ of vegetable mixture with ½ cup rice.

**Approximate analysis per serving:**
Calories  314
Protein  36 g
Carbohydrate  26 g
Fat  4 g
Saturated Fat  1 g
Polyunsaturated Fat  1 g
Sodium  107 mg
Cholesterol  85 mg

# Company Chicken Salad

½ cup reduced-calorie mayonnaise
1 tablespoon white wine vinegar
1 tablespoon low-sodium soy sauce
2 teaspoons lemon juice
½ teaspoon curry powder
½ teaspoon ground ginger
2 cups diced cooked chicken breast (skinned before cooking and cooked without salt)
1 cup seedless green grapes
½ (8-ounce) can sliced water chestnuts, drained
¼ cup chopped pecans
2 tablespoons diced celery

**Approximate analysis per serving:**
Calories  298
Protein  26 g
Carbohydrate  14 g
Fat  16 g
Saturated Fat  1 g
Polyunsaturated Fat  2 g
Sodium  392 mg
Cholesterol  76 mg

Combine first 6 ingredients in a medium bowl, stirring until well blended. Add chicken, grapes, water chestnuts, pecans, and celery to mayonnaise mixture. Toss lightly to coat well. Cover and refrigerate 2 to 3 hours before serving. **Yield:** 4 servings. **Serving size:** 1 cup.

# Chicken Florentine

1 (10-ounce) package frozen chopped spinach
2 tablespoons corn oil margarine
3 tablespoons all-purpose flour
1½ cups skim milk
½ cup (2 ounces) shredded Swiss cheese
¾ teaspoon salt
⅛ teaspoon red pepper
2 cups diced cooked chicken breast (skinned before cooking and cooked without salt)
⅓ cup fine, dry breadcrumbs

**Approximate analysis per serving:**
Calories  369
Protein  35 g
Carbohydrate  20 g
Fat  16 g
Saturated Fat  5 g
Polyunsaturated Fat  3 g
Sodium  716 mg
Cholesterol  85 mg

Cook spinach according to package directions, and drain well. Place in a 1½-quart casserole; set aside.

Melt margarine in a medium saucepan over low heat; add flour, stirring until smooth. Cook 1 minute, stirring constantly. Gradually add milk; cook over medium heat, stirring constantly, until mixture is thickened and bubbly.

Stir in cheese, salt, and pepper; cook over low heat, stirring constantly, until cheese melts. Remove from heat, and add chicken.

Pour creamed chicken mixture over spinach in casserole. Sprinkle with breadcrumbs, and bake at 350° for 15 minutes or until top is lightly browned and mixture is bubbly. **Yield:** 4 servings. **Serving size:** 1 cup

# Sweet-and-Sour Chicken

1   (15½-ounce) can unsweetened pineapple chunks, undrained
¼   cup firmly packed brown sugar
1   tablespoon cornstarch
¼   teaspoon salt
¼   cup vinegar
3   tablespoons low-sodium soy sauce
3   cups diced cooked chicken breast (skinned before cooking and cooked without salt)
½   cup diagonally sliced celery
½   cup chopped green pepper
⅓   cup sliced onion
2   tablespoons diced pimiento
2½ cups hot cooked rice (cooked without salt or fat)

**Approximate analysis per serving:**
Calories   353
Protein   32 g
Carbohydrate   46 g
Fat   4 g
Saturated Fat   1 g
Polyunsaturated Fat   1 g
Sodium   430 mg
Cholesterol   80 mg

Drain pineapple, reserving juice. Set pineapple chunks aside. Combine brown sugar, cornstarch, and salt in a large saucepan. Add pineapple juice, vinegar, and soy sauce, stirring until well blended. Bring to a boil over high heat, stirring constantly. Reduce heat to medium, and cook until mixture thickens. Remove from heat, and add chicken, pineapple chunks, celery, green pepper, and onion. Continue to cook over medium heat 5 minutes, stirring constantly. Add pimiento, and cook 1 additional minute. Serve chicken mixture over rice. **Yield:** 5 servings. **Serving size:** ¾ cup chicken mixture with ½ cup rice.

# Vegetable-Stuffed Turkey Tenderloin

1½ slices whole wheat bread
Vegetable cooking spray
½   teaspoon garlic powder
2   (¾-pound) turkey breast tenderloins
⅓   cup ready-to-serve chicken broth
2   tablespoons chopped onion
2   tablespoons chopped celery
2   tablespoons chopped sweet red pepper
⅛   teaspoon salt
⅛   teaspoon pepper
¼   cup ready-to-serve chicken broth
1   tablespoon minced fresh parsley

**Approximate analysis per serving:**
Calories   218
Protein   37 g
Carbohydrate   6 g
Fat   4 g
Saturated Fat   1 g
Polyunsaturated Fat   1 g
Sodium   185 mg
Cholesterol   82 mg

Trim crust from bread, and cut bread into ½-inch cubes. Coat an 8-inch square baking pan with cooking spray. Arrange bread cubes in a single layer in pan. Lightly spray bread cubes with cooking spray, and sprinkle evenly with garlic powder. Bake at 200° for 1 hour, stirring every 15 minutes. Remove from oven, and set aside.

Cut a lengthwise slit along thickest side of each turkey tenderloin to make a pocket for stuffing. Combine toasted bread cubes, ⅓ cup broth, and next 3 ingredients, stirring well to moisten. Stuff mixture evenly into tenderloin pockets, and secure with wooden picks. Transfer stuffed tenderloins to a shallow baking dish coated with cooking spray. Sprinkle evenly with salt and pepper.

Bake, uncovered, at 350° for 50 minutes or until turkey is no longer pink and stuffing is thoroughly heated. Baste with ¼ cup broth at 15-minute intervals. Remove from oven, and sprinkle evenly with parsley. Remove wooden picks, and cut each tenderloin into 8 slices to serve. **Yield:** 4 servings. **Serving size:** 4 slices

# Turkey Tenderloin Amandine (*photograph on page 189*)

1   tablespoon corn oil margarine
2   (¾-pound) turkey breast tenderloins
¼   teaspoon grated lemon rind
1   tablespoon lemon juice
1   tablespoon sliced almonds

**Approximate analysis per serving:**
Calories   278
Protein   38 g
Carbohydrate   7 g
Fat   13 g
Saturated Fat   2 g
Polyunsaturated Fat   2 g
Sodium   151 mg
Cholesterol   85 mg

Melt margarine in a nonstick skillet over medium heat. Add turkey, and brown evenly on both sides. Add lemon rind and juice. Cover and continue to cook 15 minutes or until turkey is no longer pink, turning once.

Transfer turkey tenderloins to a small serving platter, and keep warm. Add almonds to skillet, and sauté until lightly browned. Pour almond mixture over tenderloins, and cut in half to serve. **Yield:** 2 servings. **Serving size:** 1 turkey tenderloin half.

# Braised Turkey Breast Cutlets

2   teaspoons corn oil margarine
2   teaspoons vegetable oil
2   cloves garlic, halved
8   (2-ounce) turkey breast cutlets
1½ cups sliced fresh mushrooms
½   cup Chablis or other dry white wine
¼   cup sliced green onions
⅛   teaspoon salt
⅛   teaspoon pepper

**Approximate analysis per serving:**
Calories   199
Protein   25 g
Carbohydrate   3 g
Fat   7 g
Saturated Fat   1 g
Polyunsaturated Fat   3 g
Sodium   137 mg
Cholesterol   56 mg

Heat margarine and oil in a large skillet over medium-high heat. Add garlic, and sauté until lightly browned. Discard garlic, and add turkey to skillet. Cook turkey 2 minutes; turn and cook 1 additional minute. Add mushrooms, wine, onions, salt, and pepper. Cover and bring to a boil. Reduce heat, and simmer 3 to 4 minutes or until turkey is no longer pink and vegetables are tender. **Yield:** 4 servings. **Serving size:** 2 cutlets with ¼ of vegetables.

# Breaded Turkey Breast Cutlets

1    egg white
3    tablespoons water, divided
¼    cup fine, dry breadcrumbs
⅛    teaspoon salt
4    (2-ounce) turkey breast cutlets
1    tablespoon vegetable oil

**Approximate analysis per serving:**
Calories   246
Protein   28 g
Carbohydrate   10 g
Fat   10 g
Saturated Fat   2 g
Polyunsaturated Fat   4 g
Sodium   284 mg
Cholesterol   56 mg

Combine egg white and 1 tablespoon water, stirring with a fork to blend. Combine breadcrumbs and salt, stirring well. Dip turkey in egg white mixture, and dredge in breadcrumb mixture.

Heat oil in a large skillet. Add turkey cutlets, and brown evenly on both sides. Reduce heat, and add remaining 2 tablespoons water to skillet. Cover and simmer 10 minutes or until meat is no longer pink. **Yield:** 2 servings. **Serving size:** 2 cutlets.

# Turkey Patties in Chunky Tomato Sauce

1    pound ground fresh turkey
1    egg white
⅓    cup fine, dry breadcrumbs
½    teaspoon garlic powder
⅛    teaspoon pepper
Vegetable cooking spray
Chunky Tomato Sauce (recipe follows)
¼    cup grated fresh Parmesan cheese

**Approximate analysis per serving:**
Calories   192
Protein   24 g
Carbohydrate   16 g
Fat   4 g
Saturated Fat   1 g
Polyunsaturated Fat   1 g
Sodium   277 mg
Cholesterol   71 mg

Combine turkey, egg white, breadcrumbs, garlic powder, and pepper in a medium bowl; stir until well combined. Shape mixture into 6 patties, and place on rack of a broiler pan coated with cooking spray. Bake at 350° for 15 to 20 minutes.

Transfer patties to a shallow baking dish, and pour Chunky Tomato Sauce over top. Bake at 350° for 15 minutes. Top with cheese, and bake an additional 4 minutes or until cheese melts. **Yield:** 6 patties. **Serving size:** 1 patty plus ½ cup Chunky Tomato Sauce.

**Chunky Tomato Sauce:**

1   (14½-ounce) can Italian-style tomatoes, undrained
1   cup water
1   (6-ounce) can tomato paste
1   medium onion, sliced
¼   cup minced fresh parsley
1   clove garlic, minced
1   bay leaf
½   teaspoon sugar
½   teaspoon dried whole basil
½   teaspoon dried whole thyme
¼   teaspoon pepper

Combine all ingredients in a large saucepan, stirring until well combined; bring to a boil. Reduce heat, and simmer, uncovered, 45 minutes or until thickened, stirring frequently. Remove bay leaf before serving. **Yield:** 3 cups.

# Turkey Pita Sandwiches *(photograph on page 20)*

¼   cup plain low-fat yogurt
¼   cup reduced-calorie mayonnaise
2   tablespoons Dijon mustard
2   (6-inch) whole wheat pita bread rounds, cut in half
½   medium cucumber, peeled and thinly sliced
1   cup shredded lettuce
½   cup chopped fresh broccoli
½   cup coarsely chopped tomato
½   cup shredded carrot
½   cup (2 ounces) shredded part-skim mozzarella
       cheese
¼   pound thinly sliced cooked turkey breast, cut into
       ¼-inch strips (skinned before cooking and
       cooked without salt)

**Approximate analysis per serving:**
Calories   208
Protein   16 g
Carbohydrate   17 g
Fat   8 g
Saturated Fat   2 g
Polyunsaturated Fat   tr.
Sodium   430 mg
Cholesterol   32 mg

Combine first 3 ingredients in a large bowl, stirring until well blended. Spread 1 tablespoon yogurt mixture inside each pita bread half. Add vegetables, cheese, and turkey to remaining yogurt mixture in bowl; toss gently to coat well. Spoon mixture evenly into pita bread halves. **Yield:** 4 servings. **Serving size:** 1 sandwich half.

# Turkey Reuben Sandwiches

1    tablespoon plus 1 teaspoon prepared mustard
4    slices rye bread
2    (2-ounce) slices cooked turkey breast (skinned
        before cooking and cooked without salt)
1    (1-ounce) slice Swiss cheese, halved
¼    cup sauerkraut, drained
Vegetable cooking spray

**Approximate analysis
per serving:**
Calories   265
Protein   26 g
Carbohydrate   26 g
Fat   7 g
Saturated Fat   3 g
Polyunsaturated Fat   1 g
Sodium   669 mg
Cholesterol   52 mg

Spread mustard evenly on each slice of bread. Place 1 turkey slice on 2 bread slices. Top each with cheese slice, 2 tablespoons sauerkraut, and a slice of rye bread.

Coat a large skillet with cooking spray; place over medium heat until hot. Add sandwiches, and cook 3 to 4 minutes on each side or until bread is evenly toasted. Serve sandwiches immediately. **Yield:** 2 sandwiches. **Serving size:** 1 sandwich.

# Apricot-Glazed Cornish Hens

2    (1- to 1¼-pound) Cornish hens, skinned
¼    cup chopped celery
2    tablespoons chopped onion
2    teaspoons corn oil margarine, melted
2    tablespoons all-fruit apricot spread
2    teaspoons hot water

**Approximate analysis
per serving:**
Calories   268
Protein   41 g
Carbohydrate   4 g
Fat   9 g
Saturated Fat   2 g
Polyunsaturated Fat   3 g
Sodium   151 mg
Cholesterol   149 mg

Remove giblets from hens, and reserve for use in another recipe. Rinse hens with cold water, and pat dry.

Place half each of celery and onion in cavity of each hen. Close cavities, and secure with wooden picks; truss. Brush hens evenly with margarine, and place breast side up on a rack in a shallow roasting pan. Make a tent of aluminum foil, and place over breast portion of each hen. Bake at 400° for 1 hour or until done.

Remove hens from oven, and remove foil. Combine apricot spread and hot water, stirring until blended. Brush hens evenly with apricot glaze mixture, and broil 6 inches from heat 3 minutes or until lightly browned. Using an electric knife, split each hen in half lengthwise before serving. **Yield:** 4 servings. **Serving size:** 1 hen half.

# *Meats*

Lean cuts of meat may be less tender than meats you're accustomed to buying, so consider appropriate changes in cooking them. Cook over low heat just until tender and do not pierce the meat with a fork or knife. Both these steps will help to retain juiciness and promote tenderness. To achieve an even more tender meat product, consider braising. Braising means to brown the meat, and then simmer slowly in a small amount of water, wine, or fruit juice (sometimes only a couple of tablespoons) in a covered skillet, usually turning the meat only once. Another aid in tenderizing leaner cuts is to marinate. Marinades can be as simple as a commercially bottled oil-free Italian salad dressing, or you can create your own. Start with a few fruit berries (blueberries, strawberries, or raspberries), and let them sit in white or wine vinegar at room temperature for several days until a fruit-flavored vinegar is formed. Then use this vinegar as the base for your marinade, knowing that you are beginning with a cholesterol-free, sodium-free ingredient.

# Greek-Style Beef

1    (1½-pound) lean boneless round roast
2    tablespoons olive oil
1½ cups water, divided
1    (14½-ounce) can whole tomatoes, undrained
1    (8-ounce) can tomato sauce
⅓    cup red cooking wine
¼    cup red wine vinegar
3    whole cloves
2    cloves garlic, minced
1    (3-inch) stick cinnamon
1    bay leaf
1½ teaspoons brown sugar
½    teaspoon salt
⅛    teaspoon pepper
8    small yellow onions
¼    cup chopped fresh parsley
1½ teaspoons all-purpose flour
3    cups hot cooked noodles (cooked without salt or
       fat)

**Approximate analysis
per serving:**
Calories   440
Protein   38 g
Carbohydrate   43 g
Fat   13 g
Saturated Fat   4 g
Polyunsaturated Fat   1 g
Sodium   586 mg
Cholesterol   89 mg

Trim fat from roast, and cut roast into 1-inch cubes. Heat oil in an ovenproof Dutch oven over medium heat until hot. Add meat, and cook, stirring constantly, until evenly browned. Add 1 cup water, tomatoes, tomato sauce, wine, vinegar, cloves, garlic, cinnamon, bay leaf, brown sugar, salt, and pepper to Dutch oven, stirring gently to mix.

Peel onions, and cut a small x in stem ends. Arrange onions on top of meat in Dutch oven. Cover and bring to a boil. Transfer to oven, and bake at 300° for 1½ hours or until meat is tender. Add parsley during last 15 minutes of baking. Remove from oven.

Combine remaining ½ cup water and flour, stirring until well blended. Gently stir into meat mixture, and cook over medium heat until liquid thickens. Remove whole spices and bay leaf before serving. Serve meat mixture over noodles. **Yield:** 6 servings. **Serving size:** 1 cup meat mixture with ½ cup noodles.

# Pot Roast

2 pounds lean boneless round roast
1 teaspoon pepper
1 tablespoon vegetable oil
2 cups water
1 cup Burgundy or other dry red wine
¼ cup chopped fresh parsley
1 teaspoon salt
1 teaspoon Worcestershire sauce
4 whole cloves
4 medium potatoes, unpeeled and cut into quarters
4 medium carrots, scraped and cut into 1-inch pieces
2½ cups coarsely chopped onion
2 cups canned, undrained tomatoes
1 cup diced celery
Fresh parsley sprigs (optional)

**Approximate analysis per serving:**
Calories 428
Protein 45 g
Carbohydrate 30 g
Fat 11 g
Saturated Fat 4 g
Polyunsaturated Fat 2 g
Sodium 624 mg
Cholesterol 119 mg

Trim fat from roast, and rub roast with pepper. Heat oil in a Dutch oven over medium heat until hot. Add meat, and cook 1 to 2 minutes on each side to brown evenly. Add water, wine, chopped parsley, salt, Worcestershire sauce, cloves, potato, carrot, onion, tomatoes, and celery to Dutch oven, stirring gently to mix. (Liquid should just cover vegetables; add additional water, if necessary.) Cover and bring to a boil. Reduce heat, and simmer 2½ hours or until meat is tender.

Transfer meat and vegetables to a serving platter. Garnish with parsley sprigs, if desired. Slice meat into 4½-ounce servings. Divide vegetables into 1 cup servings. **Yield:** 6 servings. **Serving size:** 4½ ounces meat with 1 cup vegetables.

# Sirloin Tip Roast with Peppercorns

1    (2½-pound) lean boneless sirloin tip roast
2    cloves garlic, crushed
2    teaspoons crushed black peppercorns
½    cup water
2    tablespoons all-purpose flour
⅛    teaspoon salt

Trim fat from roast. Combine garlic and peppercorns; press half of mixture into each side of roast. Place roast in a 13- x 9- x 2-inch baking dish, and add ½ cup water. Insert meat thermometer into thickest part of meat. Bake, uncovered, at 300° for 1 hour or until meat thermometer registers 140° for rare or 160° for medium. Let roast stand 20 minutes before carving.

Transfer meat juices to a 1-cup glass measure, and chill. Skim and discard fat from surface; add water to juices to yield ¾ cup. Combine ¼ cup meat juice mixture and flour in a small saucepan, stirring until well blended. Gradually stir in remaining ½ cup meat juice mixture and salt. Cook over medium heat, stirring constantly, until gravy is thickened. Slice meat into 3-ounce servings, and top each with 1 tablespoon plus 1½ teaspoons gravy. **Yield:** 8 servings. **Serving size:** 3 ounces meat with 1 tablespoon plus 1½ teaspoons gravy.

**Approximate analysis per serving:**
Calories   205
Protein   28 g
Carbohydrate   2 g
Fat   9 g
Saturated Fat   4 g
Polyunsaturated Fat   tr.
Sodium   69 mg
Cholesterol   83 mg

# Marinated Filet Mignon

½    cup commercial oil-free Italian dressing
½    cup vinegar
¼    cup Worcestershire sauce
1    tablespoon dry mustard
2    tablespoons lemon juice
2    tablespoons low-sodium soy sauce
1    teaspoon pepper
1    teaspoon dried parsley flakes
6    (4-ounce) beef tenderloin steaks, well trimmed
Vegetable cooking spray

**Approximate analysis per serving:**
Calories 215
Protein   24 g
Carbohydrate   3 g
Fat   11 g
Saturated Fat   5 g
Polyunsaturated Fat   1 g
Sodium   339 mg
Cholesterol   84 mg

Combine first 8 ingredients in a heavy-duty zip-top plastic bag. Place steaks in bag, and secure tightly; turn bag to coat steaks thoroughly with marinade.

Marinate in refrigerator 3 hours. Remove steaks from marinade, reserving marinade.

Lightly coat grill rack with cooking spray. Grill steaks over hot coals 5 to 7 minutes on each side or to desired degree of doneness, basting frequently with marinade. **Yield:** 6 servings. **Serving size:** 1 tenderloin steak.

# Barbecued Round Steak

1   pound lean boneless round steak
1   tablespoon vegetable oil
¾   cup vinegar
½   cup catsup
2   tablespoons Worcestershire sauce
1   clove garlic, minced
1   teaspoon sugar
1   teaspoon dry mustard
1   teaspoon paprika
½   teaspoon salt
¼   teaspoon pepper

**Approximate analysis
per serving:**
Calories   178
Protein   21 g
Carbohydrate   9 g
Fat   7 g
Saturated Fat   2 g
Polyunsaturated Fat   2 g
Sodium   477 mg
Cholesterol   60 mg

Trim fat from steak, and cut steak crosswise into 1-inch-wide strips. Heat oil in a large skillet over medium heat until hot. Add meat, and cook, stirring constantly, until meat is evenly browned. Drain meat, and pat dry with paper towels. Transfer meat to an 8-inch square baking dish, and set aside.

Wipe pan drippings from skillet with paper towels. Combine vinegar and remaining ingredients in skillet. Bring to a boil. Reduce heat, and simmer, uncovered, 3 minutes. Pour sauce over meat. Cover and bake at 350° for 1 hour or until meat is tender. Slice meat into 2¼-ounce servings, and top each serving with ¼ cup sauce. **Yield:** 6 servings. **Serving size:** 2¼ ounces meat with ¼ cup sauce.

# Creole Steak

Vegetable cooking spray
1    pound lean boneless round steak, well trimmed
1    large onion, chopped
1    medium-size green pepper, chopped
2    tablespoons all-purpose flour
2    (16-ounce) cans whole tomatoes, undrained and
        chopped
1    cup water
¼    cup chopped fresh parsley
1    clove garlic, minced
1    bay leaf
¼    teaspoon sugar
¼    teaspoon salt
3    cups hot cooked rice (cooked without salt or fat)

**Approximate analysis
per serving:**
Calories   269
Protein   24 g
Carbohydrate   32 g
Fat   4 g
Saturated Fat  2 g
Polyunsaturated Fat   tr.
Sodium   266 mg
Cholesterol   60 mg

Coat a large skillet with cooking spray; place over medium heat until hot. Add meat, and brown evenly on both sides. Remove meat from skillet, and drain well on paper towels.

Coat skillet with cooking spray. Add onion, green pepper, and flour. Cook over medium heat, stirring constantly, until vegetables are tender and flour is browned. Add tomatoes, water, parsley, garlic, bay leaf, sugar, and salt to skillet. Cook over low heat  30 minutes. If more liquid is needed, add an additional ¼ cup water. Add meat to sauce in skillet, and continue to cook over low heat 1 hour or until meat is tender. Remove bay leaf before serving. Cut meat into 6 equal pieces. Serve meat with sauce over rice. **Yield:** 6 servings. **Serving size:** 1 piece of meat with ⅙ of sauce and ½ cup rice.

# Beef Stroganoff

1   pound lean boneless round steak, well trimmed
Vegetable cooking spray
½   cup sliced onion
2   (4-ounce) cans sliced mushrooms, drained
2   beef-flavored bouillon cubes
1½ cups boiling water
2   tablespoons catsup
¼   teaspoon pepper
¾   cup water
3   tablespoons all-purpose flour
1   (8-ounce) carton low-fat sour cream
3   cups hot cooked noodles (cooked without salt or
      fat)

**Approximate analysis
per serving:**
Calories   277
Protein   25 g
Carbohydrate   17 g
Fat   11 g
Saturated Fat   8 g
Polyunsaturated Fat   tr.
Sodium   534 mg
Cholesterol   70 mg

Partially freeze steak, and slice diagonally across grain into 3- x ¼-inch strips.

Coat a large skillet with cooking spray, and place over medium heat until hot. Add meat, and cook, stirring constantly, until evenly browned. Remove meat from skillet, and set aside.

Add onion and mushrooms to skillet. Sauté until vegetables are tender. Dissolve bouillon cubes in 1½ cups boiling water, and add to skillet with catsup and pepper, stirring well. Return browned meat to skillet; reduce heat to low, and cook until mixture is thoroughly heated, stirring occasionally.

Combine ¾ cup water and flour, stirring until well blended. Stir into meat mixture, and cook over medium heat until mixture thickens, stirring constantly. Reduce heat to low, and add sour cream. Stir gently to blend. Serve meat mixture over noodles. **Yield:** 6 servings. **Serving size:** ½ cup meat mixture with ½ cup noodles.

# Beef Burgundy

1     pound lean boneless sirloin steak
1     tablespoon vegetable oil
1     clove garlic, minced
1     large onion, sliced
½     pound fresh mushrooms, sliced
¼     cup all-purpose flour
½     teaspoon salt
⅛     teaspoon ground thyme
⅛     teaspoon ground marjoram
⅛     teaspoon pepper
2     cups ready-to-serve beef broth
2     cups Burgundy or other dry red wine
2     cups hot cooked noodles (cooked without salt or
        fat)

**Approximate analysis per serving:**
Calories   501
Protein   36 g
Carbohydrate   34 g
Fat   15 g
Saturated Fat   5 g
Polyunsaturated Fat   2 g
Sodium   721 mg
Cholesterol   89 mg

Trim fat from steak, and cut steak into 2- x ¾-inch strips. Heat oil in a large skillet over medium heat until hot. Add meat and garlic, and cook, stirring frequently, until evenly browned. Add onion, and cook until transparent, stirring frequently. Add mushrooms, and cook 1 minute, stirring constantly.

Combine flour and seasonings, stirring until well blended. Add to beef mixture in skillet with broth and wine, stirring to combine and loosen particles on bottom of skillet.

Cover and cook over medium heat 1 hour or until meat is tender. Serve meat mixture over noodles. **Yield:** 4 servings. **Serving size:** 1 cup meat mixture with ½ cup noodles.

# Beef-Zucchini Parmesan

1   pound lean ground round
2   medium onions, chopped
1   (16-ounce) can whole tomatoes, drained
1   (8-ounce) can tomato sauce
1   (6-ounce) can tomato paste
1   medium-size green pepper, chopped
½   cup (2 ounces) shredded reduced-fat Cheddar
      cheese
½   teaspoon dried whole oregano
¼   teaspoon salt
¼   teaspoon garlic salt
¼   teaspoon pepper
4   medium zucchini, cut into ¼-inch slices
¼   cup grated Parmesan cheese

**Approximate analysis
per serving:**
Calories   274
Protein   29 g
Carbohydrate   21 g
Fat   9 g
Saturated Fat   5 g
Polyunsaturated Fat   tr.
Sodium   575 mg
Cholesterol   72 mg

Combine meat and onion in a large skillet. Cook over low heat, stirring constantly, until meat is browned and onion is tender. Add tomatoes, tomato sauce, tomato paste, and green pepper. Cook over medium heat 10 minutes, stirring occasionally. Stir in Cheddar cheese and next 4 ingredients. Add zucchini, and simmer 10 minutes.

Spoon beef-zucchini mixture into an ungreased 9-inch square baking dish, and sprinkle with Parmesan cheese. Bake at 350° for 45 minutes. Serve hot. **Yield:** 6 servings. **Serving size:** ⅙ of casserole.

*Parmesan cheese is a frequently used ingredient in this book — and for good reason. It has such a strong, distinctive taste that a little bit goes a long way in flavoring any recipe. Parmesan is higher than most cheeses in protein and calcium, but it is also high in sodium, so grating a small amount provides a touch of flavor with a minimal amount of sodium.*

# Meat Loaf with Oatmeal

1½ cups minced onion
½   cup chopped green pepper
¼   cup uncooked oatmeal
¼   cup skim milk
3   tablespoons catsup
3   tablespoons Worcestershire sauce
½   teaspoon salt
⅛   teaspoon pepper
⅛   teaspoon ground marjoram
⅛   teaspoon ground thyme
1   pound lean ground round
Homemade Tomato Sauce (recipe follows)

**Approximate analysis
per serving:**
Calories   168
Protein   22 g
Carbohydrate   9 g
Fat   4 g
Saturated Fat   2 g
Polyunsaturated Fat   tr.
Sodium   394 mg
Cholesterol   60 mg

Combine first 10 ingredients in a large bowl, stirring until well combined.

Crumble meat into bowl, and stir well to mix. Place mixture in an 8-inch loafpan. Bake at 350° for 1 hour.

Remove meat loaf from pan; let stand 5 minutes before cutting into 6 equal slices. Serve each slice with 2 tablespoons Homemade Tomato Sauce. **Yield:** 6 servings. **Serving size:** 1 slice meat loaf.

**Homemade Tomato Sauce:**

¼   cup plus 2 tablespoons chopped onion
1   tablespoon chopped green pepper
½   teaspoon corn oil margarine, melted
½   cup tomato sauce
½   teaspoon sugar
1½ teaspoons Worcestershire sauce
1   drop hot sauce
⅛   teaspoon salt

Sauté onion and green pepper in margarine in a small skillet until vegetables are tender. Stir in tomato sauce and remaining ingredients; bring to a boil. Remove from heat, and serve hot. **Yield:** ¾ cup.

# Cabbage Rolls

12  large cabbage leaves
¾  pound lean ground round
2  tablespoons uncooked rice
½  cup plus 2 tablespoons minced onion, divided
1  tablespoon sugar
¼  cup plus 1 tablespoon lemon juice, divided
¼  teaspoon salt
¼  teaspoon pepper
½  teaspoon paprika, divided
1  tablespoon vegetable oil
½  cup water
⅛  teaspoon pepper
2  (8-ounce) cans tomato sauce
3  tablespoons sugar

**Approximate analysis per serving:**
Calories  204
Protein  14 g
Carbohydrate  20 g
Fat  8 g
Saturated Fat  3 g
Polyunsaturated Fat  1 g
Sodium  557 mg
Cholesterol  42 mg

Cook cabbage leaves in boiling water to cover until barely tender. Drain leaves and cool.

Combine meat, rice, 2 tablespoons onion, 1 tablespoon sugar, 1 tablespoon lemon juice, salt, ¼ teaspoon pepper, and ¼ teaspoon paprika, stirring well to mix. Place 3 tablespoons meat mixture in center of each cabbage leaf; fold ends over, and roll up. Set cabbage rolls aside.

Heat oil in a Dutch oven over medium heat until hot. Add remaining ½ cup onion, and sauté until tender. Stir in water, remaining ¼ teaspoon paprika, and ⅛ teaspoon pepper. Place cabbage rolls, seam side down, on top of onion mixture. Combine tomato sauce, remaining ¼ cup lemon juice, and 3 tablespoons sugar, stirring until well blended; pour over cabbage rolls. Cover and cook over low heat 1 hour or until cabbage is tender and meat is done. **Yield:** 1 dozen cabbage rolls. **Serving size:** 2 cabbage rolls.

# Stuffed Peppers

8    medium-size green peppers
1    pound lean ground round
½    cup chopped onion
1    (12-ounce) can whole kernel corn, drained
1    (8-ounce) can tomato sauce
2    teaspoons Worcestershire sauce
½    teaspoon salt
½    cup fine, dry breadcrumbs
1    cup (4 ounces) shredded reduced-fat Cheddar
      cheese

**Approximate analysis per serving:**
Calories   215
Protein   21 g
Carbohydrate   20 g
Fat   6 g
Saturated Fat   3 g
Polyunsaturated Fat   1 g
Sodium   677 mg
Cholesterol   51 mg

Cut off tops of green peppers; remove seeds and membranes. Wash peppers, and cook in boiling water to cover 5 minutes; drain and set aside.

Cook meat and onion in a large nonstick skillet over medium heat until meat is browned and onion is tender, stirring constantly to crumble meat. Add corn and next 3 ingredients, stirring to mix. Simmer 5 minutes or until mixture is thoroughly heated. Stuff each pepper with ½ cup meat mixture.

Place peppers in a 12- x 8- x 2-inch baking dish. Sprinkle tops of peppers with breadcrumbs. Pour hot water to a depth of ½-inch into dish. Bake, uncovered, at 350° for 15 to 20 minutes. Sprinkle tops of peppers with cheese during the last 5 minutes of baking. **Yield:** 8 servings. **Serving size:** 1 stuffed pepper.

# Crusty Pork Chops with Peas

2   lean boneless, butterflied pork chops (about ¾ pound)
½   cup dry breadcrumbs
¼   cup grated Parmesan cheese
⅛   teaspoon salt
⅛   teaspoon pepper
¼   cup skim milk
1   tablespoon vegetable oil
1   cup ready-to-serve beef broth
2   tablespoons Rhine or other dry white wine
1   teaspoon lemon juice
1   (10-ounce) package frozen English peas
¼   cup water
1   teaspoon cornstarch
Lemon twists (optional)

**Approximate analysis per serving:**
Calories   342
Protein   30 g
Carbohydrate   21 g
Fat   14 g
Saturated Fat   5 g
Polyunsaturated Fat   3 g
Sodium   566 mg
Cholesterol   73 mg

Trim fat from pork chops, and cut each butterflied pork chop in half lengthwise. Combine breadcrumbs, cheese, salt, and pepper, stirring well to mix. Dip chops in milk, and dredge in breadcrumb mixture. Freeze pork chops 20 minutes to set coating.

Heat oil in a large nonstick skillet over medium heat until hot. Add chops, and cook 10 minutes or until evenly browned, turning once. Add broth; cover and cook 40 minutes or until chops are tender. Transfer to a serving platter, and keep warm.

Add wine and lemon juice to skillet, and bring to a boil. Boil 2 minutes. Add peas; cover and cook over medium heat 5 minutes or until tender. Remove peas from skillet with a slotted spoon, reserving wine mixture in skillet. Spoon peas around chops on serving platter.

Combine water and cornstarch, stirring until well blended. Add to skillet, and bring to a boil, stirring constantly. Boil 1 minute or until mixture thickens.

Pour wine mixture over chops, and, if desired, garnish with lemon twists. **Yield:** 4 servings. **Serving size:** 1 pork chop half with ¼ peas and wine mixture.

# Pork Chops with Stuffing

1    cup fine, dry breadcrumbs
1    cup diced apple
⅓    cup skim milk
2    tablespoons minced celery
2    teaspoons minced fresh parsley
1    teaspoon poultry seasoning
1    teaspoon grated onion
¼    teaspoon salt
¼    teaspoon pepper
8    (¼-pound) lean pork chops, well trimmed
¼    teaspoon salt

**Approximate analysis per serving:**
Calories   234
Protein   20 g
Carbohydrate   13 g
Fat   11 g
Saturated Fat   4 g
Polyunsaturated Fat   2 g
Sodium   271 mg
Cholesterol   64 mg

Combine first 9 ingredients, stirring well to mix. Place ⅓ cup stuffing mixture in a mound in a 13- x 9- x 2-inch baking pan. Cover mound with a pork chop. Repeat procedure with remaining stuffing mixture and chops.

Sprinkle ¼ teaspoon salt evenly over pork chops. Cover and bake at 350° for 1 hour. Uncover and bake an additional 15 minutes or until pork chops are tender and stuffing is done. **Yield:** 8 servings. **Serving size:** 1 pork chop with ⅓ cup stuffing.

*Pork producers are raising leaner animals in the 80s than they were raising in the 60s—about 50 percent leaner. And you can reduce the saturated fat in pork even more by carefully trimming off all the visible fat.*

*When serving pork know that you are serving a nutritiously rich food; three ounces of a lean pork chop serve up a generous amount of protein and calcium as well as minerals and vitamins.*

# Skillet Pork and Apples

Vegetable cooking spray
4  (¼-pound) lean pork chops, well trimmed
2  large apples, peeled, cored, and cut into rings
1  teaspoon sugar
⅛  teaspoon ground cinnamon
⅛  teaspoon ground cloves
½  cup Chablis or other dry white wine
¼  teaspoon salt
⅛  teaspoon pepper

**Approximate analysis per serving:**
Calories  245
Protein  19 g
Carbohydrate  15 g
Fat  10 g
Saturated Fat  4 g
Polyunsaturated Fat  1 g
Sodium  174 mg
Cholesterol  63 mg

Coat a 10-inch skillet with cooking spray; place over medium heat until hot. Add pork chops, and cook until evenly browned, turning once. Cover and continue to cook over medium heat 35 to 40 minutes. (Add a small amount of water to prevent sticking, if necessary.) Remove chops from skillet, and keep warm.

Add apple rings, sugar, cinnamon, and cloves to skillet; sauté until lightly browned. Remove from skillet, and set aside. Add wine, salt, and pepper to skillet, and stir until smooth. Return apples and pork chops to skillet, and cook over medium heat 10 minutes or until thoroughly heated. **Yield:** 4 servings. **Serving size:** 1 pork chop with ¼ of cooked apple.

*By adding fiber to your diet, you can actually increase the amount of fat your body throws off—a good reason to add fruit to your diet in addition to the flavor boost fruit lends to any dish. Apples are particularly high in pectin, a type of fiber. This fiber as well as guar gum found in beans and the fiber in oats and carrots have all proved to be cholesterol-lowering agents.*

# Lamb Curry

1    pound lean boneless lamb
Vegetable cooking spray
1    cup sliced onion
1    cup diced celery
2    small cloves garlic
4    cups peeled, diced apples
1    teaspoon salt
½    teaspoon curry powder
3    cups hot cooked rice (cooked without salt or fat)

**Approximate analysis
per serving:**
Calories    265
Protein    18 g
Carbohydrate    39 g
Fat    4 g
Saturated Fat    2 g
Polyunsaturated Fat    tr.
Sodium    380 mg
Cholesterol    51 mg

Trim and discard fat from lamb, and cut lamb into 1-inch cubes. Coat a large skillet with cooking spray; place over medium heat until hot. Add lamb, and cook, stirring constantly, until evenly browned. Add onion, celery, and garlic; cook 5 minutes or until vegetables are tender. Remove garlic cloves. Add apple, salt, and curry powder to skillet, stirring gently to mix. Add water to cover, and cook, covered, 45 minutes or until lamb is tender. Serve lamb mixture over rice. **Yield:** 6 cups. **Serving size:** 1 cup lamb mixture with ½ cup rice.

# *Grains and Legumes*

In your efforts to lower cholesterol, grains and legumes will be among your best allies. In addition to being rich in both soluble and insoluble fiber, they are a good source of complete protein when served together, and they are generously endowed with essential vitamins and minerals, including iron. Also, the variety of both grains and legumes is never ending. Take rice, for instance. Researchers are suggesting that rice fiber offers as many health benefits as oat bran, and the new varieties available in the market are numerous. Two of the newest are long-grain rices that are known as "gourmet" rices or aromatics, both of which are distinguished by their aroma and nut-like flavor. Wild pecan rice is aptly named for the nut it smells like when cooking, while Texmati rice is known for its popcorn-like aroma.

# Vegetable-Rice Combo

2    cups water
½    cup uncooked brown rice
¼    teaspoon salt
2    cups cauliflower flowerets
1    cup julienned carrot
1    cup frozen English peas
1    cup shredded reduced-fat Cheddar cheese

**Approximate analysis per serving:**
Calories   182
Protein   11 g
Carbohydrate   25 g
Fat   5 g
Saturated Fat   2 g
Polyunsaturated Fat   tr.
Sodium   318 mg
Cholesterol   16 mg

Combine water, rice, and salt in a medium saucepan. Cover and bring to boil; reduce heat, and simmer 25 minutes or until all liquid is absorbed. Transfer rice to a 1-quart casserole, and keep warm.

Arrange cauliflower, carrot, and peas in a steaming rack. Place over boiling water; cover and steam 15 minutes or until vegetables are tender. Drain.

Layer steamed vegetables on top of rice, and sprinkle with cheese.

Bake at 350° for 10 minutes or until cheese melts. **Yield:** 5 servings. **Serving size:** 1 cup.

# Orange Rice

¾    cup chopped onion
1    clove garlic, minced
1    tablespoon corn oil margarine, melted
2    (14½-ounce) cans ready-to-serve chicken broth
1    teaspoon curry powder
1½ cups uncooked brown rice
½    cup golden raisins
1    tablespoon grated orange rind
1    cup orange juice
½    teaspoon salt

**Approximate analysis per serving:**
Calories   205
Protein   6 g
Carbohydrate   40 g
Fat   3 g
Saturated Fat   1 g
Polyunsaturated Fat   1 g
Sodium   490 mg
Cholesterol   0

Sauté onion and garlic in margarine in a large saucepan until tender. Stir in broth and curry powder; cover and bring to a boil. Add rice, raisins, orange rind, orange juice, and salt. Reduce heat, cover and simmer 1 hour and 10 minutes or until all liquid is absorbed. **Yield:** 8 servings. **Serving size:** ½ cup.

# Sautéed Rice and Vegetables

1   cup uncooked brown rice
1   cup chopped onion
½   cup chopped green pepper
½   cup chopped carrot
¼   cup sliced fresh mushrooms
1   clove garlic, minced
1   tablespoon vegetable oil
1   teaspoon salt
¼   teaspoon paprika
¼   teaspoon dried whole marjoram
¼   teaspoon dried whole rosemary
¼   teaspoon pepper
1½  cups ready-to-serve chicken broth

**Approximate analysis per serving:**
Calories   119
Protein   3 g
Carbohydrate   21 g
Fat   3 g
Saturated Fat   tr.
Polyunsaturated Fat   1g
Sodium   393 mg
Cholesterol   0

Cook rice according to package directions, omitting salt and fat. Set aside.

Sauté onion, green pepper, carrot, mushrooms, and garlic in oil 5 minutes or until tender. Stir in salt, paprika, marjoram, rosemary, and pepper.

Add cooked rice and broth. Cover and bring to a boil. Reduce heat, and simmer 20 minutes. **Yield:** 8 servings. **Serving size:** 1 cup.

# Risotto

¼   cup chopped celery
3   tablespoons minced onion
2   teaspoons corn oil margarine, melted
1½  cups ready-to-serve chicken broth
½   cup uncooked brown rice
1   tablespoon dried parsley flakes
⅛   teaspoon pepper

**Approximate analysis per serving:**
Calories   162
Protein   5 g
Carbohydrate   13 g
Fat   4 g
Saturated Fat   1 g
Polyunsaturated Fat   1 g
Sodium   437 mg
Cholesterol   0

Sauté celery and onion in margarine until tender. Add broth, rice, parsley, and pepper. Cover and bring to a boil. Reduce heat, and simmer 45 minutes or until all liquid is absorbed. **Yield:** 3 servings. **Serving size**: ⅓ cup.

# Mexican Bulgur  *(photograph on page 137)*

1¼ cups uncooked bulgur wheat
½  cup diced green pepper
⅓  cup chopped green onions
1  clove garlic, minced
1  tablespoon vegetable oil
1  (15-ounce) can red kidney beans, drained
1  (14½-ounce) can whole tomatoes, undrained and
    chopped
1  teaspoon paprika
½  teaspoon salt
⅛  teaspoon red pepper
⅛  teaspoon black pepper

**Approximate analysis per serving:**
Calories   321
Protein   12 g
Carbohydrate   62 g
Fat   4 g
Saturated Fat   tr.
Polyunsaturated Fat   2 g
Sodium   630 mg
Cholesterol   0

Sauté bulgur, green pepper, onions, and garlic in oil in a large skillet 2 minutes. Stir in beans, tomatoes, paprika, salt, red pepper, and black pepper. Cover and bring to a boil; reduce heat, and simmer 15 minutes or until all liquid is absorbed. **Yield:** 5 servings. **Serving size:** 1 cup.

*The flavor and color of the Southwest tempt the appetite in this hearty meal of Mexican Bulgur (opposite page), Turkey Tacos (page 76), and Hot Spiced Cider (page 49).*

# Tabbouleh

1½ cups boiling water
1   cup uncooked bulgur
3   medium tomatoes, chopped
1   (18-ounce) can garbanzo beans, drained
1½ cups minced fresh parsley
½   cup finely chopped green onions
½   cup diced green pepper
½   cup lemon juice
2   tablespoons olive oil
1   clove garlic, crushed
1   teaspoon salt
¼   teaspoon pepper

**Approximate analysis
per serving:**
Calories   209
Protein   7 g
Carbohydrate   37 g
Fat   5 g
Saturated Fat   1 g
Polyunsaturated Fat   1 g
Sodium   485 mg
Cholesterol   0

Combine boiling water and bulgur, stirring well. Cover and let stand 30 minutes. If necessary, shake in strainer and squeeze to remove excess water.

Transfer bulgur to a large bowl; add tomato and remaining ingredients, tossing lightly to mix. Cover and chill at least 1 hour. **Yield:** 8 servings. **Serving size:** 1 cup.

*Increasing fiber in your diet can be a delicious experience when you serve taste pleasers like Winter Fruit Compote (page 187), Vegetable Slaw (page 160), and Seasoned Lentils (page 140).*

# Pea and Pepper Casserole

1    cup diced lean cooked ham
1    cup sliced onion
1    cup chopped green pepper
Vegetable cooking spray
½    cup hot water
3    (16-ounce) cans black-eyed peas, undrained
2    cups cooked elbow macaroni
¼    teaspoon salt
½    teaspoon pepper

**Approximate analysis per serving:**
Calories   324
Protein   22 g
Carbohydrate   55 g
Fat   3 g
Saturated Fat   1 g
Polyunsaturated Fat   1 g
Sodium   325 mg
Cholesterol   11 mg

Combine ham, onion, and green pepper in a large skillet coated with cooking spray. Cook over medium heat until browned, stirring frequently.

Add hot water, and simmer 1 minute. Remove from heat, and stir in peas, macaroni, salt, and pepper.

Spoon mixture into a 2-quart casserole coated with cooking spray, and bake, uncovered, at 350° for 25 minutes. **Yield:** 8 servings. **Serving size:** 1 cup.

# Seasoned Lentils    *(photograph on page 138)*

2¼ cups dried lentils
5    cups water
1    large onion
1    bay leaf
3    whole cloves
¼    teaspoon ground ginger
2    tablespoons corn oil margarine
1    teaspoon salt
Additional bay leaves (optional)
Sliced purple onion (optional)

**Approximate analysis per serving:**
Calories   147
Protein   9 g
Carbohydrate   23 g
Fat   2 g
Saturated Fat   tr.
Polyunsaturated Fat   1 g
Sodium   197 mg
Cholesterol   0

Sort and wash lentils; place in a 3-quart saucepan. Cover beans with 5 cups water; add whole onion, 1 bay leaf, cloves, and ginger. Cover and bring to a boil. Reduce heat, and simmer 30 to 40 minutes or until beans are tender. Add margarine and salt during last 15 minutes of cooking time. Remove onion, bay leaf, and cloves before serving. If desired, garnish with additional bay leaves and sliced onion. **Yield:** 12 servings. **Serving size:** ½ cup.

# Baked Beans

1   (16-ounce) can vegetarian beans prepared with
      tomato sauce
¼   cup chopped green pepper
¼   cup catsup
2   tablespoons dark brown sugar
2   tablespoons chopped onion
½   teaspoon dry mustard
Vegetable cooking spray

**Approximate analysis
per serving:**
Calories   113
Protein   4 g
Carbohydrate   23 g
Fat   1 g
Saturated Fat   tr.
Polyunsaturated Fat   tr.
Sodium   396 mg
Cholesterol   0

Combine all ingredients except cooking spray, stirring
well to mix. Pour bean mixture into an 8-inch square baking dish coated with cooking spray. Bake mixture, uncovered, at 350° for 40 minutes. **Yield:** 6 servings. **Serving
size:** ⅓ cup.

# Navy Bean-Stuffed Tomatoes

6   firm medium-size tomatoes
Vegetable cooking spray
2   cloves garlic
1   tablespoon olive oil
2   cups well-drained, canned white navy beans
¼   teaspoon salt
1   teaspoon vinegar
¼   teaspoon pepper
½   teaspoon dried whole basil

**Approximate analysis
per serving:**
Calories   146
Protein   6 g
Carbohydrate   25 g
Fat   3 g
Saturated Fat   tr.
Polyunsaturated Fat   tr.
Sodium   291 mg
Cholesterol   0

Trim off stem end of tomatoes. Scoop out pulp, removing seeds and leaving shells intact. Chop pulp, and place
in a strainer to drain. Arrange tomato shells in a 12- x 8- x
2-inch baking dish coated with cooking spray. Broil shells
4 to 5 inches from heat 5 minutes. Invert shells on paper
towels to drain. Set aside.
Sauté garlic in olive oil in a large heavy skillet 1 minute.
Add navy beans and salt to skillet. Cook over medium heat
2 minutes, stirring gently. Remove from heat, and add
tomato pulp, vinegar, and pepper, stirring gently to mix.
Stuff ¾ cup bean mixture into each tomato shell, and
sprinkle with basil. Serve warm or chilled. **Yield:** 6
servings. **Serving size:** 1 stuffed tomato.

# Three-Bean Salad

1   (16-ounce) can red kidney beans
1   (16-ounce) can cut green beans
1   (16-ounce) can cut wax beans
1   medium onion, thinly sliced
⅓   cup chopped green pepper
½   cup cider vinegar
¼   cup sugar
2   tablespoons vegetable oil
½   teaspoon salt
½   teaspoon pepper

**Approximate analysis per serving:**
Calories  76
Protein  3 g
Carbohydrate  12 g
Fat  2 g
Saturated Fat  tr.
Polyunsaturated Fat  1 g
Sodium  289 mg
Cholesterol  0

Drain beans; rinse well, and drain again. Combine beans, onion, and green pepper in a large bowl. Combine vinegar and remaining ingredients, stirring until well blended. Add to bean mixture, tossing lightly to mix well. Cover and refrigerate at least 8 hours. **Yield:** 7 servings. **Serving size:** ½ cup.

# Cajun Bean Soup

1   cup dried navy beans
1   cup dried red kidney beans
2   quarts water
4   ounces lean ham, chopped
1   (16-ounce) can whole tomatoes, undrained and chopped
1   large onion, chopped
1   clove garlic, minced
2½  teaspoons pepper
⅛   teaspoon red pepper
½   teaspoon dried whole thyme

**Approximate analysis per serving:**
Calories  142
Protein  10 g
Carbohydrate  24 g
Fat  1 g
Saturated Fat  tr.
Polyunsaturated Fat  tr.
Sodium  293 mg
Cholesterol  5 mg

Sort and wash beans; place in a large Dutch oven. Cover with water 2 inches above beans; let soak overnight.

Drain beans well. Add 2 quarts water and ham. Cover and bring to a boil. Reduce heat, and simmer 2½ to 3 hours or until beans are tender. Stir in tomatoes and remaining ingredients. Cover and simmer 30 minutes, stirring occasionally. **Yield:** 3 quarts. **Serving size:** 1 cup.

# *Vegetables*

It's a shame that the parental refrain, "Eat your vegetables," gave these treasures such bad press so early in so many lives. Vegetables come in such a variety of colors, shapes, and tastes that they don't deserve to be lumped into one nondescript category. As the health-conscious cook knows, vegetables are rich in nutritive value, high in both soluble and insoluble fiber, low in fat and calories, completely devoid of cholesterol, plus they come in all colors of the rainbow and are beautiful to look at. Because vegetables offer the most nutritive value, color, texture, and flavor when they are eaten raw or just barely cooked, they adapt well to the most contemporary fat-free cooking methods such as microwaving and stir-frying. Steaming too allows vegetables to retain most of their natural qualities. Whenever possible, cook and serve vegetables with their skins on because the skin retains and adds fiber to your diet.

# Harvard Beets

⅓ cup sugar
1½ teaspoons cornstarch
¼ cup water
3 tablespoons vinegar
1 (15-ounce) can sliced beets, drained
2 whole cloves

Combine sugar and cornstarch in a 1-quart saucepan, stirring until well blended. Stir in water and vinegar. Cover and bring to a boil; boil 5 minutes. Add beets and cloves; reduce heat, and cook until vegetables are thoroughly heated. Remove cloves before serving. **Yield:** 4 servings. **Serving size:** ½ cup.

**Approximate analysis per serving:**
Calories   104
Protein   1 g
Carbohydrate   26 g
Fat   tr.
Saturated Fat   tr.
Polyunsaturated Fat   tr.
Sodium   324 mg
Cholesterol   0

# Scalloped Cabbage

1 tablespoon corn oil margarine
1 tablespoon all-purpose flour
1½ cups skim milk
½ teaspoon salt
¼ teaspoon pepper
2 cups shredded cabbage
Vegetable cooking spray
2 tablespoons fine, dry breadcrumbs
2 tablespoons uncooked, unprocessed oat bran
Paprika (optional)

Melt margarine in a 1-quart saucepan over low heat; add flour, stirring until smooth. Cook 1 minute, stirring constantly. Gradually add milk; cook over medium heat, stirring constantly, until mixture is thickened and bubbly. Stir in salt and pepper. Remove from heat, and set aside.

Place cabbage in an 8-inch square baking pan coated with cooking spray. Pour white sauce evenly over top of cabbage, and sprinkle with breadcrumbs and oat bran. Bake at 350° for 25 minutes. Garnish with paprika, if desired. **Yield:** 4 servings. **Serving size:** ½ cup.

**Approximate analysis per serving:**
Calories   98
Protein   5 g
Carbohydrate   12 g
Fat   4 g
Saturated Fat   1 g
Polyunsaturated Fat   1 g
Sodium   356 mg
Cholesterol   2 mg

# Red Cabbage and Apples

2   cups finely shredded red cabbage
1   cup sliced onion
⅓   cup vinegar
¼   cup sugar
1   teaspoon corn oil margarine
¼   teaspoon salt
1   cup thinly sliced unpeeled apple

Combine all ingredients except apple in a large skillet. Cover and bring to a boil. Reduce heat, and simmer 5 minutes. Stir in apple, and continue to simmer 2 to 3 minutes. **Yield:** 6 servings. **Serving size:** ½ cup.

**Approximate analysis per serving:**
Calories   68
Protein   1 g
Carbohydrate   16 g
Fat   1 g
Saturated Fat   tr.
Polyunsaturated Fat   1 g
Sodium   84 mg
Cholesterol   0

# Carrots and Snow Peas   *(photograph on cover)*

1   teaspoon corn oil margarine
1½ cups diagonally sliced carrot
3   tablespoons water
1   (6-ounce) package frozen snow pea pods
¼   teaspoon salt
⅛   teaspoon pepper

Melt margarine in a medium saucepan over medium heat. Add carrot slices and water. Cover and cook over medium heat 6 to 8 minutes or until carrot slices are crisp-tender.

Trim ends of snow peas, if desired, and add to saucepan with salt and pepper. Continue to cook, stirring frequently, just until snow peas are thoroughly heated. Remove from heat, and serve, using a slotted spoon. **Yield:** 4 servings. **Serving size**: ½ cup.

**Approximate analysis per serving:**
Calories   39
Protein   2 g
Carbohydrate   7 g
Fat   1 g
Saturated Fat   tr.
Polyunsaturated Fat   tr.
Sodium   23 mg
Cholesterol   0

# Carrots and Zucchini

3    medium carrots, scraped and cut into julienne strips
      (about 2 cups)
1    small onion, sliced
3    medium zucchini, cut into julienne strips (about 2
      cups)
½    teaspoon salt
1    tablespoon corn oil margarine, melted

Combine carrot and onion in a medium saucepan; add water to barely cover vegetables. Cover and bring to a boil. Reduce heat, and simmer 5 minutes. Add zucchini and salt, and continue to simmer, covered, 5 minutes. Drain off liquid. Drizzle vegetables with margarine and serve hot. **Yield:** 8 servings. **Serving size:** ½ cup.

**Approximate analysis per serving:**
Calories   45
Protein   1 g
Carbohydrate   6 g
Fat   2 g
Saturated Fat   tr.
Polyunsaturated Fat   1 g
Sodium   150 mg
Cholesterol   0

# Orange-Glazed Carrots

5    medium carrots, scraped and cut into diagonal
      slices
¼    cup water
¼    teaspoon salt
¼    cup orange juice
2    teaspoons sugar
1    teaspoon cornstarch
1    teaspoon corn oil margarine, melted
¼    teaspoon ground ginger

Combine carrot slices, water, and salt in a medium saucepan. Cover and cook over medium heat 15 minutes or just until tender (do not drain).

Combine orange juice, sugar, cornstarch, margarine, and ginger, stirring until well blended; pour over carrot slices in saucepan.

Continue to cook over medium heat, stirring occasionally, 8 minutes or until mixture thickens. **Yield:** 4 servings. **Serving size:** ½ cup.

**Approximate analysis per serving:**
Calories   62
Protein   1 g
Carbohydrate   13 g
Fat   1 g
Saturated Fat   tr.
Polyunsaturated Fat   tr.
Sodium   162 mg
Cholesterol   0

# New Potatoes with Dill

1    pound unpeeled new potatoes
1    teaspoon corn oil margarine, melted
½    teaspoon salt
½    teaspoon dried whole dillweed

**Approximate analysis
per serving:**
Calories   100
Protein   3 g
Carbohydrate   21 g
Fat   1 g
Saturated Fat   tr.
Polyunsaturated Fat   tr.
Sodium   259 mg
Cholesterol   0

Combine new potatoes and water to cover in a medium saucepan. Cover and bring to a boil. Reduce heat, and simmer 20 minutes or until fork tender. Drain and cool slightly. Cut potatoes into bite-size cubes, and set aside.

Combine margarine, salt, and dillweed in a medium bowl, stirring well. Add potatoes, and toss gently to coat well. Let stand 5 minutes before serving to allow flavors to blend. **Yield:** 4 servings. **Serving size:** ½ cup

# Sweet Potato Casserole   *(photograph on page 147)*

1½  cups cooked, mashed sweet potatoes
¼    cup orange juice
¼    cup skim milk
¼    cup sugar
1    teaspoon vanilla extract
2    tablespoons brown sugar
1    tablespoon all-purpose flour
1    tablespoon corn oil margarine
2    tablespoons chopped pecans

**Approximate analysis
per serving:**
Calories   186
Protein   2 g
Carbohydrate   35 g
Fat   5 g
Saturated Fat   1 g
Polyunsaturated Fat   1 g
Sodium   43 mg
Cholesterol   tr.

Combine mashed sweet potato, orange juice, milk, sugar, and vanilla in a medium bowl. Beat at high speed of an electric mixer until smooth. Spoon sweet potato mixture into a 1-quart casserole.

Combine brown sugar and flour in a small bowl; cut in margarine with a fork. Stir in pecans, and sprinkle mixture over potatoes. Bake, uncovered, at 375° for 20 to 25 minutes or until lightly browned. **Yield:** 5 servings. **Serving size:** ½ cup.

# Golden Mashed Potatoes

4    large potatoes, peeled and cubed (about 5½
      cups)
2    medium carrots, scraped and chopped (about 1½
      cups)
2    cups water
¼    cup skim milk
2    teaspoons corn oil margarine
½    teaspoon salt
⅛    teaspoon white pepper

**Approximate analysis
per serving:**
Calories  68
Protein  2 g
Carbohydrate  13 g
Fat  1 g
Saturated Fat  tr.
Polyunsaturated Fat  tr.
Sodium  148 mg
Cholesterol  tr.

Combine potato, carrot, and water in a 3-quart sauce-pan. Cover and cook over medium heat 20 minutes or until vegetables are tender. Drain vegetables, reserving 1 cup cooking liquid.

Transfer cooked vegetables to a large bowl. Add reserved cooking liquid, milk, margarine, salt, and pepper. Beat at low speed of an electric mixer. Increase speed to medium, and beat until mixture is smooth (carrot will remain in small golden bits). **Yield:** 8 servings. **Serving size:** ½ cup.

# Microwave Stuffed Potatoes

2    medium baking potatoes
½    cup plain low-fat yogurt
¼    cup skim milk
¼    teaspoon salt
¼    teaspoon pepper
2    cups sliced yellow squash
1    cup sliced fresh mushrooms
¼    cup chopped onion
½    cup (2 ounces) shredded part-skim mozzarella
      cheese
2    tablespoons chopped green onions

**Approximate analysis
per serving:**
Calories  188
Protein  9 g
Carbohydrate  33 g
Fat  3 g
Saturated Fat  2 g
Polyunsaturated Fat  tr.
Sodium  227 mg
Cholesterol  9 mg

Wash potatoes, and pat dry; prick each potato several times with a fork. Place potatoes on a double-layer of paper towels in a microwave oven. Microwave at HIGH 6 to 8 minutes. Remove from oven, and wrap each potato in aluminum foil. Let stand 10 minutes. Cut each potato in half lengthwise. Scoop out pulp, leaving a ¼-inch-thick shell. Set shells aside. Combine potato pulp, yogurt, milk, salt, and pepper in a medium bowl; beat at medium speed of an electric mixer until well blended. Set aside.

Combine squash, mushrooms, and ¼ cup onion in a 1-quart baking dish. Cover with heavy-duty plastic wrap, and microwave at HIGH 4 minutes or until vegetables are tender. Drain. Add microwaved vegetables to potato pulp mixture, stirring gently to mix. Stuff potato shells with potato mixture.

Combine cheese and green onions; sprinkle evenly over stuffed potato halves. Return stuffed potato halves to microwave oven, placing 1 inch apart in a circle on paper towels. Microwave at MEDIUM (50% power) 2 minutes or until potatoes are thoroughly heated and cheese melts. **Yield:** 4 servings. **Serving size:** 1 stuffed potato half.

# Baked Acorn Squash

2    small acorn squash
¼    cup water
2    tablespoons brown sugar
¼    teaspoon salt
⅛    teaspoon ground cinnamon
⅛    teaspoon ground nutmeg
⅛    teaspoon grated orange rind
1    teaspoon corn oil margarine

**Approximate analysis per serving:**
Calories   90
Protein   1 g
Carbohydrate   21 g
Fat   1 g
Saturated Fat   tr.
Polyunsaturated Fat   tr.
Sodium   137 mg
Cholesterol   0

Cut squash in half lengthwise, and remove seeds. Place squash, cut side down, in a 9-inch square baking pan. Add water to pan. Cover and bake at 400° for 30 minutes. Remove from oven, and turn squash cut side up.

Combine brown sugar and next 4 ingredients in a small bowl, stirring well to mix. Cut in margarine with a fork. Spoon brown sugar mixture evenly into squash cavities. Return to oven, and bake an additional 30 minutes. **Yield:** 4 servings. **Serving size:** 1 stuffed squash half.

# Yellow Squash Casserole

4½ cups sliced yellow squash (about 8 small squash)
1    cup water
½    cup evaporated skim milk
¼    cup (2 ounces) shredded reduced-fat Cheddar
       cheese
¼    cup uncooked, unprocessed oat bran
2    tablespoons minced onion
2    teaspoons corn oil margarine, melted
1    chicken-flavored bouillon cube, crushed
¼    teaspoon pepper
¼    cup fine, dry breadcrumbs
⅛    teaspoon paprika

**Approximate analysis
per serving:**
Calories   92
Protein   5 g
Carbohydrate   11 g
Fat   3 g
Saturated Fat   1 g
Polyunsaturated Fat   1 g
Sodium   350 mg
Cholesterol   6 mg

Combine squash and water in a 1-quart saucepan. Cover and bring to a boil. Reduce heat, and simmer 15 minutes or until tender. Drain and mash squash.

Add milk, cheese, oat bran, onion, margarine, crushed bouillon cube, and pepper, stirring until well combined. Pour into a 1-quart casserole; top with breadcrumbs and paprika. Bake at 350° for 30 minutes. **Yield:** 6 servings. **Serving size:** ½ cup.

# Stewed Zucchini and Tomatoes

1    medium onion, chopped
1    tablespoon corn oil margarine, melted
3    medium zucchini, cut into ½-inch slices
1    (14½-ounce) can tomato wedges, undrained
2    teaspoons Worcestershire sauce
¼    teaspoon salt
⅛    teaspoon pepper

**Approximate analysis
per serving:**
Calories   78
Protein   3 g
Carbohydrate   11 g
Fat   3 g
Saturated Fat   1 g
Polyunsaturated Fat   1 g
Sodium   291 mg
Cholesterol   0

Sauté onion in margarine in a large skillet until transparent. Stir in zucchini. Cover and cook over medium heat 8 minutes or until zucchini is tender. Gently stir in tomato wedges, Worcestershire sauce, salt, and pepper; continue to cook over medium heat until mixture is thoroughly heated. Serve immediately. **Yield:** 5 servings. **Serving size:** 1 cup.

# Tomato-Eggplant Casserole

2    medium eggplants
1    teaspoon salt
1½  teaspoons vegetable oil
1    (28-ounce) can whole tomatoes, undrained and
       chopped
1    clove garlic, minced
½   cup uncooked, unprocessed oat bran, divided

Peel eggplants, and cut lengthwise into ⅜-inch slices. Place eggplant slices in a shallow pan. Add water to cover and salt. Soak about 15 minutes to remove bitter taste from eggplant. Drain eggplant on paper towels.

Heat oil in a large skillet over medium heat until hot. Add eggplant slices, and cook until evenly browned, turning once. Remove eggplant from skillet, and set aside.

Add tomatoes and garlic to skillet, and bring to a boil. Stir in ¼ cup oat bran to thicken tomato mixture. Remove from heat, and set aside.

Place eggplant slices in an 8-inch square baking dish. Spoon tomato mixture evenly over top, and sprinkle with remaining ¼ cup oat bran. Bake at 400° for 45 minutes. **Yield:** 8 servings. **Serving size**: ⅛ of casserole.

**Approximate analysis per serving:**
Calories   67
Protein    2 g
Carbohydrate   8 g
Fat   3 g
Saturated Fat   tr.
Polyunsaturated Fat   2 g
Sodium   372 mg
Cholesterol   0

*Using oat bran as a thickener, as was done in Tomato-Eggplant Casserole, offers a number of culinary benefits. In addition to lowering cholesterol, oat bran will add a slightly nutty flavor to any dish that includes it. Whole-grain oats contain important vitamins and minerals, including iron and calcium, and the quality of the protein in oats surpasses that of wheat and other grains.*

# Spinach-Topped Tomatoes

1    (10-ounce) package frozen chopped spinach
½    pound chopped fresh mushrooms
2    tablespoons chopped onion
1    clove garlic, minced
1    tablespoon corn oil margarine, melted
½    teaspoon dried whole basil
¼    teaspoon salt
3    medium tomatoes, halved
⅓    cup grated Parmesan cheese

**Approximate analysis per serving:**
Calories   76
Protein   5 g
Carbohydrate   7 g
Fat   4 g
Saturated Fat   1 g
Polyunsaturated Fat   1 g
Sodium   240 mg
Cholesterol   4 mg

Cook frozen spinach according to package directions. Drain thoroughly, and set aside.

Sauté mushrooms, onion, and garlic in margarine until vegetables are tender. Combine drained spinach, sautéed mixture, basil, and salt, stirring well to combine.

Top each tomato half equally with spinach mixture. Sprinkle cheese evenly over spinach topping. Bake, uncovered, at 350° for 20 minutes. **Yield:** 6 servings. **Serving size:** 1 tomato half.

# Herbed Vegetables

½    pound fresh green beans, cut into ½-inch diagonal
      pieces
1    cup chopped onion
½    teaspoon salt
½    teaspoon dried whole basil
¼    teaspoon dried whole thyme
⅛    teaspoon pepper
¾    cup water, divided
2    cups sliced yellow squash
3    cups cherry tomatoes, halved
1    tablespoon corn oil margarine

**Approximate analysis per serving:**
Calories   83
Protein   3 g
Carbohydrate   15 g
Fat   3 g
Saturated Fat   1 g
Polyunsaturated Fat   1 g
Sodium   204 mg
Cholesterol   0

Combine first 6 ingredients in a large skillet; stir in ½ cup water. Cover and bring to a boil. Reduce heat, and simmer 10 minutes.

Add squash and remaining ¼ cup water to skillet; continue to simmer, covered, 10 minutes or until squash is crisp-tender. Drain off liquid, leaving vegetables in skillet.

Add cherry tomato halves and margarine to skillet; cook over medium heat, stirring frequently, until margarine melts. Serve immediately. **Yield:** 6 servings. **Serving size:** ¾ cup.

# Fresh Vegetable Medley   *(photograph on page 155)*

½  cup chopped onion
½  cup chopped green pepper
2  teaspoons corn oil margarine, melted
1  (10-ounce) package frozen sliced okra
1  clove garlic
½  teaspoon salt
⅛  teaspoon pepper
1  cup corn, cut from cob
1  large tomato, chopped
1½ cups sliced yellow squash

**Approximate analysis per serving:**
Calories   50
Protein   2 g
Carbohydrate   9 g
Fat   2 g
Saturated Fat   tr.
Polyunsaturated Fat   1 g
Sodium   140 mg
Cholesterol   0

Sauté onion and green pepper in margarine in a large skillet 2 minutes. Add frozen okra, garlic, salt, and pepper; cook over medium heat 4 minutes, stirring gently. Add corn, and cook 3 minutes, stirring occasionally. Add tomato and squash to skillet; continue to cook over medium heat 5 minutes or until vegetables are crisp-tender, stirring occasionally. Remove from heat, and let stand 2 to 3 minutes. Remove garlic before serving. **Yield:** 8 servings. **Serving size:** ½ cup.

# Oriental Mixed Vegetables

1    (1-pound) bunch fresh broccoli
1    (2-pound) head Chinese cabbage
1    cup ready-to-serve beef broth
1    tablespoon cornstarch
2    teaspoons low-sodium soy sauce
1    cup sliced onion
2    cloves garlic, minced
1    teaspoon corn oil margarine, melted
2    cups sliced fresh mushrooms

**Approximate analysis
per serving:**
Calories   59
Protein   4 g
Carbohydrate   10 g
Fat   1 g
Saturated Fat   tr.
Polyunsaturated Fat   tr.
Sodium   315 mg
Cholesterol   0

Trim off large leaves of broccoli. Remove tough ends of lower stalks and wash broccoli thoroughly. Cut broccoli into flowerets; cut stems into ¼-inch diagonal slices. Cut cabbage crosswise into 1-inch slices.

Combine beef broth, cornstarch, and soy sauce, stirring until well blended. Set mixture aside. Sauté onion and garlic in margarine in a large skillet 2 minutes. Add mushrooms to skillet, and sauté 3 minutes. Stir in broccoli, and sauté 3 minutes, stirring constantly. Add cabbage and beef broth mixture. Cook over high heat, stirring constantly, 2 to 3 minutes or until mixture is thickened and bubbly. **Yield:** 6 cups. **Serving size:** 1 cup.

*Corn is an all-time favorite regardless of how you serve it — freshly cooked on-the-cob, as a succulent addition to Fresh Vegetable Medley (page 153), or as a high-fiber ingredient in Jalapeño Cornbread (page 177).*

# Salads
## and
# Salad
# Dressings

Serve a creative salad and you serve variety and contrast for the rest of the meal. The fresh flavor and texture of different kinds of lettuce, the crunch and color of raw vegetables or fruit, and the tart, sweet, or creamy taste of a low-fat dressing provide endless possibilities. Salads are also a good way to increase your complex carbohydrates and fiber and to try out new foods. Try a different lettuce, such as arugula or escarole; a new protein source, such as tofu and sprouts; or a salad dressing you have whipped up yourself. One benefit of a homemade salad dressing is that you can select the ingredients that go into it. For example, the Dilled Potato Salad (page 158) was originally made with mayonnaise. By substituting a combination of reduced-calorie mayonnaise and low-fat yogurt, the sodium was reduced from 1200 to 316 milligrams and the fat from 23 grams to 3 grams.

*Save calories and cholesterol by serving fruit and vegetable salads like Tangy Orange and Spinach Salad (page 163) and low-fat salad dressings like (clockwise from left) Poppy Seed Dressing (page 168), Light Russian Dressing, and Sesame-Honey Dressing (page 167).*

# Dilled Potato Salad

3    pounds new potatoes, unpeeled
½    cup plain low-fat yogurt
¼    cup reduced-calorie mayonnaise
3    green onions, thinly sliced
1    teaspoon salt
½    teaspoon dried whole dillweed

Combine potatoes and water to cover in a small Dutch oven. Bring to a boil; reduce heat, and simmer 20 minutes or until crisp-tender. Drain and let cool.

Cut potatoes into ¼-inch slices. Combine yogurt, mayonnaise, onions, salt, and dillweed in a large bowl, stirring well. Add potatoes, and toss gently to coat well. Cover and chill 2 hours before serving. **Yield:** 8 servings. **Serving size:** 1 cup.

**Approximate analysis per serving:**
Calories   177
Protein   4 g
Carbohydrate   35 g
Fat   3 g
Saturated Fat   tr.
Polyunsaturated Fat   tr.
Sodium   316 mg
Cholesterol   3 mg

# Crispy Vegetable-Tuna Salad

2    large carrots, cut into 2-inch julienne strips (about 2 cups)
½    small head cauliflower, broken into flowerets (about 1½ cups)
2    tablespoons water
1    cup frozen English peas, thawed
1    cup sliced fresh mushrooms
½    cup thinly sliced celery
1    (9¼-ounce) can white tuna in water, well drained and flaked
½    cup commercial oil-free Italian dressing
2    tablespoons lemon juice

Place carrot and cauliflower in a 2-quart casserole. Add 2 tablespoons water. Cover with heavy-duty plastic wrap and microwave at HIGH 4 minutes or until crisp-tender, stirring after 2 minutes. Stir in peas, mushrooms, and celery. Drain.

Add remaining ingredients. Toss lightly to coat well. Serve warm, or cover and chill thoroughly before serving. **Yield:** 4 servings. **Serving size:** 1 cup.

**Approximate analysis per serving:**
Calories   120
Protein   11 g
Carbohydrate   18 g
Fat   1 g
Saturated Fat   tr.
Polyunsaturated Fat   tr.
Sodium   490 mg
Cholesterol   0

# Fresh Vegetable Salad *(photograph on page 87)*

2½ cups cauliflower flowerets
2½ cups broccoli flowerets
¼ cup diced green onions
1 large tomato, diced
½ cup sliced fresh mushrooms
1 small green pepper, sliced
1 (8-ounce) bottle commercial oil-free Italian dressing
¼ cup reduced-calorie mayonnaise
2 tablespoons chili sauce
1 teaspoon dried whole dillweed
½ teaspoon salt
Tomato slices (optional)

**Approximate analysis per serving:**
Calories 75
Protein 3 g
Carbohydrate 12 g
Fat 2 g
Saturated Fat 0
Polyunsaturated Fat tr.
Sodium 362 mg
Cholesterol 2 mg

Combine first 6 ingredients in a large bowl. Pour dressing over top, and toss lightly to coat well. Cover and marinate in refrigerator 8 hours, stirring occasionally. Drain off dressing.

Combine mayonnaise, chili sauce, dillweed, and salt, stirring until well blended. Pour over vegetables in bowl; toss lightly to coat well. Cover and chill until ready to serve. Garnish salad with tomato slices, if desired. **Yield:** 8 servings. **Serving size:** 1 cup.

# Green and Gold Salad

12 cups loosely-packed torn romaine lettuce
2 medium cucumbers, cut into 32 slices
2 large sweet yellow peppers, seeded and sliced into 16 rings
2 medium carrots, scraped and shredded (1 cup)
1 cup Light Russian Dressing (see page 167)

**Approximate analysis per serving:**
Calories 86
Protein 2 g
Carbohydrate 9 g
Fat 5 g
Saturated Fat 1 g
Polyunsaturated Fat 3 g
Sodium 229 mg
Cholesterol 0

Divide lettuce evenly among 8 salad bowls. Attractively arrange 4 cucumber slices, 4 yellow pepper rings, and 2 tablespoons shredded carrot over top of each salad. Top each with 2 tablespoons Light Russian Dressing. **Yield:** 8 servings. **Serving size:** 2 cups.

# Marinated Cucumber Salad

2½ cups thinly sliced cucumber
¼ teaspoon salt
¼ cup plus 2 tablespoons vinegar
3    tablespoons sugar
1    tablespoon water

Place cucumber slices in a medium bowl, and sprinkle with salt. Combine vinegar, sugar, and water, stirring until sugar dissolves. Pour over cucumber slices. Toss lightly to coat. Cover and chill 30 minutes before serving with a slotted spoon. **Yield:** 4 servings. **Serving size:** ½ cup

**Approximate analysis per serving:**
Calories   51
Protein   tr.
Carbohydrate   13 g
Fat   tr.
Saturated Fat   tr.
Polyunsaturated Fat   tr.
Sodium   126 mg
Cholesterol   0

# Vegetable Slaw    *(photograph on page 138)*

½ cup reduced-calorie mayonnaise
¼ cup plain low-fat yogurt
2    tablespoons chopped fresh dillweed or
        1 tablespoon dried whole dillweed
1    tablespoon freshly squeezed lemon juice
½ teaspoon pepper
¼ teaspoon salt
4    cups finely shredded cabbage
1    medium tomato, diced
½ cup grated carrot
¼ cup finely chopped onion
Fresh dillweed sprigs (optional)
Carrot curls (optional)
Cherry tomatoes (optional)

Combine mayonnaise, yogurt, chopped dillweed, lemon juice, pepper, and salt in a large bowl, stirring until well blended. Stir in cabbage, tomato, grated carrot, and onion. Cover and chill at least 1 hour before serving. If desired, garnish with dillweed sprigs, carrot curls, and cherry tomatoes. **Yield:** 4 servings. **Serving size:** 1 cup.

**Approximate analysis per serving:**
Calories   123
Protein   3 g
Carbohydrate   11 g
Fat   9 g
Saturated Fat   tr.
Polyunsaturated Fat   tr.
Sodium   375 mg
Cholesterol   11 mg

# Layered Lettuce Salad

4   cups shredded lettuce
½   cup chopped green onions
1   cup cauliflower flowerets
½   cup chopped green pepper
½   cup sliced fresh mushrooms
1   (10-ounce) package frozen English peas, thawed
½   cup reduced-calorie mayonnaise
1   tablespoon lemon juice

**Approximate analysis
per serving:**
Calories  82
Protein  3 g
Carbohydrate  9 g
Fat  4 g
Saturated Fat  tr.
Polyunsaturated Fat  tr.
Sodium  255 mg
Cholesterol  5 mg

Layer first 6 ingredients in a large serving bowl. Combine mayonnaise and lemon juice, stirring to blend; spread over top of salad to seal. Cover and refrigerate 24 hours. Toss layers just before serving. **Yield:** 8 servings. **Serving size:** 1 cup.

# Pineapple-Cabbage Slaw

1   (20-ounce) can unsweetened pineapple tidbits,
      undrained
4   cups finely shredded cabbage
½   cup shredded carrot
¼   cup reduced-calorie mayonnaise
1   tablespoon lemon juice
1   tablespoon prepared horseradish
½   teaspoon celery seeds
¼   teaspoon salt
Carrot curls (optional)

**Approximate analysis
per serving:**
Calories  79
Protein  1g
Carbohydrate  15 g
Fat  3 g
Saturated Fat  tr.
Polyunsaturated Fat  tr.
Sodium  147 mg
Cholesterol  3 mg

Drain pineapple, reserving 2 tablespoons juice. Combine pineapple, cabbage, and shredded carrot in a large bowl. Combine reserved pineapple juice, mayonnaise, lemon juice, horseradish, celery seeds, and salt, stirring until well blended. Pour over vegetable-fruit mixture, and toss lightly to coat well. Cover and refrigerate at least 2 hours to allow flavors to blend. Garnish with carrot curls, if desired. **Yield:** 7 servings. **Serving size:** 1 cup.

# Orange Waldorf Salad

4   medium-size oranges
1   Red Delicious apple, unpeeled and diced
½   cup sliced celery
2   tablespoons reduced-calorie mayonnaise
⅛   teaspoon ground cinnamon
Lettuce leaves (optional)

Peel and section oranges over a large bowl to catch 2 teaspoons juice. Add orange sections, apple, and celery to bowl, tossing gently to mix. Combine mayonnaise and cinnamon, stirring to blend. Add to fruit mixture, and toss lightly to coat. Cover and refrigerate until thoroughly chilled. Serve salad on a lettuce-lined serving platter, if desired. **Yield:** 11 servings. **Serving size:** ½ cup.

**Note:** To section each orange, first peel orange with a sharp knife, cutting through rind and positioning blade between white pith of orange and fruit. Slide knife blade around fruit, using a sawing motion to detach rind, pith, and outer white membrane of fruit. Place knife blade next to one section, separating it from membrane of fruit; cut toward center of fruit along side of orange section, using a gentle sawing motion. Repeat cutting process on opposite side of section next to membrane to detach orange section. Gently remove orange section from membrane pocket. Repeat sectioning process with remaining fruit.

**Approximate analysis per serving:**
Calories   61
Protein   1 g
Carbohydrate   13 g
Fat   1 g
Saturated Fat   tr.
Polyunsaturated Fat   tr.
Sodium   104 mg
Cholesterol   1 mg

# Tangy Orange and Spinach Salad *(photograph on page 156)*

¼ cup lemon juice
1 tablespoon sugar
2 tablespoons vegetable oil
1½ teaspoons grated lemon rind
¼ teaspoon seasoned salt
¼ teaspoon dried whole marjoram
3 medium-size oranges, peeled and cut crosswise into ½-inch slices
2 cups cauliflower flowerets
2 tablespoons chopped green onions
6 cups fresh spinach

**Approximate analysis per serving:**
Calories 109
Protein 3 g
Carbohydrate 16 g
Fat 5 g
Saturated Fat 1 g
Polyunsaturated Fat 3 g
Sodium 130 mg
Cholesterol 0

Combine lemon juice, sugar, oil, lemon rind, seasoned salt, and marjoram in a large bowl, stirring well. Add orange slices, cauliflower, and green onions, tossing lightly to coat well. Cover and marinate in refrigerator 30 minutes, stirring occasionally.

Tear spinach into bite-size pieces; add to orange mixture. Toss lightly, and serve. **Yield:** 6 servings. **Serving size**: 1½ cups.

# Fruited Carrot Salad *(photograph on page 69)*

2 cups shredded carrot
1 (8-ounce) can unsweetened pineapple tidbits, undrained
½ cup chopped Red Delicious apple
½ cup orange juice
¼ cup raisins

**Approximate analysis per serving:**
Calories 54
Protein 1 g
Carbohydrate 14 g
Fat tr.
Saturated Fat tr.
Polyunsaturated Fat tr.
Sodium 11 mg
Cholesterol 0

Combine all ingredients in a 2-quart bowl, tossing gently to mix. Cover and refrigerate until ready to serve. **Yield:** 8 servings. **Serving size:** ½ cup.

# Zesty Fruit Combo

3    medium-size oranges, peeled and cut crosswise into
      ½-inch slices
2    medium pears, unpeeled and cut into bite-size
      pieces
2    medium bananas, sliced
1    cup seedless red grapes, halved
1    (8-ounce) carton vanilla low-fat yogurt
½    teaspoon grated orange rind
⅓    cup orange juice
⅛    teaspoon ground cinnamon

**Approximate analysis
per serving:**
Calories    71
Protein    1 g
Carbohydrate    16 g
Fat    1 g
Saturated Fat    tr.
Polyunsaturated Fat    tr.
Sodium    17 mg
Cholesterol    1 mg

Combine first 4 ingredients in a large bowl. Combine yogurt, orange rind, orange juice, and cinnamon, stirring until well blended.

Pour yogurt mixture over fruit, tossing lightly to coat well. Cover and chill until ready to serve. **Yield:** 14 servings. **Serving size:** ½ cup.

# Waldorf Salad    *(photograph on page 189)*

½    cup raisins
½    cup warm water
½    cup plain low-fat yogurt
¼    cup reduced-calorie mayonnaise
¼    cup nonfat buttermilk
1    medium-size Golden Delicious apple, unpeeled and
      diced
1    medium-size Red Delicious apple, unpeeled and
      diced
2    cups chopped celery
1    cup seedless green grapes, halved

**Approximate analysis
per serving:**
Calories    99
Protein    2 g
Carbohydrate    19 g
Fat    3 g
Saturated Fat    tr.
Polyunsaturated Fat    tr.
Sodium    89 mg
Cholesterol    3 mg

Combine raisins and warm water; set aside 30 minutes to plump raisins.

Combine yogurt, mayonnaise, and buttermilk in container of an electric blender; process until smooth. Transfer yogurt mixture to a medium bowl.

Drain raisins, and add to yogurt mixture with apples, celery, and grapes, tossing lightly to coat well. Cover and chill. **Yield:** 8 servings. **Serving size:** ½ cup.

# Fresh Fruit Medley

2 medium kiwifruit, peeled and sliced
1 cup cubed cantaloupe
½ cup fresh blueberries
½ cup seedless green grapes, halved
½ cup fresh strawberries, halved
4 lettuce leaves
Poppy Seed-Yogurt Dressing (recipe follows)

**Approximate analysis per serving:**
Calories   104
Protein   3 g
Carbohydrate   21 g
Fat   1 g
Saturated Fat   tr.
Polyunsaturated Fat   tr.
Sodium   26 mg
Cholesterol   2 mg

Combine fruit, stirring gently to mix. Spoon ¾ cup fruit mixture onto each of 4 lettuce-lined salad plates. Drizzle each with 2 tablespoons Poppy Seed-Yogurt Dressing. **Yield:** 4 servings. **Serving size:** ¾ cup fruit mixture with 2 tablespoons dressing.

## Poppy Seed-Yogurt Dressing:

½ teaspoon poppy seeds
1 tablespoon honey
⅛ teaspoon grated orange rind
⅛ teaspoon grated lemon rind
½ cup plain low-fat yogurt

Combine all ingredients in a small bowl, stirring well. Cover and refrigerate until dressing is thoroughly chilled. **Yield:** ½ cup.

*Nothing surpasses fresh fruits as a salad, a dessert, or a snack. Along with their sweet natural flavors and their fresh, vibrant colors, they are an appetizing source of cholesterol-lowering fiber. Most fruits too are high in vitamin C, especially kiwifruit which has twice the recommended daily amount of vitamin C required for an adult.*

# Buttermilk Salad Dressing

2    cups nonfat buttermilk
1½ cups reduced-calorie mayonnaise
2    tablespoons plus 1½ teaspoons dried parsley
        flakes
1    teaspoon onion powder
½    teaspoon garlic powder
½    teaspoon salt
¾    teaspoon pepper

**Approximate analysis
per serving:**
Calories    42
Protein    1 g
Carbohydrate    2 g
Fat    4 g
Saturated Fat    tr.
Polyunsaturated Fat    tr.
Sodium    151 mg
Cholesterol    4 mg

Combine all ingredients in a jar with a tight-fitting lid; shake vigorously. Store in refrigerator up to 6 weeks. **Yield:** 3½ cups. **Serving size:** 2 tablespoons.

**Note:** Buttermilk Salad Dressing may be served over vegetable salads.

# French Dressing

1½ cups catsup
1    small onion, sliced
½    cup vegetable oil
½    cup vinegar
⅓    cup sugar
2    tablespoons lemon juice
½    teaspoon salt
¾    teaspoon paprika
¼    teaspoon ground ginger

**Approximate analysis
per serving:**
Calories    65
Protein    tr.
Carbohydrate    7 g
Fat    4 g
Saturated Fat    1 g
Polyunsaturated Fat    3 g
Sodium    182 mg
Cholesterol    0

Combine all ingredients in container of an electric blender. Process 2 minutes or until dressing is smooth. Transfer dressing to an airtight container, and store in refrigerator until ready to use. **Yield:** 3¼ cups. **Serving size:** 2 tablespoons.

**Note:** French Dressing may be served over vegetable salads.

# Light Russian Dressing   *(photograph on page 156)*

⅔  cup water
¼  cup cider vinegar
¼  cup catsup
1   tablespoon plus 1 teaspoon grated onion
2   teaspoons sugar
1   teaspoon salt
¼  cup vegetable oil

Combine water, vinegar, catsup, onion, sugar, and salt in a small bowl, stirring until well blended. Slowly stir in oil, using a wire whisk (do not use blender). Cover and store in refrigerator. Stir well before using. **Yield:** 1½ cups. **Serving size:** 2 tablespoons.

**Note:** Light Russian Dressing may be served over vegetable salads.

**Approximate analysis per serving:**
Calories  50
Protein  tr.
Carbohydrate  2 g
Fat  4 g
Saturated Fat  tr.
Polyunsaturated Fat  2 g
Sodium  214 mg
Cholesterol  0

# Sesame-Honey Dressing   *(photograph on page 156)*

3   tablespoons sesame seeds
1   cup plain low-fat yogurt
2   tablespoons honey
¼  teaspoon grated orange rind
¼  teaspoon grated lemon rind

Place sesame seeds in a small nonstick skillet, and cook over medium-high heat, stirring constantly, 3 minutes or until lightly browned.

Transfer toasted sesame seeds to a small bowl; add yogurt and remaining ingredients, stirring well. Cover and refrigerate until thoroughly chilled. **Yield:** 1 cup. **Serving size:** 2 tablespoons.

**Note:** Sesame-Honey Dressing may be served over fruit salads.

**Approximate analysis per serving:**
Calories  53
Protein  2 g
Carbohydrate  7 g
Fat  2 g
Saturated Fat  1 g
Polyunsaturated Fat  1 g
Sodium  21 mg
Cholesterol  2 mg

# Poppy Seed Dressing *(photograph on page 156)*

½  cup sugar
¼  cup vinegar
1  teaspoon salt
1  teaspoon paprika
1  teaspoon dry mustard
2  teaspoons minced onion
1  cup vegetable oil
1  teaspoon poppy seeds

**Approximate analysis per serving:**
Calories  240
Protein  tr.
Carbohydrate  11 g
Fat  23 g
Saturated Fat  3 g
Polyunsaturated Fat  13 g
Sodium  198 mg
Cholesterol  0

Combine sugar, vinegar, salt, paprika, mustard, and onion in container of an electric blender; process on high speed until mixture is smooth. Gradually add oil in a slow, steady stream with blender on high. Process about 30 seconds or until mixture thickens. Stir in poppy seeds.

Transfer dressing to an airtight container, and store in refrigerator until ready to use. **Yield:** 1¼ cups. **Serving size:** 2 tablespoons.

**Note:** Poppy Seed Dressing may be served over fruit salads.

# *Breads and Cereals*

Breads and cereals are two of your most valuable sources of complex carbohydrates, soluble and insoluble fiber, and vitamins and minerals. When buying a commercial brand of bread or buying ingredients to make your own, buy whole wheat and other whole grains. It's the whole grains that contain the most fiber and nutrition. If you've never baked with whole wheat flour before, try some of the recipes in this chapter. Or experiment with some of your own recipes by using a mixture of half white flour and half whole wheat. Experiment too with oat bran. The fact that oat bran lowers cholesterol has been confirmed by substantial research, and it is an ingredient that can be incorporated into many of your favorite recipes, such as bread, muffins, rolls, breading for fish, stuffing for poultry, and binders for casseroles and meat loaves. Oatmeal contains the same fiber as that found in oat bran except in a lesser amount, but it is still considered healthy and an aid in lowering cholesterol.

# Honey-Wheat Raisin Bread

1¼ cups whole wheat flour
½   cup all-purpose flour
¼   cup uncooked, unprocessed oat bran
1   teaspoon baking powder
1   teaspoon baking soda
½   teaspoon salt
1   cup nonfat buttermilk
¾   cup skim milk
¼   cup honey
1   egg, beaten
3   tablespoons corn oil margarine, melted
⅓   cup chopped walnuts
⅓   cup raisins
Vegetable cooking spray

**Approximate analysis
per serving:**
Calories   128
Protein   4 g
Carbohydrate   19 g
Fat   5 g
Saturated Fat   1 g
Polyunsaturated Fat   2 g
Sodium   195 mg
Cholesterol   17 mg

Combine flours, oat bran, baking powder, soda, and salt in a large bowl; make a well in center of mixture. Combine buttermilk and next 4 ingredients, stirring until well blended; add to dry ingredients, stirring just until moistened. Fold in walnuts and raisins.

Spoon batter into an 8½- x 4½- x 3-inch loafpan coated with cooking spray. Bake at 375° for 50 minutes or until a wooden pick inserted in center comes out clean. Cool bread in pan 10 minutes. Remove from pan, and cool completely on a wire rack. Cut bread into 16 slices. **Yield:** 16 servings. **Serving size:** 1 slice.

# Orange-Walnut Bread

½   cup firmly packed brown sugar
¼   cup vegetable oil
1   egg
1½ tablespoons grated orange rind
2   cups all-purpose flour
2   teaspoons baking powder
¼   teaspoon salt
¾   cup orange juice
⅓   cup chopped walnuts
Vegetable cooking spray

**Approximate analysis
per serving:**
Calories   134
Protein   2 g
Carbohydrate   19 g
Fat   6 g
Saturated Fat   1 g
Polyunsaturated Fat   3 g
Sodium   91 mg
Cholesterol   16 mg

Combine brown sugar, oil, egg, and orange rind in a large bowl; beat at medium speed of an electric mixer until well blended. Sift together flour, baking powder, and salt. Add to sugar mixture alternately with orange juice, beginning and ending with flour mixture. Stir in walnuts.

Spoon batter into an 8½- x 4½- x 3-inch loafpan coated with cooking spray. Bake at 350° for 50 minutes or until a wooden pick inserted in center comes out clean. Cool bread in pan 10 minutes. Remove from pan, and cool completely on a wire rack. Cut bread into 16 slices. **Yield:** 16 servings. **Serving size:** 1 slice.

# Oatmeal-Applesauce Bread   *(photograph on page 19)*

⅔ cup firmly packed brown sugar
1   egg
1   cup unsweetened applesauce
1½ cups all-purpose flour
1½ teaspoons baking powder
1   teaspoon baking soda
1   teaspoon salt
2   teaspoons ground cinnamon
1½ cups uncooked regular oats
1   cup raisins
⅓ cup vegetable oil
Vegetable cooking spray
2   teaspoons uncooked regular oats

**Approximate analysis per serving:**
Calories   186
Protein   3 g
Carbohydrate   32 g
Fat   6 g
Saturated Fat   1 g
Polyunsaturated Fat   3 g
Sodium   222 mg
Cholesterol   16 mg

Combine brown sugar and egg in a large bowl, beating at medium speed of an electric mixer until smooth. Stir in applesauce. Sift together flour, baking powder, soda, salt, and cinnamon. Gradually add to egg mixture, stirring to blend. Add 1½ cups oats, raisins, and oil, stirring well.

Spoon batter into an 8½- x 4½- x 3-inch loafpan coated with cooking spray. Sprinkle with 2 teaspoons oats, and bake at 350° for 1 hour or until a wooden pick inserted in center comes out clean. Cool bread in pan 10 minutes. Remove from pan, and cool on a wire rack. Cut bread ino 16 slices. **Yield:** 16 servings. **Serving size:** 1 slice.

# Moist Oat Bran Muffins

2    cups uncooked, unprocessed oat bran
¼    cup firmly packed brown sugar
2    teaspoons baking powder
½    teaspoon ground cinnamon
¼    teaspoon salt
1    cup skim milk
½    cup unsweetened applesauce
2    egg whites, slightly beaten
2    tablespoons honey
2    tablespoons vegetable oil
Vegetable cooking spray

**Approximate analysis per serving:**
Calories   118
Protein   4 g
Carbohydrate   18 g
Fat   4 g
Saturated Fat   tr.
Polyunsaturated Fat   1 g
Sodium   132 mg
Cholesterol   tr.

Combine first 5 ingredients in a large bowl; make a well in center of mixture. Add milk and next 4 ingredients; stir just until dry ingredients are moistened. Spoon batter evenly into muffin pans coated with cooking spray, filling three-fourths full. Bake at 425° for 18 to 20 minutes. **Yield:** 1 dozen muffins. **Serving size:** 1 muffin.

# Cinnamon-Oatmeal Muffins

1    cup uncooked regular oats
1    cup nonfat buttermilk
1    cup all-purpose flour
1½  teaspoons baking powder
½    teaspoon baking soda
1    teaspoon ground cinnamon
⅓    cup firmly packed brown sugar
2    egg whites, slightly beaten
Vegetable cooking spray

**Approximate analysis per serving:**
Calories   94
Protein   3 g
Carbohydrate   18 g
Fat   1 g
Saturated Fat   tr.
Polyunsaturated Fat   tr.
Sodium   122 mg
Cholesterol   0

Combine oats and buttermilk in a small bowl; let stand 5 minutes.

Sift flour and next 3 ingredients together in a medium bowl; make a well in center of mixture. Add sugar and egg whites to oat mixture, stirring well. Add oat mixture to flour mixture, and stir just until moistened. Spoon batter evenly into muffin pans coated with cooking spray, filling two-thirds full. Bake at 400° for 18 minutes. **Yield:** 12 muffins. **Serving size:** 1 muffin.

# Banana-Oatmeal Muffins

1   cup whole wheat flour
⅓   cup sugar
2½ teaspoons baking powder
¼   teaspoon baking soda
¾   cup uncooked regular oats
½   cup ripe, mashed banana
1   egg, beaten
3   tablespoons vegetable oil
½   teaspoon banana extract
Vegetable cooking spray

**Approximate analysis per serving:**
Calories   125
Protein   3 g
Carbohydrate   19 g
Fat   5 g
Saturated Fat   1 g
Polyunsaturated Fat   2 g
Sodium   113 mg
Cholesterol   22 mg

Sift together flour, sugar, baking powder, and soda in a large bowl. Stir in oats. Add banana, egg, oil, and banana extract; stir just until moistened. Spoon batter evenly into muffin pans coated with cooking spray, filling two-thirds full. Bake at 400° for 20 minutes. **Yield:** 1 dozen muffins. **Serving size:** 1 muffin.

# Walnut-Bran Muffins

1¾ cups skim milk
1½ cups shreds of wheat bran cereal
½   cup uncooked, unprocessed oat bran
2   egg whites, slightly beaten
¼   cup corn oil
1   cup all-purpose flour
⅓   cup sugar
2   teaspoons baking soda
⅓   cup chopped walnuts
Vegetable cooking spray

**Approximate analysis per serving:**
Calories   125
Protein   4 g
Carbohydrate   17 g
Fat   5 g
Saturated Fat   1 g
Polyunsaturated Fat   3 g
Sodium   169 mg
Cholesterol   tr.

Combine milk, cereal, and oat bran in a small bowl; let stand 5 minutes. Stir in egg whites and oil.

Combine flour, sugar, and soda in a large bowl; make a well in center of mixture. Add cereal mixture and walnuts; stir just until moistened. Spoon batter evenly into muffin pans coated with cooking spray, filling two-thirds full. Bake at 400° for 20 minutes. **Yield:** 1½ dozen muffins. **Serving size:** 1 muffin.

# Banana-Bran Muffins

1   cup bran flakes cereal
1   cup nonfat buttermilk
2   tablespoons corn oil margarine, softened
¼   cup sugar
2   egg whites, slightly beaten
1½ cups all-purpose flour
1   teaspoon baking powder
½   teaspoon baking soda
1   teaspoon ground cinnamon
1   cup ripe, mashed banana
Vegetable cooking spray

**Approximate analysis
per serving:**
Calories   135
Protein   3 g
Carbohydrate   24 g
Fat   3 g
Saturated Fat   tr.
Polyunsaturated Fat   1 g
Sodium   138 mg
Cholesterol   0

Soak bran cereal in buttermilk 5 minutes.

Cream margarine and sugar in a large bowl, beating at medium speed of an electric mixer until smooth. Add egg whites, stirring well.

Combine flour and next 3 ingredients, stirring well; add to creamed mixture alternately with buttermilk mixture. Stir lightly after each addition. Add banana, and stir just until moistened. Spoon batter evenly into muffin pans coated with cooking spray or paper-lined muffin pans, filling two-thirds full. Bake at 400° for 12 to 15 minutes. **Yield:** 1 dozen muffins. **Serving size:** 1 muffin.

# Refrigerator Whole Wheat Muffins

5   cups whole wheat flour
2   cups all-purpose flour
2½ cups sugar
1   tablespoon plus 2 teaspoons baking powder
2   teaspoons salt
1   quart nonfat buttermilk
¾   cup vegetable oil
4   eggs, beaten
Vegetable cooking spray

**Approximate analysis
per serving:**
Calories   147
Protein   4 g
Carbohydrate   25 g
Fat   4 g
Saturated Fat   1 g
Polyunsaturated Fat   2 g
Sodium   196 mg
Cholesterol   22 mg

Combine dry ingredients in a large bowl; make a well in center of mixture. Combine buttermilk, oil, and eggs; add to dry ingredients, stirring just until moistened. Cover batter, and store in refrigerator up to 6 weeks.

When ready to bake, stir batter, and spoon evenly into muffin pans coated with cooking spray, filling half full. Bake at 350° for 30 minutes. **Yield:** 4 dozen muffins. **Serving size:** 1 muffin.

# Blueberry Muffins

2   cups all-purpose flour
⅓   cup sugar
2½  teaspoons baking powder
½   teaspoon salt
1   cup skim milk
¼   cup vegetable oil
1   egg, beaten
1   cup fresh, frozen, or canned blueberries
Vegetable cooking spray

**Approximate analysis per serving:**
Calories   150
Protein   3 g
Carbohydrate   22 g
Fat   5 g
Saturated Fat   1 g
Polyunsaturated Fat   3 g
Sodium   187 mg
Cholesterol   22 mg

Combine flour, sugar, baking powder, and salt in a large bowl; make a well in center of mixture. Combine milk, oil, and egg; add to dry ingredients, stirring just until moistened. Gently fold in blueberries.

Spoon batter evenly into muffin pans coated with cooking spray or paper-lined muffin pans, filling two-thirds full. Bake at 375° for 30 minutes or until lightly browned. **Yield:** 1 dozen muffins. **Serving size:** 1 muffin.

**Note:**   If using canned blueberries, drain, rinse, and pat dry before measuring and folding into batter. If frozen blueberries are used, measure first, then thaw, drain, and pat dry.

# Creole Muffins    *(photograph on page 87)*

2    cups all-purpose flour
¼    cup white cornmeal
3    tablespoons sugar
1    tablespoon baking powder
¼    teaspoon salt
¼    teaspoon red pepper
½    cup (2 ounces) shredded process American cheese
2    tablespoons chopped green pepper
2    tablespoons chopped onion
2    tablespoons chopped pimiento
1    cup plus 2 tablespoons skim milk
3    tablespoons vegetable oil
1    egg white, slightly beaten
Vegetable cooking spray

**Approximate analysis
per serving:**
Calories   147
Protein   4 g
Carbohydrate   21 g
Fat   5 g
Saturated Fat   1 g
Polyunsaturated Fat   2 g
Sodium   260 mg
Cholesterol   3 mg

Combine first 6 ingredients in a large bowl, stirring well. Add cheese, green pepper, onion, and pimiento; stir until well combined. Combine milk, oil, and egg white, stirring until well blended. Add to flour mixture, stirring just until moistened. Spoon batter evenly into muffin pans coated with cooking spray. Bake at 400° for 20 minutes or until lightly browned. **Yield:** 1 dozen muffins. **Serving size:** 1 muffin.

# Low-Cholesterol Corn Sticks    *(photograph on page 70)*

1    cup cornmeal
½    cup all-purpose flour
1    teaspoon baking powder
½    teaspoon baking soda
½    teaspoon salt
1    cup nonfat buttermilk
2    tablespoons vegetable oil
Vegetable cooking spray

**Approximate analysis
per serving:**
Calories   88
Protein   2 g
Carbohydrate   14 g
Fat   3 g
Saturated Fat   tr.
Polyunsaturated Fat   1 g
Sodium   162 mg
Cholesterol   tr.

Combine dry ingredients in a large mixing bowl; stir to mix well.

Combine buttermilk and oil; add to dry ingredients, stirring just until moistened. Let batter stand 10 minutes.

Place a cast-iron corn stick pan coated with cooking spray in a 450° oven for 3 minutes or until hot. Remove pan from oven; spoon batter into pan, filling two-thirds full. Bake at 450° for 15 minutes or until lightly browned. **Yield:** 1 dozen corn sticks. **Serving size:** 1 corn stick.

# Jalapeño Cornbread *(photograph on page 155)*

1    cup cornmeal
½    teaspoon baking soda
½    teaspoon salt
1    cup canned cream-style corn
⅔    cup nonfat buttermilk
1    (4-ounce) can chopped green chiles
2    egg whites, slightly beaten
2    tablespoons vegetable oil
Vegetable cooking spray
½    cup (2 ounces) shredded reduced-fat Cheddar
       cheese

**Approximate analysis per serving:**
Calories   104
Protein   4 g
Carbohydrate   14 g
Fat   3 g
Saturated Fat   1 g
Polyunsaturated Fat   1 g
Sodium   297 mg
Cholesterol   3 mg

Combine cornmeal, soda, and salt in a large bowl, stirring well. Add corn and next 4 ingredients, stirring just until moistened.

Coat a 9-inch square baking pan with cooking spray. Place in a 425° oven for 3 minutes or until hot. Remove pan from oven, and spoon half of batter into hot pan. Sprinkle evenly with cheese, and cover with remaining batter. Bake at 425° for 30 minutes or until golden brown. Cut into 12 portions, and serve hot. **Yield:** 12 servings. **Serving size:** 1 portion.

# Vegetable-Cheese Cornbread

1    cup all-purpose flour
½    cup white cornmeal
1    tablespoon sugar
1    tablespoon baking powder
½    teaspoon salt
¾    cup skim milk
¼    cup (1 ounce) shredded sharp Cheddar cheese
1    egg white, beaten
3    tablespoons chopped green pepper
1    tablespoon chopped onion
1    tablespoon corn oil margarine, melted
Vegetable cooking spray

**Approximate analysis per serving:**
Calories   116
Protein   4 g
Carbohydrate   18 g
Fat   3 g
Saturated Fat   1 g
Polyunsaturated Fat   1 g
Sodium   286 mg
Cholesterol   4 mg

Combine first 5 ingredients in a medium bowl, stirring well. Gradually add milk, and stir well to mix. Add cheese, egg white, green pepper, onion, and margarine, stirring gently to mix.

Pour batter into an 8-inch square baking pan coated with cooking spray. Bake at 375° for 25 minutes. Cut into 9 squares, and serve hot. **Yield:** 9 servings. **Serving size:** 1 square.

# Whole Wheat Biscuits    *(photograph on page 189)*

1    cup whole wheat flour
1    cup all-purpose flour
1    tablespoon baking powder
½    teaspoon salt
¾    cup skim milk
¼    cup vegetable oil
Vegetable cooking spray

**Approximate analysis per serving:**
Calories   114
Protein   3 g
Carbohydrate   15 g
Fat   5 g
Saturated Fat   1 g
Polyunsaturated Fat   3 g
Sodium   197 mg
Cholesterol   tr.

Combine flours, baking powder, and salt; stir well to mix. Add milk and oil, stirring to form a soft dough.

Turn dough out onto a lightly floured surface, and knead lightly 2 or 3 times. Roll dough to ½-inch thickness, and cut with a 2¼-inch biscuit cutter. Place biscuits on a baking sheet coated with cooking spray. Bake at 450° for 12 minutes or until lightly browned. **Yield:** 1 dozen biscuits. **Serving size:** 1 biscuit.

# **Yummy Oatmeal Yeast Rolls** *(photograph on cover)*

1    package dry yeast
¼    cup warm water (105° to 115°)
1½   cups warm skim milk (105° to 115°)
⅓    cup vegetable oil
¼    cup sugar
2¼   teaspoons salt
4    cups all-purpose flour, divided
1½   cups uncooked regular oats
Vegetable cooking spray
1    egg white, slightly beaten
1    tablespoon water

**Approximate analysis per serving:**
Calories   148
Protein   4 g
Carbohydrate   23 g
Fat   4 g
Saturated Fat   tr.
Polyunsaturated Fat   2 g
Sodium   243 mg
Cholesterol   tr.

Dissolve yeast in warm water; let stand 5 minutes. Combine milk, oil, sugar, and salt in a large bowl. Add 1 cup flour, yeast mixture, and oats, stirring until well combined. Gradually stir in enough remaining flour to make a soft dough. Turn dough out onto a lightly floured surface; knead 8 to 10 minutes or until smooth and elastic.

Shape dough into a ball, and place in a bowl coated with cooking spray, turning to grease top. Cover and let rise in a warm place (85°), free from drafts, 1½ hours or until doubled in bulk.

Punch dough down; cover and let rest 10 minutes. Divide dough into thirds, and shape each third into 7 rolls. Place rolls in muffin pans coated with cooking spray. Cover and let rise in a warm place, free from drafts, 1 hour or until doubled in bulk.

Combine egg white and 1 tablespoon water; stir until well blended. Gently brush egg white mixture over tops of rolls. Bake at 375° for 15 minutes or until lightly browned. Remove from pans, and serve hot. **Yield:** 21 rolls. **Serving size:** 1 roll.

# Dainty Crusty Biscuits

2    cups all-purpose flour
2½ teaspoons baking powder
½    teaspoon salt
¾    cup skim milk
⅓    cup vegetable oil

Combine flour, baking powder, and salt in a medium mixing bowl; gradually add milk and oil, stirring just until moistened.

Turn dough out onto a lightly floured surface, and knead lightly 2 or 3 times.

Pat dough to ½-inch thickness, and cut with a floured 1¾-inch biscuit cutter. Arrange biscuits with sides lightly touching on an ungreased baking sheet. Bake at 450° for 12 to 15 minutes or until lightly browned. **Yield:** 1½ dozen biscuits. **Serving size:** 1 biscuit.

**Approximate analysis per serving:**
Calories  85
Protein  2 g
Carbohydrate  10 g
Fat  4 g
Saturated Fat  1 g
Polyunsaturated Fat  2 g
Sodium  142 mg
Cholesterol  tr.

# Oatmeal Pancakes    *(photograph on page 2)*

1½ cups uncooked regular oats
½    cup all-purpose flour
1    tablespoon baking powder
¼    teaspoon salt
1¼ cups skim milk
2    egg whites, slightly beaten
2    tablespoons corn oil
Vegetable cooking spray
2    cups Strawberry Sauce (recipe follows)

Combine first 4 ingredients in a medium bowl; make a well in center of mixture. Combine milk, egg whites, and oil, stirring until well blended. Add to dry ingredients, and stir just until moistened.

For each pancake, pour 3 tablespoons batter onto a hot griddle or skillet coated with cooking spray, smoothing to distribute oats. Turn pancakes when tops are covered with bubbles and edges are lightly browned. Top each serving of pancakes with ¼ cup Strawberry Sauce. Serve immediately. **Yield:** 1 dozen pancakes. **Serving size:** 2 pancakes with ¼ cup Strawberry Sauce.

**Approximate analysis per serving:**
Calories  181
Protein  7 g
Carbohydrate  24 g
Fat  6 g
Saturated Fat  1 g
Polyunsaturated Fat  3 g
Sodium  338 mg
Cholesterol  1 mg

**Strawberry Sauce:**

4   cups fresh strawberries, washed, hulled, halved, and divided
½   cup sugar
½   cup plus 2 tablespoons orange juice, divided
1   teaspoon lemon juice
1½ teaspoons cornstarch

Combine 2 cups halved strawberries, sugar, 2 tablespoons orange juice, and lemon juice in a small saucepan. Cook over medium-high heat, stirring constantly, 3 to 5 minutes or until sugar dissolves and strawberries begin to soften. Remove from heat, and transfer mixture to container of an electric blender; cover and process until slightly pureed.

Combine cornstarch and remaining ½ cup orange juice in saucepan; stir until dissolved. Add pureed strawberry mixture, and cook over medium-high heat, stirring frequently, 5 minutes or until clear and slightly thickened. Remove from heat, and stir in remaining halved strawberries. Serve warm over pancakes, or let cool to serve as a topping for fresh fruit or desserts. Store in an airtight container. **Yield:** 3 cups. **Serving size:** ¼ cup.

**Approximate analysis per serving:**
Calories   27
Protein   tr.
Carbohydrate   7 g
Fat   tr.
Saturated Fat   tr.
Polyunsaturated Fat   tr.
Sodium   tr.
Cholesterol   0

# Fruited Oatmeal   *(photograph on page 19)*

1⅓ cups skim milk
⅔   cup uncooked quick-cooking oats
1   small apple, unpeeled and shredded
¼   cup raisins
1   tablespoon brown sugar
½   teaspoon ground cinnamon
¼   teaspoon salt
Diced unpeeled apple (optional)

Combine milk and oats in a small saucepan, stirring well; bring to a boil. Reduce heat, and simmer 1 minute, stirring constantly. Stir in shredded apple, raisins, brown sugar, cinnamon, and salt. Cover and remove from heat. Let stand until mixture reaches desired consistency. Sprinkle oatmeal with diced apple, if desired. **Yield:** 2 servings. **Serving size:** 1 cup.

**Approximate analysis per serving:**
Calories   258
Protein   10 g
Carbohydrate   52 g
Fat   2 g
Saturated Fat   tr.
Polyunsaturated Fat   tr.
Sodium   296 mg
Cholesterol   2 mg

# Swiss-Style Oatmeal

1    tablespoon lemon juice
1    medium apple, unpeeled, cored, and shredded
¾    cup skim milk
¾    cup uncooked quick-cooking oats
¼    cup raisins
1    tablespoon brown sugar
½    teaspoon ground cinnamon
¼    teaspoon salt
Fresh blueberries, strawberry, banana, and apple slices
        (optional)

Sprinkle lemon juice over shredded apple in a medium bowl; stir to coat well. Add milk and remaining ingredients except fresh fruit, stirring until combined. Serve immediately, or cover and store in refrigerator up to 2 days. If desired, garnish each serving with fresh fruit. **Yield:** 3 servings. **Serving size:** ⅔ cup.

**Approximate analysis per serving:**
Calories   177
Protein   6 g
Carbohydrate   37 g
Fat   2 g
Saturated Fat   tr.
Polyunsaturated Fat   tr.
Sodium   198 mg
Cholesterol   1 mg

# Peanut Butter and Honey Oat Bran

1    cup water
⅓    cup uncooked, unprocessed oat bran
1    tablespoon creamy peanut butter
⅛    teaspoon salt
1    tablespoon honey
Skim milk (optional)

Combine water, oat bran, peanut butter, and salt in a 4-cup glass measure, stirring well. Cover with heavy-duty plastic wrap. Microwave at HIGH 2 to 2½-minutes or until mixture begins to thicken. Remove from microwave, and stir well to eliminate lumps. Spoon hot cereal into serving bowls, and swirl 1½ teaspoons honey into each serving. Serve with skim milk, if desired. **Yield:** 2 servings. **Serving size:** ⅔ cup.

**Approximate analysis per serving:**
Calories   132
Protein   5 g
Carbohydrate   17 g
Fat   5 g
Saturated Fat   1 g
Polyunsaturated Fat   1 g
Sodium   233 mg
Cholesterol   0

# Desserts

Adjusting recipes to make them healthier can be fun, but changing dessert recipes may be the greatest challenge. A proper balance between the tenderizing effect of sugar, fat, and egg yolk and the firming effect of the flour and egg white must be achieved. This balance may require some experimentation, and moderation in serving size must still be the rule. Emphasizing fruits as part of the ingredients in desserts offers several nutritional benefits: it increases vitamin and fiber content while helping to decrease calories. In addition, it reduces the need for sugar to achieve the sweet taste we associate with desserts. In fact, the natural sweetness of most fruits makes them a delight to serve alone or with a dollop of non-fat or low-fat yogurt on top. For a favorite summertime dessert, crank up the ice cream freezer and try our Peach Ice Cream (page 194) — a low-fat version made with egg whites and skim milk.

# Meringue Shells with Fruit

4   egg whites
¼   teaspoon cream of tartar
1¼ teaspoons vanilla extract, divided
1   cup plus 3 tablespoons sugar, divided
2   cups fresh blueberries or other fresh fruit
1   cup plain low-fat yogurt

Beat egg whites (at room temperature) in a large bowl at high speed of an electric mixer until foamy. Add cream of tartar and ¼ teaspoon vanilla; beat until soft peaks form. Gradually add 1 cup sugar, 1 tablespoon at a time, beating until stiff peaks form.

Spoon meringue mixture into 8 mounds on a baking sheet lined with unglazed brown paper. Shape meringue mixture into circles, using the back of a spoon and mounding the sides at least ½ inch higher than centers. Bake at 275° for 1 hour or until lightly browned. Let cool.

Carefully transfer meringue shells to serving plates, and fill each shell with ¼ cup blueberries. Combine yogurt, remaining 3 tablespoons sugar, and remaining 1 teaspoon vanilla; stir until well blended, and drizzle 2 tablespoons over blueberries. **Yield:** 8 servings. **Serving size:** 1 filled shell with 2 tablespoons yogurt mixture.

**Approximate analysis per serving:**
Calories   139
Protein   4 g
Carbohydrate   32 g
Fat   tr.
Saturated Fat   tr.
Polyunsaturated Fat   tr.
Sodium   53 mg
Cholesterol   1 mg

# Apple Meringue

½   cup sugar
¼   cup water
8   cups unpeeled, sliced apples
¼   cup orange juice
2   egg whites
½   teaspoon vanilla extract
⅛   teaspoon cream of tartar
¼   cup sugar

**Approximate analysis per serving:**
Calories   117
Protein   1 g
Carbohydrate   29 g
Fat   tr.
Saturated Fat   tr.
Polyunsaturated Fat   tr.
Sodium   14 mg
Cholesterol   0

Combine ½ cup sugar and water in a Dutch oven, stirring well. Bring to a boil. Add apples to sugar mixture. Cover and return to a boil. Reduce heat, and simmer 15 minutes or until apples are tender. Stir gently once or twice to coat apples and cook evenly. Transfer apples to a 9-inch square baking pan, using a slotted spoon. Sprinkle apples evenly with orange juice. Set aside.

Beat egg whites (at room temperature) in a small bowl at high speed of an electric mixer until foamy. Add vanilla and cream of tartar; beat until soft peaks form. Gradually add ¼ cup sugar, 1 tablespoon at a time, beating until stiff peaks form. Gently spread over apples in pan, and bake at 325° for 15 minutes or until lightly browned. Cut into 9 portions, and serve warm. **Yield:** 9 servings. **Serving size:** 1 portion.

# Peach Rum Mousse *(photograph on page 189)*

---

1   (16-ounce) can sliced peaches in light syrup,
      undrained
1   envelope unflavored gelatin
¼   cup honey
¼   teaspoon almond extract
1   tablespoon lemon juice
1   cup vanilla low-fat yogurt
1½ teaspoons rum flavoring
Fresh mint sprigs (optional)

**Approximate analysis per serving:**
Calories   116
Protein   4 g
Carbohydrate   25 g
Fat   1 g
Saturated Fat   tr.
Polyunsaturated Fat   tr.
Sodium   55 mg
Cholesterol   2 mg

Drain peaches, reserving syrup. Place syrup in a small saucepan; sprinkle gelatin over syrup, and let stand 1 minute. Place peaches, honey, and almond extract in container of an electric blender. Cover and process until smooth. Set aside.

Add lemon juice to gelatin mixture; cook over low heat, stirring until gelatin is dissolved. Remove from heat, and add yogurt and rum flavoring. Add mixture to pureed peaches in blender; cover and process until well blended.

Spoon mousse evenly into 6 serving dishes, and chill until slightly thickened. Garnish each serving with fresh mint sprigs, if desired. **Yield:** 3 cups. **Serving size:** ½ cup.

# Cherry Streusel

1   (16-ounce) can pitted sour red cherries, undrained
½   cup sugar
1   egg white, slightly beaten
2   tablespoons skim milk
1   tablespoon vanilla extract
½   cup all-purpose flour
¼   cup firmly packed brown sugar
¼   cup corn oil margarine
½   cup chopped walnuts

**Approximate analysis per serving:**
Calories   154
Protein   2 g
Carbohydrate   22 g
Fat   7 g
Saturated Fat   1 g
Polyunsaturated Fat   3 g
Sodium   61 mg
Cholesterol   tr.

   Combine cherries and ½ cup sugar in an 8-inch square baking pan, stirring well.
   Combine egg white, milk, and vanilla, stirring well to blend. Pour over cherries. Combine flour and brown sugar in a small bowl, stirring well to mix. Cut in margarine with a pastry blender until mixture resembles coarse meal. Stir in walnuts. Sprinkle crumb mixture over top. Bake at 350° for 40 to 50 minutes or until golden brown. Serve warm. **Yield:** 12 servings. **Serving size:** ½ cup.

# Apple-Oatmeal Crisp

4   cups unpeeled, chopped apples
3   tablespoons sugar
1   tablespoon lemon juice
Vegetable cooking spray
1   cup uncooked regular oats
½   cup firmly packed dark brown sugar
⅓   cup all-purpose flour
¼   cup corn oil margarine, melted
1   teaspoon ground cinnamon
¼   teaspoon salt

**Approximate analysis per serving:**
Calories   187
Protein   2 g
Carbohydrate   32 g
Fat   6 g
Saturated Fat   1 g
Polyunsaturated Fat   2 g
Sodium   123 mg
Cholesterol   0

   Combine apples, 3 tablespoons sugar, and lemon juice. Toss gently, and spoon mixture into a 9-inch square baking dish coated lightly with cooking spray. Combine oats, brown sugar, flour, margarine, cinnamon, and salt; stir until well combined. Sprinkle evenly over apple mixture. Bake at 375° for 30 minutes or until golden brown. Serve warm. **Yield:** 9 servings. **Serving size:** ½ cup.

# Winter Fruit Compote  *(photograph on page 138)*

4   whole allspice
2   whole cloves
3   cups water
⅓   cup sugar
1   (12-ounce) package dried figlets, stems removed
1   (6-ounce) package dried apricots
¼   cup golden raisins
3   thin slices lemon, halved crosswise
3   thin slices orange, halved crosswise
½   teaspoon vanilla extract
1   medium pear, unpeeled
½   cup plus 2 tablespoons Yogurt Dessert Topping
      (recipe follows)
Apricot roses (optional)
Pear slices (optional)

Combine allspice and cloves in a cheesecloth bag; tie securely, and set aside.

Combine water, sugar, and spice bag in a large saucepan; cover and bring to a boil. Add figlets; reduce heat to medium. Cover and cook 10 minutes. Add dried apricots and next 3 ingredients; continue to cook, covered, 5 minutes. Remove from heat; remove spice bag. Stir in vanilla. Slice pear, and gently fold into fruit mixture. Spoon ½ cup fruit mixture into each of 10 dessert dishes. Dollop each serving with 1 tablespoon Yogurt Dessert Topping and, if desired, garnish with apricot roses and pear slices. **Yield:** 10 servings. **Serving size:** ½ cup fruit mixture with 1 tablespoon Yogurt Dessert Topping.

**Approximate analysis per serving:**
Calories   189
Protein   3 g
Carbohydrate   48 g
Fat   1 g
Saturated Fat   tr.
Polyunsaturated Fat   tr.
Sodium   18 mg
Cholesterol   1 mg

## Yogurt Dessert Topping:

1   cup plain nonfat yogurt
2   tablespoons sugar
½   teaspoon vanilla extract

Combine all ingredients, stirring until well blended. Cover and refrigerate until thoroughly chilled. **Yield:** 1 cup. **Serving size:** 1 tablespoon.

**Approximate analysis per serving:**
Calories   15
Protein   1 g
Carbohydrate   3 g
Fat   tr.
Saturated Fat   tr.
Polyunsaturated Fat   tr.
Sodium   10 mg
Cholesterol   1 mg

# Festive Oranges   *(photograph on pages 190-191)*

4   large oranges, divided
⅓   cup water
⅓   cup Grand Marnier or other orange-flavored liqueur
¼   cup sugar
2   teaspoons lemon juice
¼   teaspoon cream of tartar

Remove a thin layer of peel from 2 oranges, using a small sharp knife or vegetable peeler. (Be careful not to include bitter white pith.) Cut peel into julienne strips. Remove 2 teaspoons grated orange rind from 1 orange. Set orange strips, grated rind, and whole oranges aside.

Combine water, liqueur, sugar, lemon juice, and cream of tartar in a heavy saucepan; bring to a boil, stirring occasionally to dissolve sugar. Add orange strips and grated rind; simmer until syrup is reduced by one-third and orange strips and rind are caramelized. Remove syrup and caramelized pieces from heat, and let cool.

Using a sharp knife and holding oranges over a bowl to catch juice, remove and discard all remaining peel and pith from 4 whole oranges. Add juice to syrup, stirring well. Cut each orange crosswise into ¼-inch-thick slices. Arrange orange slices in a single layer in a shallow dish. Spoon syrup evenly over orange slices to distribute caramelized orange strips and rind. Cover and chill at least 4 hours. Serve orange slices with syrup on individual dessert plates. **Yield:** 4 servings. **Serving size:** 1 cup.

**Note:** Oranges may be sectioned rather than sliced and served in individual sherbet dishes.

**Approximate analysis per serving:**
Calories   145
Protein   1 g
Carbohydrate   37 g
Fat   tr.
Saturated Fat   tr.
Polyunsaturated Fat   tr.
Sodium   15 mg
Cholesterol   0

*Impress a friend with an elegant, low-fat dinner of Turkey Tenderloin Amandine (page 113), Sweet Potato Casserole (page 147), steamed brussels sprouts, Waldorf Salad (page 164), Whole Wheat Biscuits (page 178), and Peach Rum Mousse (page 185).*

*Rejoice! There really are wonderful low-fat, low-cholesterol desserts: (clockwise from left front) Festive Oranges (page 188), Chocolate Buttermilk Cake (page 200), Angel Food Cake (pages 200), Tangy Grapefruit Sorbet (page 195), and Chewy Gingersnaps (page 205) served with Apricot-Yogurt Spread (page 42).*

# Fresh Peach Dessert

12  vanilla wafers
1   tablespoon corn oil margarine, melted
¼   teaspoon ground cinnamon
¼   cup sugar
3   tablespoons cornstarch
1   (12-ounce) can peach nectar
1   tablespoon lemon juice
⅛   teaspoon ground nutmeg
¼   teaspoon almond extract
4   cups peeled, sliced fresh peaches
1   cup vanilla low-fat yogurt

**Approximate analysis per serving:**
Calories   163
Protein   3 g
Carbohydrate   33 g
Fat   3 g
Saturated Fat   1 g
Polyunsaturated Fat   1 g
Sodium   55 mg
Cholesterol   4 mg

Place vanilla wafers between 2 sheets of wax paper, and crush with a rolling pin to yield ¾ cup crumbs. Combine cookie crumbs, margarine, and cinnamon, stirring well to mix; spread evenly on a baking sheet, and bake at 375° for 7 minutes or until lightly toasted. Set aside.

Combine sugar and cornstarch in a large saucepan, stirring well to blend. Add peach nectar, lemon juice, nutmeg, and almond extract, and bring to a boil. Reduce heat, and simmer, stirring constantly, until thickened and clear. Remove from heat, and let cool. Add peaches, stirring gently to coat.

Layer cookie crumbs and peach mixture evenly in 8 individual custard or sherbet dishes. Cover and chill thoroughly. Top each dessert with 2 tablespoons vanilla yogurt just before serving. **Yield:** 8 servings. **Serving size:** ¾ cup.

*Delight your party guests with an array of appealing appetizers like Cranberry Punch (page 50), Cracker Bread (page 41) for dipping into Yogurt Cheese Spread (page 42), and Creamy Fruit Dip (page 44) to serve with various fruits.*

# Peach Ice Cream

2    cups skim milk
1    cup sugar
4    egg whites, slightly beaten
1    quart sliced fresh or frozen peaches, mashed
1    (13-ounce) can evaporated skim milk
1    teaspoon almond extract

Combine 2 cups skim milk and sugar in a Dutch oven; cook over medium heat, stirring constantly, until sugar dissolves. Gradually add egg whites to milk mixture, stirring constantly. Reduce heat to low, and cook, stirring constantly, 3 minutes. Remove from heat, and stir in peaches, evaporated skim milk, and almond extract.

Pour mixture into freezer can of a 1-gallon hand-turned or electric ice cream freezer; freeze according to manufacturer's instructions. Let ripen about 1 hour before serving. **Yield:** 3 quarts. **Serving size:** 1 cup.

**Approximate analysis per serving:**
Calories   183
Protein   5 g
Carbohydrate   42 g
Fat   tr.
Saturated Fat   tr.
Polyunsaturated Fat   tr.
Sodium   78 mg
Cholesterol   2 mg

# Apricot Ice

1    (16-ounce) can apricot halves in light syrup, undrained
1    (12-ounce) can apricot nectar
⅓    cup sugar
1    teaspoon lemon juice

Combine all ingredients in container of an electric blender. Cover and process until smooth. Pour evenly into freezer trays or an 8-inch square baking pan. Freeze until firm, stirring several times during freezing process. Break frozen mixture into large pieces, and place in a medium bowl; beat at low speed of an electric mixer until smooth. Spoon evenly into chilled individual dessert dishes; freeze until ready to serve. **Yield:** 3 cups. **Serving size:** ½ cup.

**Approximate analysis per serving:**
Calories   73
Protein   1 g
Carbohydrate   18 g
Fat   tr.
Saturated Fat   0
Polyunsaturated Fat   0
Sodium   2 mg
Cholesterol   0

# Tangy Grapefruit Sorbet  *(photograph on pages 190-191)*

½ cup cold water
1   tablespoon unflavored gelatin
1   cup pink grapefruit juice
⅔ cup diced pink grapefruit sections
¼ cup sugar
1   tablespoon lemon juice
Fresh kiwifruit slices (optional)
Fresh mint sprigs (optional)

**Approximate analysis
per serving:**
Calories   61
Protein   2 g
Carbohydrate   14 g
Fat   0
Saturated Fat   0
Polyunsaturated Fat   0
Sodium   4 mg
Cholesterol   0

Combine water and gelatin in a large saucepan; cook over low heat, stirring until dissolved. Remove from heat, and stir in grapefruit juice, diced grapefruit, sugar, and lemon juice. Pour grapefruit mixture into freezer trays or an 8-inch square baking pan, and freeze until almost firm.

Position knife blade in food processor bowl. Break frozen mixture into large pieces, and place in processor bowl; process several seconds or until fluffy but not thawed. Return to freezer trays, and freeze until firm. Use an ice cream scoop to serve. If desired, garnish each serving with kiwifruit slices and a mint sprig. **Yield:** 3 cups. **Serving size:** ½ cup.

*Grapefruit, with its clean, fresh taste, is a natural ingredient for a sorbet, which is a fruit-flavored ice often served as a palate refresher between courses. In addition to cholesterol-lowering fiber, grapefruit is very rich in vitamin C and potassium, and pink grapefruit is also high in vitamin A.*

# Applesauce Cake

1    cup unsweetened applesauce
¾    cup firmly packed brown sugar
½    cup corn oil
1¾  cups all-purpose flour
1    teaspoon baking soda
1    teaspoon ground cinnamon
½    teaspoon salt
½    teaspoon ground cloves
⅓    cup raisins
⅓    cup chopped walnuts
Vegetable cooking spray

**Approximate analysis
per serving:**
Calories   337
Protein   4 g
Carbohydrate   49 g
Fat   16 g
Saturated Fat   2 g
Polyunsaturated Fat   10 g
Sodium   209 mg
Cholesterol   0

Combine applesauce, brown sugar, and oil; stir until well blended. Set aside. Sift flour and next 4 ingredients together in a large bowl. Add raisins and walnuts, stirring to coat well. Stir in applesauce mixture.

Spoon batter into an 8-inch square baking dish coated with cooking spray. Bake at 350° for 40 minutes or until a wooden pick inserted in center of cake comes out clean. Cool and cut into 9 squares. **Yield:** 9 servings. **Serving size:** 1 square.

# Fresh Apple-Walnut Cake

2    cups all-purpose flour
1¼  cups sugar
1    teaspoon baking soda
1    teaspoon salt
1    teaspoon ground cinnamon
½    teaspoon baking powder
½    cup corn oil
¼    cup apple juice
2    eggs, beaten
1    egg white
2    cups peeled, cubed apple
½    cup chopped walnuts
Vegetable cooking spray

**Approximate analysis
per serving:**
Calories   195
Protein   3 g
Carbohydrate   27 g
Fat   9 g
Saturated Fat   1 g
Polyunsaturated Fat   5 g
Sodium   176 mg
Cholesterol   29 mg

Sift first 6 ingredients together in a 2-quart bowl; make a well in center of mixture. Add oil, apple juice, eggs, and egg white, stirring just until dry ingredients are moistened. Fold in apple and walnuts. Spoon batter into a 13- x 9- x 2-inch baking pan coated with cooking spray. Bake at 350° for 40 minutes or until a wooden pick inserted in center comes out clean. Cool completely in pan, and cut into 18 portions. **Yield:** 18 servings. **Serving size:** 1 portion.

# Peach Dessert Cake

½   cup corn oil margarine, softened
¾   cup sugar, divided
1    egg
1    egg white
1    teaspoon vanilla extract
1    cup all-purpose flour
1    teaspoon baking powder
¼    teaspoon salt
¼    cup skim milk
Vegetable cooking spray
4    medium-size fresh peaches, peeled, seeded, and
       sliced
½    teaspoon ground cinnamon

**Approximate analysis per serving:**
Calories   176
Protein   2 g
Carbohydrate   23 g
Fat   9 g
Saturated Fat   2 g
Polyunsaturated Fat   3 g
Sodium   143 mg
Cholesterol   22 mg

Cream margarine in a large bowl; add ½ cup sugar, beating until light and fluffy (about 5 minutes). Add egg, egg white, and vanilla; beat until well blended. Sift together flour, baking powder, and salt. Add to creamed mixture alternately with milk, beginning and ending with flour mixture.

Spoon half of batter into an 8-inch square baking pan coated with cooking spray. Arrange peach slices over top, and spread with remaining batter. Combine remaining ¼ cup sugar and cinnamon; stir well to blend. Sprinkle mixture over top of batter. Bake at 350° for 40 minutes or until a wooden pick inserted in center comes out clean. Cool completely in pan, and cut into 12 portions. **Yield:** 12 servings. **Serving size:** 1 portion.

# Orange-Glazed Citrus Cake

Vegetable cooking spray
¼   cup chopped walnuts, divided
1    large orange
1    cup golden raisins
2    cups all-purpose flour
1    cup sugar
1    teaspoon baking soda
1    teaspoon salt
½   cup corn oil margarine, softened
1    cup skim milk, divided
1    egg
1    egg white
1    cup powdered sugar

**Approximate analysis per serving:**
Calories   176
Protein   2 g
Carbohydrate   30 g
Fat   6 g
Saturated Fat   1 g
Polyunsaturated Fat   2 g
Sodium   174 mg
Cholesterol   11 mg

Coat a 10-inch nonstick Bundt pan with cooking spray. Sprinkle with 2 tablespoons walnuts, and set aside.

Squeeze 1 tablespoon juice from orange; set juice aside. Remove seeds and pith from orange; place orange pulp and rind in bowl of food processor fitted with knife blade. Add raisins; cover and process until coarsely ground. Set aside.

Sift flour, 1 cup sugar, soda, and salt together in a large bowl. Add margarine and ¾ cup milk. Beat at medium speed of an electric mixer 2 minutes or until well blended. Add egg, egg white, and remaining ¼ cup milk. Beat 2 minutes. Fold in orange-raisin mixture and remaining 2 tablespoons walnuts.

Pour batter into prepared pan, and bake at 350° for 45 minutes to 1 hour or until cake springs back when lightly touched. Remove from pan, and let cool. Combine powdered sugar and reserved orange juice, beating until well blended. Drizzle over top of cake. Cut cake into 24 slices.
**Yield:** 24 servings. **Serving size:** 1 slice.

# Prune Cake

1 cup sugar
½ cup vegetable oil
2 egg whites
1 egg
2 cups all-purpose flour
1½ teaspoons baking powder
1 teaspoon baking soda
1 teaspoon ground cinnamon
1 teaspoon ground nutmeg
½ teaspoon salt
1 cup nonfat buttermilk
1 cup chopped pitted prunes
¼ cup chopped pecans
Vegetable cooking spray

**Approximate analysis per serving:**
Calories 185
Protein 2 g
Carbohydrate 29 g
Fat 7 g
Saturated Fat 1 g
Polyunsaturated Fat 3 g
Sodium 157 mg
Cholesterol 11 mg

Combine sugar, oil, egg whites, and egg in a large bowl; beat at medium speed of an electric mixer 2 minutes or until smooth. Sift together flour, baking powder, soda, cinnamon, nutmeg, and salt. Add to sugar mixture alternately with buttermilk, beginning and ending with flour mixture. Mix well after each addition. Stir in chopped prunes and chopped pecans.

Spoon batter into a 13- x 9- x 2-inch baking pan coated with cooking spray. Bake at 350° for 30 minutes or until a wooden pick inserted in center comes out clean. Cool completely in pan, and cut into 24 portions. **Yield:** 24 servings. **Serving size:** 1 portion.

# Chocolate Buttermilk Cake　*(photograph on pages 190-191)*

1⅔ cups all-purpose flour
1　cup sugar
⅓　cup cocoa
1　teaspoon baking soda
½　teaspoon salt
1　cup nonfat buttermilk
⅓　cup vegetable oil
1　teaspoon vanilla extract
Vegetable cooking spray
1　teaspoon sifted powdered sugar
Fresh raspberries (optional)

**Approximate analysis per serving:**
Calories　146
Protein　2 g
Carbohydrate　21 g
Fat　7 g
Saturated Fat　1 g
Polyunsaturated Fat　4 g
Sodium　116 mg
Cholesterol　0

　　Sift first 5 ingredients together in a large bowl; make a well in center of mixture. Add buttermilk, oil, and vanilla, stirring until smooth. Spoon batter into a 9-inch round cakepan coated with cooking spray, and bake at 375° for 20 minutes or until a wooden pick inserted in center comes out clean. Cool completely in pan. Sprinkle lightly with powdered sugar, and garnish with raspberries, if desired. Cut into 18 portions to serve. **Yield:** 18 servings. **Serving size:** 1 portion.

# Angel Food Cake　*(photograph on pages 190-191)*

12 egg whites
¼　teaspoon salt
1½ teaspoons cream of tartar
1½ teaspoons vanilla extract
¼　teaspoon almond extract
1½ cups sugar, divided
1　cup sifted cake flour
Sliced fresh peaches (optional)
Fresh strawberries (optional)

**Approximate analysis per serving:**
Calories　107
Protein　3 g
Carbohydrate　24 g
Fat　tr.
Saturated Fat　0
Polyunsaturated Fat　0
Sodium　87 mg
Cholesterol　0

　　Beat egg whites (at room temperature) and salt in a large bowl at high speed of an electric mixer until foamy. Add cream of tartar and flavorings; beat until soft peaks form. Gradually add ¾ cup sugar, 1 tablespoon at a time, beating until stiff peaks form.

Sift flour and remaining ¾ cup sugar together 3 times. Sift flour mixture over egg white mixture, one-fourth at a time; fold well after each addition.

Spoon batter into an ungreased 10-inch tube pan. Bake at 375° for 30 to 35 minutes or until cake springs back when lightly touched. Invert cake, and let cool completely. Remove cake from pan. Transfer to cake plate, and garnish with peaches and strawberries, if desired. Cut into 16 slices to serve. **Yield:** 16 servings. **Serving size:** 1 slice.

# Low-Cholesterol Pound Cake *(photograph on back cover)*

1   cup corn oil margarine, softened
2   cups sugar
¾   cup egg substitute
3   cups sifted all-purpose flour
½   teaspoon baking powder
¼   teaspoon salt
1   cup skim milk
1   teaspoon lemon extract
1   teaspoon vanilla extract
Vegetable cooking spray
1   teaspoon sifted powdered sugar
Lemon slices (optional)

**Approximate analysis per serving:**
Calories   152
Protein   2 g
Carbohydrate   21 g
Fat   7 g
Saturated Fat   1 g
Polyunsaturated Fat   2 g
Sodium   109 mg
Cholesterol   tr.

Cream margarine in a large bowl; gradually add 2 cups sugar, beating at medium speed of an electric mixer until light and fluffy (about 5 minutes). Add egg substitute, ¼ cup at a time, beating well after each addition.

Sift together flour, baking powder, and salt. Add to creamed mixture alternately with milk, beginning and ending with flour mixture. Mix just until blended after each addition. Stir in flavorings.

Pour batter into a 10-inch nonstick Bundt pan coated with cooking spray. Bake at 325° for 1 hour and 15 minutes or until a wooden pick inserted in center comes out clean. Remove from pan immediately, and let cool. Transfer cake to a serving plate, and sprinkle lightly with powdered sugar. Garnish base of cake with lemon slices, if desired. Cut cake into 32 slices. **Yield:** 32 servings. **Serving size:** 1 slice.

# Gingerbread

1½ cups all-purpose flour
½   cup sugar
2   teaspoons baking powder
1   teaspoon ground ginger
½   teaspoon ground cinnamon
¼   teaspoon salt
¼   teaspoon ground cloves
½   cup boiling water
⅓   cup molasses
¼   cup corn oil
Vegetable cooking spray
1   cup unsweetened applesauce

**Approximate analysis per serving:**
Calories   117
Protein   1 g
Carbohydrate   20 g
Fat   4 g
Saturated Fat   tr.
Polyunsaturated Fat   2 g
Sodium   92 mg
Cholesterol   0

Sift first 7 ingredients together in a medium bowl; make a well in center of mixture. Combine water, molasses, and oil, stirring well; add to flour mixture, beating at medium speed of an electric mixer until batter is smooth.

Spoon batter into an 8-inch square baking pan coated with cooking spray. Bake at 325° for 25 to 30 minutes or until a wooden pick inserted in center comes out clean. Cut into 16 squares, and top each serving with 1 tablespoon applesauce. **Yield:** 16 servings. **Serving size:** 1 square with 1 tablespoon applesauce.

# Fruit Squares

1   cup chopped mixed dried fruit
1   cup sugar
1   cup water
1   teaspoon ground cinnamon
¼   teaspoon salt
¼   teaspoon ground cloves
½   cup corn oil margarine, softened
1   teaspoon baking soda
2   cups all-purpose flour
½   cup chopped pecans
1½ teaspoons vanilla extract, divided
Vegetable cooking spray
2   cups powdered sugar
2   tablespoons skim milk

**Approximate analysis per serving:**
Calories   95
Protein   1 g
Carbohydrate   17 g
Fat   3 g
Saturated Fat   tr.
Polyunsaturated Fat   1 g
Sodium   52 mg
Cholesterol   tr.

Combine dried fruit, 1 cup sugar, water, cinnamon, salt, and cloves in a large saucepan. Bring to a boil, and boil 4 minutes; add margarine, stirring until melted. Remove from heat, and stir in soda. Let cool. Add flour, pecans, and 1 teaspoon vanilla, stirring until well combined.

Spoon mixture into an 18- x 12- x 1-inch jellyroll pan coated with cooking spray. Bake at 350° for 20 minutes or until a wooden pick inserted in center comes out clean. Cool completely in pan.

Combine powdered sugar, milk, and remaining ½ teaspoon vanilla; beat until smooth. Spread frosting evenly over top. Allow frosting to set before cutting into squares. **Yield:** 4 dozen servings. **Serving size:** 1 square.

# Easy Spiced Fruit Squares *(photograph on page 20)*

2 teaspoons baking soda
¼ cup warm water
3 cups all-purpose flour
2 cups unsweetened applesauce
1½ cups sugar
½ cup vegetable oil
2 teaspoons ground cinnamon
1 teaspoon ground nutmeg
1 teaspoon grated orange rind
1 teaspoon vanilla extract
½ teaspoon ground cloves
¼ teaspoon salt
1 cup raisins
½ cup chopped dates
Vegetable cooking spray

**Approximate analysis per serving:**
Calories  144
Protein  1 g
Carbohydrate  27 g
Fat  4 g
Saturated Fat  tr.
Polyunsaturated Fat  2 g
Sodium  72 mg
Cholesterol  0

Dissolve soda in warm water, stirring well. Set aside.

Combine flour and next 9 ingredients in a large bowl, stirring until well combined. Stir in soda mixture, and fold in raisins and dates.

Spoon batter into a 13- x 9- x 2-inch baking pan coated with cooking spray. Bake at 300° for 1 hour or until a wooden pick inserted in center comes out clean. Cool completely in pan, and cut into 30 squares. **Yield:** 30 servings. **Serving size:** 1 square.

# Date Bars

2   cups chopped dates
1   cup water
3   tablespoons freshly squeezed lemon juice
1   cup uncooked regular oats
¾   cup all-purpose flour
½   cup firmly packed brown sugar
⅓   cup corn oil margarine
Vegetable cooking spray

**Approximate analysis per serving:**
Calories   108
Protein   1 g
Carbohydrate   20 g
Fat   3 g
Saturated Fat   1 g
Polyunsaturated Fat   1 g
Sodium   34 mg
Cholesterol   0

Combine first 3 ingredients in a heavy saucepan. Bring to a boil. Reduce heat, and simmer, stirring frequently, until mixture thickens. Remove from heat, and let cool.

Combine oats, flour, and brown sugar in a small bowl, stirring well to mix. Cut in margarine with a pastry blender until mixture resembles coarse meal. Pat half of oat mixture evenly into a 9-inch square baking pan coated with cooking spray. Spread date filling over oat layer, and top with remaining oat mixture. Bake at 375° for 45 minutes; cool completely in pan, and cut into 24 bars. **Yield:** 24 servings. **Serving size:** 1 bar.

*One nutrition fact to remember about dried fruits: they are a concentrated source of food elements, both good and bad. On the one hand, dried fruits are extremely high in iron and dietary fiber, while on the other hand, they are high in sugar and calories. Dried fruits are low in fat, so they make good treats to keep in the refrigerator for nibblers who are trying to lower their cholesterol. However, small snack-size portions are best.*

# Chewy Gingersnaps *(photograph on pages 190-191)*

½ cup corn oil margarine, softened
⅔ cup plus 1 tablespoon sugar, divided
½ cup molasses
1 egg
2¾ cups all-purpose flour
2 teaspoons baking soda
1 teaspoon ground ginger
½ teaspoon salt
½ teaspoon ground cloves
¾ teaspoon ground cinnamon,
   divided
Vegetable cooking spray

**Approximate analysis per serving:**
Calories   109
Protein   1 g
Carbohydrate   17 g
Fat   4 g
Saturated Fat   1 g
Polyunsaturated Fat   1 g
Sodium   148 mg
Cholesterol   10 mg

Cream margarine in a large bowl; gradually add ⅔ cup sugar, beating well. Add molasses and egg, and beat until blended. Sift together flour, soda, ginger, salt, cloves, and ½ teaspoon cinnamon; gradually add to creamed mixture, beating well after each addition. Cover and chill dough thoroughly.

Shape dough into balls, using 1 tablespoon dough for each cookie. Combine remaining 1 tablespoon sugar and ¼ teaspoon cinnamon, stirring to blend. Dip tops of cookies in mixture.

Place cookies, sugar side up, about 3 inches apart on cookie sheets coated with cooking spray. Bake at 375° for 10 to 12 minutes. (Cookies will puff while baking and flatten upon cooling.) Transfer to wire racks to cool. **Yield:** 4½ dozen cookies. **Serving size:** 2 cookies.

**Note:** Each Chewy Gingersnap may be topped with 1 teaspoon Apricot-Yogurt Spread (see recipe with analysis page 42).

# Crispy Oatmeal Cookies

½  cup corn oil margarine, softened
1  cup sugar
1  cup firmly packed brown sugar
1  teaspoon vanilla extract
1  egg
1  egg white
2  cups all-purpose flour
1¼ teaspoons baking powder
1¼ teaspoons baking soda
2  cups uncooked quick-cooking oats
2  cups crisp rice cereal
½  cup raisins
Vegetable cooking spray

**Approximate analysis per serving:**
Calories   121
Protein   2 g
Carbohydrate   22 g
Fat   3 g
Saturated Fat   1 g
Polyunsaturated Fat   1 g
Sodium   98 mg
Cholesterol   7 mg

Cream margarine in a large bowl; add sugars and vanilla, beating until light and fluffy. Add egg and egg white; beat well.

Sift together flour, baking powder, and soda; gradually add to creamed mixture, mixing well. Stir in oats, cereal, and raisins. Drop by heaping teaspoonfuls onto cookie sheets coated with cooking spray. Bake at 325° for 18 minutes or until lightly browned. Cool on wire racks. **Yield:** 6 dozen cookies. **Serving size**: 2 cookies.

# Oatmeal-Pumpkin Cookies

½  cup corn oil margarine, softened
½  cup sugar
½  cup firmly packed brown sugar
1  egg
1  cup canned pumpkin
½  teaspoon lemon extract
½  teaspoon vanilla extract
1½ cups all-purpose flour
1  teaspoon ground cinnamon
½  teaspoon baking soda
1½ cups uncooked quick-cooking oats
⅓  cup chopped walnuts
Vegetable cooking spray

**Approximate analysis per serving:**
Calories   132
Protein   2 g
Carbohydrate   19 g
Fat   6 g
Saturated Fat   1 g
Polyunsaturated Fat   2 g
Sodium   70 mg
Cholesterol   11 mg

Cream margarine in a bowl; add sugars, beating until light and fluffy (about 5 minutes). Add egg; beat well. Add pumpkin and flavorings; beat until well blended.

Sift flour, cinnamon, and soda together in a medium bowl. Stir in oats. Gradually add to creamed mixture, mixing well. Stir in walnuts. Cover and chill 30 minutes.

Drop dough by tablespoonfuls onto cookie sheets coated with cooking spray. Bake at 375° for 15 minutes or until lightly browned. Transfer to wire racks to cool. **Yield:** 4 dozen cookies. **Serving size:** 2 cookies.

# Oatmeal-Raisin Cookies

⅓  cup corn oil margarine, softened
½  cup firmly packed brown sugar
1  egg
½  teaspoon grated orange rind
2  cups all-purpose flour
2½ teaspoons baking powder
1½ teaspoons ground nutmeg
½  teaspoon baking soda
½  cup skim milk
¼  cup frozen orange juice concentrate, thawed and
    undiluted
1  cup uncooked regular oats
½  cup raisins
¼  cup chopped pecans
Vegetable cooking spray

**Approximate analysis per serving:**
Calories   130
Protein   3 g
Carbohydrate   21 g
Fat   4 g
Saturated Fat   1 g
Polyunsaturated Fat   1 g
Sodium   121 mg
Cholesterol   13 mg

Cream margarine in a large bowl; add sugar, beating until light and fluffy. Add egg and orange rind, beating well. Combine flour, baking powder, nutmeg, and soda. Add to creamed mixture alternately with milk and orange juice concentrate, beginning and ending with flour mixture. Stir in oats, raisins, and pecans.

Drop dough by teaspoonfuls onto cookie sheets coated with cooking spray. Bake at 350° for 12 to 15 minutes or until lightly browned. Transfer to wire racks to cool. **Yield:** 5 dozen cookies. **Serving size:** 3 cookies.

# Chocolate Meringue Cookies

2    egg whites
⅛    teaspoon salt
¼    teaspoon cream of tartar
½    cup sugar
½    teaspoon vinegar
½    teaspoon vanilla extract
¼    cup cocoa
1    tablespoon cornstarch

**Approximate analysis per serving:**
Calories   42
Protein   1 g
Carbohydrate   10 g
Fat   tr.
Saturated Fat   tr.
Polyunsaturated Fat   0
Sodium   22 mg
Cholesterol   0

Preheat oven to 250° for 15 minutes. Beat egg whites (at room temperature) and salt in a medium bowl at high speed of an electric mixer until foamy. Add cream of tartar, and beat until soft peaks form. Gradually add sugar, 1 tablespoon at a time, beating until stiff peaks form. Add vinegar and vanilla, beat until blended. Combine cocoa and cornstarch; gently fold into egg whites.

Drop mixture by tablespoonfuls onto cookie sheets lined with unglazed brown paper. Reduce temperature to 225°, and bake for 1½ hours or until meringue is dry. Turn oven off, and let cookies cool 1 hour before opening oven door. Carefully remove cookies from brown paper, and store in an airtight container. **Yield:** 2 dozen cookies. **Serving size:** 2 cookies.

# *Appendix*

# Glossary

**Aerobic exercise**. Physical activity that conditions the cardiovascular system by using large muscle groups in continuous motion that creates an increased demand for oxygen over an extended time.

**Artery**. A vessel that carries oxygenated blood from the heart to the tissues.

**Atherosclerosis**. A type of artery disease characterized by the accumulation of fatty material on the inner walls of the artery, causing the walls to thicken. As the interior of the artery becomes smaller, the blood supply to the heart muscle is reduced.

**Calorie**. A unit of heat that measures the amount of energy in food. Calories are provided to the body by carbohydrates, protein, fat, and alcohol.

**Carbohydrate**. A primary foodstuff that supplies 4 calories per gram.

**Cholesterol**. A fat-like substance which is found only in foods of animal origin (dietary cholesterol) and produced by the liver and stored in the body (blood cholesterol). It is used for the manufacture of hormones, the formation of cell walls, and other necessary functions in the body.

**Coronary heart disease**. Heart ailment usually caused by a narrowing of the coronary arteries due to a build up of fat and cholesterol on the artery walls. (This process is called atherosclerosis. When blood flow is completely stopped, the result is a heart attack.)

**Diabetes mellitus**. A disease in which the body cannot utilize carbohydrates normally because of inadequate production or use of insulin.

**Dietary fiber**. A nondigestible component of complex carbohydrates that is useful in digestion.

**Fat**. A compound containing glycerol and fatty acids that is used as a source of energy. Fat provides 9 calories per gram and helps in the absorption of certain vitamins.

**Total fat**. The sum of the saturated, monounsaturated, and polyunsaturated fats present in food.

**Saturated fat**. A type of fat found mostly in animal foods such as meat and whole-milk dairy products.

**Unsaturated fat**. There are two types of unsaturated fat: monounsaturated and polyunsaturated. Both are usually liquid at room temperature.

**Gram (g)**. A metric unit of weight. There are about 28 grams in 1 ounce.

**Heart attack**. The sudden cessation of blood flow to the heart muscle.

**High blood pressure**. Hypertension, or the elevation of blood pressure above the normal range.

**Hydrogenation**. A process that converts liquid vegetable oils into a more solid (saturated) fat. Examples are stick margarines and vegetable shortening.

**Lipoprotein**. Fatty protein substances that carry fat and cholesterol through the blood.

**High density lipoproteins (HDLs)**. Sometimes called the "good cholesterol," carry cholesterol away from body cells and tissues to the liver where it can be recycled or excreted.

**Low density lipoproteins (LDLs)**. Sometimes called the "bad cholesterol," deposit cholesterol on the artery walls.

**Milligrams (mg)**. A metric unit of weight. There are 1,000 milligrams in 1 gram.

**Milligrams/deciliter (mg/dl)**. A measurement that expresses concentration; for example, the weight of cholesterol (in milligrams) in a deciliter of blood. (A deciliter is approximately one-tenth of a quart.)

**Obesity**. Excess body fat; usually defined as 20 percent above desirable body weight.

**Plaque**. An accumulation of fat, cholesterol, and other substances that build up in the arteries hindering the flow of blood.

**Protein**. An essential nutrient that supplies 4 calories per gram and helps to build muscle, bone, skin, and blood.

**Registered dietitian (R.D.)**. Nutrition counselor that has been certified by the American Dietetic Association. To become registered, a dietitian must have successfully passed an examination and completed a planned course of study.

**Risk factor**. A characteristic behavior, condition, or trait related to the increased chance of developing a disease.

**Soluble fiber**. The type fiber found in some fruits and vegetables, oats, barley, and legumes which is useful as an aid in reducing blood cholesterol.

# Weight Chart
## of Persons 20 years and older*

| Height | Weight (without clothing) | |
| :---: | :---: | :---: |
| (without shoes) | **Normal range** | **Obesity level**** |
| **Men** | | |
| 5'3" | 118-141 | 169 |
| 5'4" | 122-145 | 174 |
| 5'5" | 126-149 | 179 |
| 5'6" | 130-155 | 186 |
| 5'7" | 134-161 | 193 |
| 5'8" | 139-166 | 199 |
| 5'9" | 143-170 | 204 |
| 5'10" | 147-174 | 209 |
| 5'11" | 150-176 | 214 |
| 6'0" | 154-183 | 220 |
| 6'1" | 158-189 | 226 |
| 6'2" | 162-192 | 230 |
| 6'3" | 165-195 | 234 |
| **Women** | | |
| 5'0" | 100-118 | 142 |
| 5'1" | 104-121 | 145 |
| 5'2" | 107-125 | 150 |
| 5'3" | 110-128 | 154 |
| 5'4" | 113-132 | 158 |
| 5'5" | 116-135 | 162 |
| 5'6" | 120-139 | 167 |
| 5'7" | 123-142 | 170 |
| 5'8" | 126-146 | 175 |
| 5'9" | 130-156 | 181 |
| 5'10" | 133-156 | 187 |
| 5'11" | 137-166 | 193 |
| 6'0" | 141-166 | 199 |

*This chart is one of several widely-accepted tables showing weight ranges for healthy adults. The weight ranges listed in different charts may vary by several pounds.

**A weight above 20 percent of upper normal is generally considered the obesity level. Source: U. S. Department of Agriculture Home and Garden Bulletin No. 74.

# Herb and Spice Chart

When you eliminate fats such as bacon drippings, fatback, butter, or margarine, you may find the food tastes bland. Zest can be added by using more herbs and spices. The list below will be helpful in seasoning your food.

| Food | Herbs/Spices |
|---|---|
| **Soup** | bay, chervil, French tarragon, marjoram, parsley, rosemary, savory |
| **Poultry** | garlic, oregano, rosemary, sage, savory |
| **Beef** | bay, chives, cloves, cumin, garlic, hot pepper, marjoram, rosemary, savory |
| **Lamb** | garlic, marjoram, oregano, rosemary, thyme (make little slits in lamb to be roasted and insert herbs) |
| **Pork** | coriander, cumin, garlic, ginger, hot pepper, pepper, sage, savory, thyme |
| **Cheese** | basil, chervil, chives, curry, dill, fennel, garlic chives, marjoram, oregano, parsley, sage, thyme |
| **Fish** | chervil, dill, fennel, French tarragon, garlic, parsley, thyme |
| **Fruits** | anise, cinnamon, cloves, coriander, ginger, lemon verbena, mint, rose geranium, sweet cicely |
| **Bread** | caraway, marjoram, oregano, poppy seed, rosemary, thyme |
| **Vegetables** | basil, burnet, chervil, chives, dill, French tarragon, marjoram, mint, parsley, pepper, thyme |
| **Salads** | basil, borage, burnet, chives, French tarragon, garlic chives, parsley, rocket-salad, sorrel (These are best used fresh or added to salad dressing. Otherwise, use herb vinegars for extra flavor.) |

# Still Need Help?

Trying to turn the recommendations in this book into a total change in lifestyle can be a difficult task. You may need some help from a nutrition counselor. Registered Dietitians (R.D.s) are specially trained nutrition counselors. An R.D. can help you translate your low-saturated-fat, low-cholesterol diet into daily menus and help you make life-long changes in your eating habits. How do you find an R.D.? If your physician is unable to refer you to a Registered Dietitian, here are ways to find good nutrition counseling.

• Your local American Heart Association may be able to refer you to an R.D.

• Some hospital out-patient clinics offer nutrition counseling. Contact the hospital dietetics department for information.

• Check the yellow pages under Health Care Services. Make sure to look for the R.D. designation.

• Ask your Public Health Department.

• Contact the nutrition department of your local university or extension service.

• Call the American Dietetic Association (1-800-621-6469).

• Contact nutrition information offices affiliated with universities in various areas of the United States. These may be listed in the yellow pages under nutritionists or dietitians.

# Sample Food Diary

| Meal | Amount | Preparation Method | Calories (kcal) | Fat (g) | Cholesterol (mg) | Sodium (mg) |
|---|---|---|---|---|---|---|
| **Breakfast** | | | | | | |
| Doughnut | 1 | fried | 156 | 7.4 | 24 | 200 |
| Coffee with | 1 cup | — | — | — | — | — |
| whole milk | 2 tablespoons | — | 19 | 11 | 4 | 15 |
| **Lunch** | | | | | | |
| Hamburger | ¼ pound | fried | 213 | 13.7 | 70 | 42 |
| Bun | 1 | toasted | 136 | 3.4 | 13 | 112 |
| Catsup | 1 tablespoon | — | 18 | 0.1 | 0 | 178 |
| Mustard | 1 tablespoon | — | 12 | 0.7 | 0 | 196 |
| Potatoes | ½ cup | fried | 228 | 12.0 | 0 | 190 |
| Cola | 12 ounces | — | 144 | 0 | 0 | 14 |
| **Snack** | | | | | | |
| Butter crackers | 4 | — | 68 | 4.0 | — | 128 |
| Cola | 12 ounces | — | 144 | 0 | 0 | 14 |
| **Dinner** | | | | | | |
| Spaghetti | 1 cup | boiled | 192 | 0.6 | 0 | 2 |
| Meatballs | 2 (2-ounce) | fried | 213 | 13.7 | 70 | 42 |
| Lettuce salad | 1 cup | — | 7 | 0.1 | 0 | 5 |
| French dressing | 1 tablespoon | — | 96 | 9.4 | 8 | 250 |
| French bread | 1 slice | — | 73 | 0.5 | 1 | 145 |
| Butter | 1 teaspoon | — | 34 | 3.8 | 10 | tr. |
| Yellow cake | 1 slice | baked | 227 | 9 | 80 | 404 |
| **Snack** | | | | | | |
| Cola | 12 ounces | — | 144 | 0 | 0 | 14 |
| Chocolate | | | | | | |
| chip cookies | 2 | — | 138 | 9.2 | 14 | 60 |
| **Total** | | | **2262** | **881** | **280** | **1911** |

# My Food Diary

| Meal | Amount | Preparation Method | Calories (kcal) | Fat (g) | Cholesterol (mg) | Sodium (mg) |
|------|--------|--------------------|-----------------|---------|------------------|-------------|
| **Breakfast** | | | | | | |
| | | | | | | |
| | | | | | | |
| | | | | | | |
| | | | | | | |
| | | | | | | |
| **Lunch** | | | | | | |
| | | | | | | |
| | | | | | | |
| | | | | | | |
| | | | | | | |
| | | | | | | |
| | | | | | | |
| **Snack** | | | | | | |
| | | | | | | |
| | | | | | | |
| **Dinner** | | | | | | |
| | | | | | | |
| | | | | | | |
| | | | | | | |
| | | | | | | |
| | | | | | | |
| | | | | | | |
| **Snack** | | | | | | |
| | | | | | | |
| | | | | | | |
| | | | | | | |
| **Total** | | | | | | |

# Calorie / Nutrient Chart

| Food | Approximate Measure | Food Energy (calories) | Protein (grams) | Fat (grams) | Carbohydrates (grams) | Cholesterol (milligrams) | Sodium (milligrams) |
|---|---|---|---|---|---|---|---|
| Apple | | | | | | | |
| Fresh, with skin | 1 medium | 81 | 0.2 | 0.5 | 21.0 | 0 | 0 |
| Juice, unsweetened | ½ cup | 58 | 0.1 | 0.1 | 14.5 | 0 | 4 |
| Applesauce, unsweetened | ½ cup | 52 | 0.2 | 0.1 | 13.8 | 0 | 2 |
| Apricot | | | | | | | |
| Canned, in light syrup | ½ cup | 75 | 0.7 | 0.1 | 19.0 | — | 1 |
| Dried, uncooked | 1 each | 17 | 0.3 | 0.0 | 4.3 | 0 | 1 |
| Fresh | 1 each | 18 | 0.4 | 0.1 | 4.1 | 0 | 0 |
| Nectar | ½ cup | 70 | 0.5 | 0.1 | 18.0 | 0 | 4 |
| Artichoke, fresh, cooked | 1 each | 53 | 2.6 | 0.2 | 12.4 | 0 | 79 |
| Asparagus, fresh, cooked | ½ cup | 23 | 2.3 | 0.3 | 4.0 | 0 | 4 |
| Arugula | 3 ounces | 20 | 2.2 | 0.3 | 3.3 | 0 | — |
| Avocado | 1 medium | 322 | 3.9 | 30.6 | 14.8 | 0 | 20 |
| | | | | | | | |
| Bacon | | | | | | | |
| Canadian-style | 1 ounce | 52 | 6.9 | 2.4 | 0.3 | 16 | 438 |
| Cured, broiled | 1 slice | 29 | 1.4 | 2.6 | 0.1 | 4 | 95 |
| Bamboo shoots, cooked | ½ cup | 7 | 0.9 | 0.1 | 1.1 | 0 | 2 |
| Banana | | | | | | | |
| Mashed | ½ cup | 101 | 1.1 | 0.5 | 25.8 | 0 | 1 |
| Whole | 1 medium | 109 | 1.2 | 0.5 | 27.6 | 0 | 1 |
| Barley, dry | ½ cup | 349 | 8.1 | 1.0 | 78.8 | 0 | 3 |
| Bean sprouts, raw | ½ cup | 16 | 1.6 | 0.1 | 3.1 | 0 | 3 |
| Beans | | | | | | | |
| Black, cooked | ½ cup | 114 | 7.6 | 0.5 | 20.4 | 0 | 1 |
| Garbanzo, cooked | ½ cup | 134 | 7.3 | 2.1 | 22.5 | 0 | 6 |
| Great Northern, cooked | ½ cup | 132 | 9.3 | 0.5 | 23.7 | 0 | 2 |
| Green, canned, regular pack | ½ cup | 18 | 1.0 | 0.1 | 4.2 | 0 | 442 |
| Green, fresh, cooked | ½ cup | 22 | 1.2 | 0.2 | 4.9 | 0 | 2 |
| Kidney, cooked | ½ cup | 112 | 7.7 | 0.4 | 20.2 | 0 | 2 |
| Lima, frozen, baby | ½ cup | 94 | 6 | 0.3 | 17.5 | 0 | 26 |
| Pinto, cooked | ½ cup | 117 | 7.0 | 0.4 | 21.9 | 0 | 2 |
| Red, cooked | ½ cup | 112 | 7.7 | 0.4 | 20.2 | 0 | 2 |
| Yellow or wax, canned, regular pack | ½ cup | 17 | 0.9 | 0.2 | 3.6 | — | 208 |
| Beef, trimmed of fat | | | | | | | |
| Flank steak, broiled | 3 ounces | 207 | 21.6 | 12.7 | 0.0 | 60 | 71 |
| Ground, extra-lean | 3 ounces | 213 | 22.5 | 13.7 | 0.0 | 70 | 42 |
| Liver, braised | 3 ounces | 137 | 20.7 | 4.2 | 2.9 | 331 | 60 |
| Roast | 3 ounces | 204 | 23.1 | 11.7 | 0.0 | 69 | 63 |
| Round, bottom, braised | 3 ounces | 189 | 26.9 | 8.2 | 0.0 | 82 | 43 |
| Round, eye of, cooked | 3 ounces | 156 | 24.7 | 5.5 | 0.0 | 59 | 53 |
| Sirloin, broiled | 3 ounces | 177 | 25.8 | 7.4 | 0.0 | 76 | 56 |

| Food | Approximate Measure | Food Energy (calories) | Protein (grams) | Fat (grams) | Carbohydrates (grams) | Cholesterol (milligrams) | Sodium (milligrams) |
|---|---|---|---|---|---|---|---|
| **Beverages** | | | | | | | |
| Beer | 12 fluid ounces | 146 | 1.1 | 0.0 | 13.1 | 0 | 18 |
| Beer, light | 12 fluid ounces | 99 | 0.7 | 0.0 | 4.6 | 0 | 11 |
| Champagne | 6 fluid ounces | 134 | 0.5 | 0.0 | 2.1 | 0 | 7 |
| Coffee, black | 1 cup | 5 | 0.2 | 0.0 | 0.9 | 0 | 5 |
| Coffee liqueur | 1 fluid ounce | 99 | 0.0 | 0.1 | 13.9 | 0 | 2 |
| Cognac brandy | 1 fluid ounce | 72 | — | — | — | — | — |
| Crème de menthe liqueur | 1 tablespoon | 62 | 0.0 | 0.1 | 7.0 | 0 | 1 |
| Gin, rum, vodka, or whiskey, 80 proof | 1 fluid ounce | 68 | 0.0 | 0.0 | 0.0 | 0 | 0.0 |
| Sherry, sweet | 1 fluid ounce | 39 | 0.1 | 0.0 | 2.0 | 0 | 4 |
| Vermouth, dry | 1 fluid ounce | 33 | 0.0 | 0.0 | 1.6 | 0 | 5 |
| Vermouth, sweet | 1 fluid ounce | 43 | 0.0 | 0.0 | 4.5 | 0 | 8 |
| Wine, red | 6 fluid ounces | 116 | 0.3 | 0.0 | 0.4 | 0 | 16 |
| Wine, white, dry | 6 fluid ounces | 113 | 0.2 | 0.0 | 1.1 | 0 | 7.5 |
| **Beets** | | | | | | | |
| Canned, regular pack | ½ cup | 30 | 0.8 | 0.1 | 7.2 | — | 209 |
| Fresh, diced, cooked | ½ cup | 26 | 0.9 | 0.4 | 5.7 | 0 | 42 |
| Blackberries, fresh | ½ cup | 37 | 0.5 | 0.3 | 9.2 | 0 | 0 |
| Blueberries, fresh | ½ cup | 41 | 0.5 | 0.3 | 10.2 | 0 | 4 |
| **Bouillon, dry** | | | | | | | |
| Beef-flavored cubes | 1 cube | 3 | 0.1 | 0.0 | 0.2 | — | 400 |
| Beef-flavored granules | 1 teaspoon | 5 | 0.0 | 0.5 | 0.0 | — | 461 |
| Chicken-flavored cubes | 1 cube | 7 | 0.2 | 0.1 | 0.5 | — | 800 |
| Chicken-flavored granules | 1 teaspoon | 5 | 0.2 | 0.5 | 0.2 | — | 381 |
| **Bran** | | | | | | | |
| Oat, dry uncooked | ½ cup | 153 | 8.0 | 3.0 | 23.5 | 0 | 1 |
| Wheat, raw | ½ cup | 59 | 4.0 | 1.3 | 7.5 | 0 | 3 |
| **Bread** | | | | | | | |
| Bagel, plain | 1 each | 161 | 5.9 | 1.5 | 30.5 | — | 196 |
| Bun, hamburger or hot dog | 1 each | 136 | 3.2 | 3.4 | 22.4 | 13 | 112 |
| English muffin | 1 each | 174 | 5.3 | 1.4 | 34.6 | 0 | 334 |
| French/vienna | 1 slice | 73 | 2.3 | 0.5 | 13.9 | 1 | 145 |
| Pita, whole wheat | 1 medium | 122 | 2.4 | 0.9 | 23.5 | 0 | — |
| Pumpernickel | 1 slice | 76 | 2.8 | 0.4 | 16.4 | 0 | 176 |
| Raisin | 1 slice | 66 | 1.6 | 0.7 | 13.4 | 1 | 91 |
| Rye | 1 slice | 61 | 2.3 | 0.3 | 13.0 | 0 | 139 |
| White | 1 slice | 67 | 2.2 | 0.8 | 12.6 | 1 | 127 |
| Whole wheat | 1 slice | 61 | 2.6 | 0.8 | 11.9 | 1 | 132 |
| Breadcrumbs, fine, dry | ½ cup | 196 | 6.3 | 2.2 | 36.7 | 2 | 368 |
| Broccoli, fresh, chopped, cooked | ½ cup | 26 | 2.8 | 0.1 | 4.9 | 0 | 22 |
| Broth, beef, homemade | 1 cup | 22 | 0.5 | 0.0 | 1.9 | 0 | 7 |

| Food | Approximate Measure | Food Energy (calories) | Protein (grams) | Fat (grams) | Carbohydrates (grams) | Cholesterol (milligrams) | Sodium (milligrams) |
|---|---|---|---|---|---|---|---|
| Brussels sprouts, fresh, cooked | ½ cup | 30 | 2.0 | 0.4 | 6.8 | 0 | 16 |
| Bulgur, uncooked | ½ cup | 301 | 9.5 | 1.3 | 64.3 | 0 | 3 |
| Butter | | | | | | | |
|   Regular | 1 tablespoon | 102 | 0.1 | 11.5 | 0.0 | 31 | 117 |
|   Unsalted | 1 tablespoon | 102 | 0.1 | 11.5 | 0.0 | 31 | 2 |
|   Whipped | 1 tablespoon | 68 | 0.1 | 7.7 | 0.0 | 21 | 78 |
| Cabbage | | | | | | | |
|   Bok choy | 1 cup | 9 | 1.0 | 0.1 | 1.5 | 0 | 45 |
|   Common varieties, raw, shredded | ½ cup | 8 | 0.4 | 0.1 | 1.9 | 0 | 6 |
| Cake, without frosting | | | | | | | |
|   Angel food | 1 (2-ounce) slice | 166 | 3.3 | 0.1 | 38.1 | — | 56 |
|   Pound | 1 (1-ounce) slice | 305 | 3.6 | 17.5 | 33.7 | 134 | 245 |
|   Sponge, cut into 12 slices | 1 piece | 183 | 3.6 | 5.0 | 30.8 | 221 | 99 |
|   Yellow, cut into 12 slices | 1 piece | 227 | 3.6 | 9.0 | 33.0 | 80 | 404 |
| Candy | | | | | | | |
|   Fudge, chocolate | 1 ounce | 113 | 0.8 | 3.4 | 21.3 | 0 | 54 |
|   Gumdrops | 1 ounce | 98 | 0.0 | 0.2 | 24.8 | 0 | 10 |
|   Hard | 1 each | 27 | 0.0 | 0.0 | 6.8 | 0 | 2 |
|   Jelly beans | 1 ounce | 104 | 0.0 | 0.1 | 26.4 | 0 | 3 |
|   Marshmallows, large | 1 each | 26 | 0.2 | 0.0 | 6.4 | 0 | 3 |
|   Milk chocolate | 1 ounce | 149 | 2.0 | 7.9 | 16.9 | 6 | 23 |
| Cantaloupe, raw, diced | ½ cup | 28 | 0.7 | 0.2 | 6.7 | 0 | 7 |
| Capers | 1 tablespoon | 4 | 0.4 | 0.0 | 0.6 | 0 | 670 |
| Carrot | | | | | | | |
|   Raw | 1 medium | 30 | 0.7 | 0.1 | 7.1 | 0 | 25 |
|   Cooked, sliced | ½ cup | 35 | 0.8 | 0.1 | 8.1 | 0 | 51 |
| Catsup | | | | | | | |
|   Regular | 1 tablespoon | 18 | 0.3 | 0.1 | 4.3 | 0 | 178 |
|   No-salt-added | 1 tablespoon | 15 | 0.0 | 0.0 | 4.0 | — | 6 |
| Cauliflower | | | | | | | |
|   Raw, flowerets | ½ cup | 10 | 0.8 | 0.1 | 2.1 | 0 | 6 |
|   Cooked, flowerets | ½ cup | 15 | 1.2 | 0.1 | 2.8 | 0 | 4 |
| Caviar | 1 tablespoon | 54 | 5.8 | 2.8 | 0.8 | 65 | 374 |
| Celery | | | | | | | |
|   Raw, diced | ½ cup | 10 | 0.4 | 0.1 | 2.2 | 0 | 53 |
|   Cooked | ½ cup | 11 | 0.4 | 0.1 | 2.6 | 0 | 48 |
| Cereal | | | | | | | |
|   Bran, whole | ½ cup | 106 | 6.1 | 0.7 | 31.6 | 0 | 480 |
|   Bran flakes | ½ cup | 64 | 2.5 | 0.4 | 15.3 | 0 | 182 |
|   Corn flakes | ½ cup | 44 | 0.9 | 0.0 | 9.8 | 0 | 140 |
|   Granola | ½ cup | 251 | 5.7 | 9.8 | 37.7 | 0 | 116 |

| Food | Approximate Measure | Food Energy (calories) | Protein (grams) | Fat (grams) | Carbohydrates (grams) | Cholesterol (milligrams) | Sodium (milligrams) |
|---|---|---|---|---|---|---|---|
| **Cereal** *(continued)* | | | | | | | |
| Crispy rice | ½ cup | 55 | 0.9 | 0.1 | 12.4 | 0 | 103 |
| Whole-grain wheat flakes | ½ cup | 79 | 1.9 | 0.2 | 18.6 | 0 | 150 |
| Puffed wheat | ½ cup | 28 | 1.6 | 0.1 | 5.5 | — | 2 |
| Raisin bran | ½ cup | 77 | 2.7 | 0.5 | 18.6 | 0 | 179 |
| Shredded wheat miniatures | ½ cup | 76 | 2.3 | 0.5 | 17.0 | 0 | 2 |
| Toasted oat cereal | ½ cup | 44 | 1.7 | 0.7 | 7.8 | 0 | 123 |
| **Cheese** | | | | | | | |
| American, processed, skim | 1 ounce | 69 | 6.0 | 5.0 | 1.0 | 10 | — |
| American, processed | 1 ounce | 106 | 6.3 | 8.9 | 0.5 | 27 | 405 |
| Blue | 1 ounce | 100 | 6.0 | 8.1 | 0.7 | 21 | 395 |
| Brie | 1 ounce | 95 | 5.9 | 7.8 | 0.1 | 28 | 178 |
| Cheddar | 1 ounce | 114 | 7.0 | 9.4 | 0.3 | 30 | 176 |
| Cheddar, 40% less fat | 1 ounce | 71 | 5.0 | 4.1 | 6.0 | — | 150 |
| Cottage, dry curd, no-salt-added | ½ cup | 62 | 12.5 | 0.3 | 1.3 | 5 | 9 |
| Cottage, lowfat, (1% milk-fat) | ½ cup | 81 | 14.0 | 1.1 | 3.1 | 5 | 459 |
| Cottage, lowfat, (2% milk-fat) | ½ cup | 102 | 15.5 | 2.2 | 4.1 | 9 | 459 |
| Cottage, (4% milk-fat) | ½ cup | 108 | 13.1 | 4.7 | 2.8 | 16 | 425 |
| Cream, light | 1 ounce | 60 | 3.0 | 5.0 | 2.0 | — | 159 |
| Farmers | 1 ounce | 40 | 4.0 | 3.0 | 1.0 | — | — |
| Feta | 1 ounce | 75 | 4.0 | 6.0 | 1.2 | 25 | 316 |
| Fontina | 1 ounce | 110 | 7.3 | 8.8 | 0.4 | 33 | — |
| Gruyère | 1 ounce | 117 | 8.4 | 9.2 | 0.1 | 31 | 95 |
| Monterey Jack | 1 ounce | 64 | 9.9 | 3.0 | 1.0 | 9 | 64 |
| Mozzarella, part-skim | 1 ounce | 72 | 6.9 | 4.5 | 0.8 | 16 | 132 |
| Mozzarella, whole milk | 1 ounce | 80 | 5.5 | 6.1 | 0.6 | 22 | 106 |
| Muenster | 1 ounce | 104 | 6.6 | 8.5 | 0.3 | 27 | 178 |
| Neufchâtel | 1 ounce | 74 | 2.8 | 6.6 | 0.8 | 22 | 113 |
| Parmesan, grated | 1 ounce | 111 | 10.1 | 7.3 | 0.9 | 19 | 454 |
| Provolone | 1 ounce | 100 | 7.2 | 7.5 | 0.6 | 20 | 248 |
| Ricotta, part-skim | 1 ounce | 39 | 3.2 | 2.2 | 1.5 | 9 | 35 |
| Romano, grated | 1 ounce | 110 | 9.0 | 7.6 | 1.0 | 29 | 340 |
| Swiss | 1 ounce | 107 | 8.1 | 7.8 | 1.0 | 26 | 74 |
| **Cherries** | | | | | | | |
| Fresh, sweet | ½ cup | 52 | 0.9 | 0.7 | 12.0 | 0 | 0 |
| Sour, sweetened | ½ cup | 127 | 1.0 | 1.1 | 33.1 | 0 | 10 |
| Sour, unsweetened | ½ cup | 36 | 0.7 | 0.3 | 8.5 | 0 | 1 |
| **Chicken, skinned, boned and roasted** | | | | | | | |
| White meat | 3 ounces | 140 | 26.4 | 3.0 | 0.0 | 72 | 63 |
| Dark meat | 3 ounces | 174 | 23.3 | 8.3 | 0.0 | 79 | 79 |
| Liver | 3 ounces | 134 | 20.7 | 4.6 | 0.7 | 537 | 43 |
| **Chives, raw, chopped** | 1 tablespoon | 1 | 0.1 | 0.0 | 0.1 | 0 | 0 |

| Food | Approximate Measure | Food Energy (calories) | Protein (grams) | Fat (grams) | Carbohydrates (grams) | Cholesterol (milligrams) | Sodium (milligrams) |
|---|---|---|---|---|---|---|---|
| **Chocolate** | | | | | | | |
| Semisweet | 1 ounce | 144 | 1.2 | 10.1 | 16.2 | 0 | 1 |
| Sweet | 1 ounce | 150 | 1.2 | 9.9 | 16.4 | 0 | 9 |
| Syrup, fudge | 1 tablespoon | 65 | 0.9 | 2.5 | 9.6 | — | 22 |
| Unsweetened, baking | 1 ounce | 141 | 3.1 | 14.7 | 8.5 | 0 | 1 |
| **Chutney** | 1 tablespoon | 41 | 0.2 | 0.0 | 10.5 | — | 34 |
| **Cilantro, fresh, minced** | 1 tablespoon | 1 | 0.1 | 0.0 | 0.3 | 0 | 1 |
| **Clams** | | | | | | | |
| Canned, drained | ½ cup | 118 | 20.4 | 1.6 | 4.1 | 54 | 90 |
| Raw | ½ cup | 92 | 15.8 | 1.2 | 3.2 | 42 | 69 |
| **Cocoa powder, unsweetened** | 1 tablespoon | 24 | 1.6 | 0.7 | 2.6 | — | 0 |
| **Coconut** | | | | | | | |
| Fresh, grated | 1 cup | 526 | 5.5 | 51.4 | 18.8 | 0 | 30 |
| Dried, unsweetened, shredded | 1 cup | 526 | 5.5 | 51.4 | 18.8 | 0 | 30 |
| Dried, sweetened, shredded | 1 cup | 463 | 2.7 | 32.8 | 44.0 | 0 | 242 |
| **Cookies** | | | | | | | |
| Chocolate | 1 each | 72 | 1.0 | 3.4 | 9.4 | 13 | 61 |
| Chocolate chip, homemade | 1 each | 69 | 0.9 | 4.6 | 6.8 | 7 | 30 |
| Oatmeal, plain | 1 each | 57 | 0.9 | 2.7 | 7.2 | 9 | 46 |
| Sandwich, with creme | 1 each | 40 | 0.3 | 1.7 | 6.0 | — | 41 |
| Vanilla wafers | 1 each | 19 | 0.2 | 0.9 | 2.5 | — | 16 |
| **Corn** | | | | | | | |
| Cream-style, regular pack | ½ cup | 92 | 2.2 | 0.5 | 23.2 | 0 | 365 |
| Fresh, kernels, cooked | ½ cup | 89 | 2.6 | 1.0 | 20.6 | 0 | 14 |
| **Cornmeal** | | | | | | | |
| Enriched, dry | 1 cup | 453 | 10.9 | 1.7 | 95.2 | 0 | 1 |
| Self-rising | 1 cup | 465 | 11.4 | 4.3 | 95.8 | 0 | 1849 |
| **Cornstarch** | 1 tablespoon | 29 | 0.0 | 0.0 | 7.0 | 0 | 0 |
| **Couscous, cooked** | ½ cup | 98 | 3.5 | 0.0 | 20.6 | — | — |
| **Crab** | | | | | | | |
| Blue, cooked | 3 ounces | 87 | 17.2 | 1.5 | 0.0 | 85 | 237 |
| Imitation | 3 ounces | 75 | 10.2 | 0.0 | 8.4 | — | — |
| **Crackers** | | | | | | | |
| Animal | 1 each | 14 | 0.2 | 0.4 | 2.3 | — | 11 |
| Butter | 1 each | 17 | 0.0 | 1.0 | 2.0 | — | 32 |
| Graham, plain | 1 each | 54 | 1.1 | 1.3 | 10.3 | 0 | 94 |
| Melba rounds, plain | 1 each | 11 | 0.4 | 0.2 | 2.0 | — | 26 |
| Saltine | 1 each | 13 | 0.3 | 0.3 | 2.0 | — | 43 |
| Whole wheat | 1 each | 27 | 0.5 | 1.0 | 3.5 | — | 50 |
| **Cranberry** | | | | | | | |
| Fresh, whole | ½ cup | 23 | 0.2 | 0.1 | 6.0 | 0 | 0 |
| Juice cocktail, reduced-calorie | ½ cup | 24 | 0.0 | 0.0 | 5.9 | — | 4 |
| Juice cocktail, regular | ½ cup | 75 | 0.0 | 0.1 | 19.2 | 0 | 5 |

| Food | Approximate Measure | Food Energy (calories) | Protein (grams) | Fat (grams) | Carbohydrates (grams) | Cholesterol (milligrams) | Sodium (milligrams) |
|---|---|---|---|---|---|---|---|
| Cranberry *(continued)* | | | | | | | |
| Sauce, sweetened | ¼ cup | 105 | 0.1 | 0.1 | 26.9 | 0 | 20 |
| Cream | | | | | | | |
| Half-and-half | 1 tablespoon | 20 | 0.5 | 1.7 | 0.7 | 6 | 6 |
| Sour | 1 tablespoon | 31 | 0.5 | 0.3 | 0.6 | 6 | 8 |
| Sour, reduced-calorie | 1 tablespoon | 20 | 0.4 | 1.8 | 0.6 | 6 | 6 |
| Creamer, non-dairy | 1 teaspoon | 11 | 0.1 | 0.7 | 1.1 | 0 | 4 |
| Croutons, seasoned | 1 ounce | 139 | 3.0 | 5.0 | 18.9 | — | — |
| Cucumbers, raw, whole | 1 medium | 32 | 1.3 | 0.3 | 7.1 | 0 | 5 |
| Currants | 1 tablespoon | 25 | 0.3 | 0.2 | 6.1 | — | 3 |
| | | | | | | | |
| Dates, pitted, unsweetened | 5 each | 114 | 0.8 | 0.2 | 30.5 | 0 | 1 |
| Doughnut | | | | | | | |
| Cake type | 1 each | 156 | 1.8 | 7.4 | 20.6 | 24 | 200 |
| Plain, yeast | 1 each | 166 | 2.5 | 10.7 | 15.1 | 10 | 94 |
| | | | | | | | |
| Egg | | | | | | | |
| White | 1 each | 16 | 3.2 | 0.0 | 0.4 | 0 | 49 |
| Whole | 1 each | 74 | 6.4 | 5.1 | 0.6 | 207 | 67 |
| Yolk | 1 each | 63 | 2.8 | 5.6 | 0.0 | 272 | 8 |
| Substitute | ¼ cup | 30 | 6.0 | 0.0 | 1.0 | 0 | 90 |
| Eggplant, cooked without salt | ½ cup | 13 | 0.4 | 0.1 | 3.2 | 0 | 1 |
| Extracts | | | | | | | |
| Almond | 1 teaspoon | 10 | — | — | — | — | — |
| Coconut | 1 teaspoon | 6 | — | — | — | — | — |
| Peppermint | 1 teaspoon | 22 | — | — | — | — | — |
| Vanilla | 1 teaspoon | 12 | — | — | — | — | — |
| | | | | | | | |
| Fennel, leaves, raw | ½ cup | 13 | 1.2 | 0.2 | 2.3 | 0 | 4 |
| Figs | | | | | | | |
| Fresh | 1 medium | 37 | 0.4 | 0.2 | 9.9 | 0 | 1 |
| Dried | 1 each | 48 | 0.6 | 0.2 | 12.2 | 0 | 2 |
| Fish, cooked | | | | | | | |
| Catfish, farm-raised | 3 ounces | 195 | 15.4 | 11.3 | 6.8 | 69 | 238 |
| Cod | 3 ounces | 89 | 19.4 | 0.7 | 0.0 | 47 | 66 |
| Flounder | 3 ounces | 100 | 20.5 | 1.3 | 0.0 | 58 | 89 |
| Grouper | 3 ounces | 100 | 21.1 | 1.1 | 0.0 | 40 | 45 |
| Haddock | 3 ounces | 95 | 20.6 | 0.8 | 0.0 | 63 | 74 |
| Halibut | 3 ounces | 119 | 22.7 | 2.5 | 0.0 | 35 | 59 |
| Mackerel | 3 ounces | 134 | 20.1 | 5.4 | 0.0 | 62 | 56 |
| Perch | 3 ounces | 100 | 21.1 | 1.0 | 0.0 | 98 | 67 |
| Pompano | 3 ounces | 179 | 20.1 | 10.3 | 0.0 | 54 | 65 |
| Snapper | 3 ounces | 109 | 22.4 | 1.5 | 0.0 | 40 | 48 |
| Salmon | 3 ounces | 184 | 23.2 | 9.3 | 0.0 | 74 | 56 |

| Food | Approximate Measure | Food Energy (calories) | Protein (grams) | Fat (grams) | Carbohydrates (grams) | Cholesterol (milligrams) | Sodium (milligrams) |
|---|---|---|---|---|---|---|---|
| **Fish** *(continued)* | | | | | | | |
| Sole | 3 ounces | 100 | 20.5 | 1.3 | 0.0 | 58 | 89 |
| Swordfish | 3 ounces | 132 | 21.6 | 4.4 | 0.0 | 43 | 98 |
| Trout | 3 ounces | 128 | 22.4 | 3.7 | 0.0 | 62 | 29 |
| Tuna, canned in water | 6½ ounces | 251 | 49.1 | 4.5 | 0.0 | 77 | 722 |
| Tuna, canned in oil | 6½ ounces | 343 | 48.9 | 14.9 | 0.0 | 57 | 730 |
| **Flour** | | | | | | | |
| All-purpose, unsifted | 1 cup | 499 | 14.4 | 1.4 | 104.1 | 0 | 3 |
| Bread, sifted | 1 cup | 420 | 13.6 | 1.3 | 85.8 | 0 | 2 |
| Buckwheat, light, unsifted | 1 cup | 340 | 6.3 | 1.2 | 77.9 | 0 | 2 |
| Cake, sifted | 1 cup | 349 | 7.2 | 0.8 | 76.2 | 0 | 2 |
| Rye, light, sifted | 1 cup | 314 | 8.2 | 0.9 | 68.6 | 0 | 1 |
| Whole wheat, unsifted | 1 cup | 400 | 16.0 | 2.4 | 85.2 | 0 | 4 |
| **Frankfurter** | | | | | | | |
| All-meat | 1 each | 130 | 5.8 | 11.2 | 1.1 | 29 | 484 |
| Turkey franks | 1 each | 63 | 3.8 | 5.3 | 0.1 | — | 299 |
| Fruit bits, dried | 1 ounce | 93 | 1.3 | 0.0 | 20.0 | 0 | 24 |
| Fruit cocktail, canned, packed in juice | ½ cup | 57 | 0.6 | 0.0 | 14.6 | 0 | 5 |
| **Garlic**, raw | 1 clove | 4 | 0.2 | 0.0 | 1.0 | 0 | 1 |
| **Gelatin** | | | | | | | |
| Flavored, prepared with water | ½ cup | 80 | 2.0 | — | 18.9 | — | 90 |
| Unflavored | 1 teaspoon | 10 | 2.6 | 0.0 | 0.0 | — | 3 |
| Grape juice | ½ cup | 77 | 0.7 | 0.1 | 18.9 | 0 | 4 |
| **Grapefruit** | | | | | | | |
| Juice, unsweetened | ½ cup | 47 | 0.6 | 0.1 | 11.1 | 0 | 1 |
| Raw | 1 medium | 77 | 1.5 | 0.2 | 19.3 | 0 | 0 |
| Grapes, green, seedless | 1 cup | 114 | 1.1 | 0.9 | 28.4 | 0 | 3 |
| Grits, cooked | ½ cup | 73 | 1.6 | 0.2 | 15.7 | 0 | 0 |
| **Ham** | | | | | | | |
| Cured, roasted, extra-lean | 3 ounces | 123 | 17.8 | 4.7 | 1.3 | 45 | 1023 |
| Honey | 1 tablespoon | 64 | 0.1 | 0.0 | 17.5 | 0 | 1 |
| Honeydew, raw, diced | 1 cup | 59 | 0.8 | 0.2 | 15.6 | 0 | 17 |
| Horseradish, prepared | 1 tablespoon | 6 | 0.2 | 0.0 | 1.4 | 0 | 14 |
| **Ice cream**, vanilla, regular | ½ cup | 134 | 2.3 | 7.2 | 15.9 | 30 | 58 |
| Ice milk, vanilla | ½ cup | 92 | 2.6 | 2.8 | 14.5 | 9 | 52 |
| **Jams and Jellies** | | | | | | | |
| Regular | 1 tablespoon | 51 | 0.0 | 0.0 | 13.2 | 0 | 3 |

| Food | Approximate Measure | Food Energy (calories) | Protein (grams) | Fat (grams) | Carbohydrates (grams) | Cholesterol (milligrams) | Sodium (milligrams) |
|---|---|---|---|---|---|---|---|
| **Jams and Jellies** *(continued)* | | | | | | | |
| Reduced-calorie | 1 tablespoon | 29 | 0.1 | 0.0 | 7.4 | 0 | 16 |
| Jicama | 1 cup | 49 | 1.6 | 0.2 | 10.5 | 0 | 7 |
| **Kiwifruit** | 1 each | 44 | 1.0 | 0.5 | 8.9 | 0 | 0 |
| **Lamb** | | | | | | | |
| Leg, roasted | 3 ounces | 158 | 24.4 | 6.0 | 0.0 | 85 | 60 |
| Loin, broiled | 3 ounces | 156 | 24.0 | 6.0 | 0.0 | 85 | 60 |
| Chop | 3 ounces | 160 | 24.0 | 6.4 | 0.0 | 85 | 60 |
| Ground, cooked | 3 ounces | 160 | 24.0 | 6.4 | 0.0 | 85 | 60 |
| Lard | 1 tablespoon | 116 | 0.0 | 12.8 | 0.0 | 12 | 0 |
| Leeks, bulb, raw | ½ cup | 32 | 0.8 | 0.2 | 7.3 | 0 | 10 |
| **Lemon** | | | | | | | |
| Fresh | 1 each | 16 | 0.6 | 0.2 | 5.2 | 0 | 1 |
| Juice | 1 tablespoon | 4 | 0.1 | 0.0 | 1.3 | 0 | 0 |
| Lemonade, sweetened | 1 cup | 99 | 0.2 | 0.0 | 26.0 | 0 | 7 |
| Lentils, cooked | ½ cup | 115 | 8.9 | 0.4 | 19.9 | 0 | 2 |
| **Lettuce** | | | | | | | |
| Boston or Bibb, shredded | 1 cup | 7 | 0.7 | 0.1 | 1.3 | 0 | 3 |
| Endive or escarole | 1 cup | 8 | 0.6 | 0.1 | 1.7 | 0 | 11 |
| Iceberg, chopped | 1 cup | 7 | 0.5 | 0.1 | 1.1 | 0 | 5 |
| Romaine, chopped | 1 cup | 9 | 0.9 | 0.1 | 1.3 | 0 | 4 |
| **Lime** | | | | | | | |
| Fresh | 1 each | 20 | 0.4 | 0.1 | 6.8 | 0 | 1 |
| Juice | 1 tablespoon | 4 | 0.1 | 0.0 | 1.4 | 0 | 0 |
| Lobster, cooked, meat only | 3 ounces | 83 | 17.4 | 0.5 | 1.1 | 61 | 323 |
| **Luncheon meats** | | | | | | | |
| Bologna | 1 slice | 74 | 2.5 | 6.9 | 0.4 | 13 | 241 |
| Deviled ham | 1 ounce | 78 | 4.3 | 6.7 | 0.0 | — | — |
| Salami | 1 ounce | 74 | 4.0 | 6.2 | 0.6 | — | 393 |
| Turkey ham | 1 ounce | 35 | 5.6 | 1.4 | 0.0 | 16 | 196 |
| Turkey pastrami | 1 ounce | 34 | 5.3 | 1.4 | 0.0 | 16 | 218 |
| Lychees, raw | 1 each | 6 | 0.1 | 0.0 | 1.6 | 0 | 0 |
| **Mango, raw** | ½ cup | 54 | 0.4 | 0.2 | 14.0 | 0 | 2 |
| **Margarine** | | | | | | | |
| Regular | 1 tablespoon | 101 | 0.1 | 11.4 | 0.1 | 0 | 133 |
| Reduced-calorie, stick | 1 tablespoon | 60 | 0.0 | 7.3 | 0.0 | 0 | 110 |
| Salt-free | 1 tablespoon | 101 | 0.1 | 11.3 | 0.1 | 0 | 0 |
| **Mayonnaise** | | | | | | | |
| Regular | 1 tablespoon | 99 | 0.2 | 10.9 | 0.4 | 8 | 78 |
| Reduced-calorie | 1 tablespoon | 44 | 0.1 | 4.6 | 0.7 | 6 | 88 |
| **Milk** | | | | | | | |
| Buttermilk, nonfat | 1 cup | 90 | 9.0 | 1.0 | 12.0 | — | 255 |

| Food | Approximate Measure | Food Energy (calories) | Protein (grams) | Fat (grams) | Carbohydrates (grams) | Cholesterol (milligrams) | Sodium (milligrams) |
|---|---|---|---|---|---|---|---|
| **Milk** *(continued)* | | | | | | | |
| Chocolate, low-fat | 1 cup | 158 | 8.1 | 2.5 | 26.1 | 8 | 153 |
| Condensed, sweetened | 1 cup | 982 | 24.2 | 26.3 | 166.5 | 104 | 389 |
| Evaporated, skim, | | | | | | | |
| canned | 1 cup | 200 | 19.3 | 0.5 | 29.1 | 10 | 294 |
| Low-fat, 2% fat | 1 cup | 122 | 8.1 | 4.7 | 11.7 | 20 | 122 |
| Low-fat, 1% fat | 1 cup | 102 | 8.0 | 2.5 | 11.6 | 10 | 122 |
| Nonfat dry | ⅓ cup | 145 | 14.5 | 0.3 | 20.8 | 8 | 214 |
| Skim | 1 cup | 86 | 8.3 | 0.4 | 11.9 | 5 | 127 |
| Whole | 1 cup | 156 | 8.0 | 8.9 | 11.3 | 34 | 120 |
| Molasses, cane, light | 1 tablespoon | 52 | 0.0 | 0.0 | 13.3 | 0 | 3 |
| **Mushrooms** | | | | | | | |
| Canned | ¼ cup | 13 | 0.1 | 0.1 | 2.5 | 0 | 1 |
| Fresh | ½ cup | 9 | 0.7 | 0.1 | 1.6 | 0 | 1 |
| Shiitake, dried | 1 each | 14 | 0.3 | 0.0 | 2.6 | 0 | 0 |
| Mussels, blue, cooked | 3 ounces | 146 | 20.2 | 3.8 | 6.3 | 48 | 314 |
| **Mustard** | | | | | | | |
| Dijon | 1 tablespoon | 18 | 0.0 | 1.0 | 1.0 | 0 | 446 |
| Prepared, yellow | 1 tablespoon | 12 | 0.7 | 0.7 | 1.0 | 0 | 196 |
| | | | | | | | |
| Nectarine, fresh | 1 each | 67 | 1.3 | 0.6 | 16.1 | 0 | 0 |
| **Nuts** | | | | | | | |
| Almonds, chopped | 1 tablespoon | 48 | 1.6 | 4.2 | 1.7 | 0 | 1 |
| Hazelnuts, chopped | 1 tablespoon | 45 | 0.9 | 4.5 | 1.1 | 0 | 0 |
| Peanuts, roasted, | 1 tablespoon | 53 | 2.4 | 4.5 | 1.7 | 0 | 1 |
| unsalted | | | | | | | |
| Pecans, chopped | 1 tablespoon | 50 | 0.6 | 5.0 | 1.4 | 0 | 0 |
| Pistachio nuts | 1 tablespoon | 46 | 1.6 | 3.9 | 2.0 | 0 | 0 |
| Walnuts, black | 1 tablespoon | 47 | 1.9 | 4.4 | 0.9 | 0 | 0 |
| | | | | | | | |
| **Oats** | | | | | | | |
| Cooked | 1 cup | 145 | 5.8 | 2.3 | 25.3 | 0 | 374 |
| Rolled, dry | ½ cup | 154 | 6.4 | 2.5 | 26.8 | 0 | — |
| **Oil** | | | | | | | |
| Vegetable | 1 tablespoon | 121 | 0.0 | 13.6 | 0.0 | 0 | 0 |
| Olive | 1 tablespoon | 119 | 0.0 | 13.5 | 0.0 | 0 | 0 |
| Sesame | 1 teaspoon | 40 | 0.0 | 4.5 | 0.0 | 0 | 0 |
| Okra, cooked | ½ cup | 26 | 1.5 | 0.1 | 5.8 | 0 | 4 |
| **Olives** | | | | | | | |
| Black | 1 medium | 5 | 0.0 | 0.4 | 0.3 | 0 | 35 |
| Green, stuffed | ½ cup | 54 | 0.7 | 4.6 | 3.8 | 0 | 606 |
| **Onions** | | | | | | | |
| Green | 1 tablespoon | 2 | 0.1 | 0.0 | 0.3 | 0 | 0 |
| Cooked, yellow or | | | | | | | |
| white | ½ cup | 15 | 0.4 | 0.1 | 3.3 | 0 | 4 |
| Raw, chopped | ½ cup | 29 | 1.0 | 0.2 | 6.2 | 0 | 2 |

| Food | Approximate Measure | Food Energy (calories) | Protein (grams) | Fat (grams) | Carbohydrates (grams) | Cholesterol (milligrams) | Sodium (milligrams) |
|---|---|---|---|---|---|---|---|
| Orange | | | | | | | |
| Fresh | 1 medium | 62 | 1.2 | 0.2 | 15.4 | 0 | 0 |
| Juice | ½ cup | 56 | 0.8 | 0.1 | 13.4 | 0 | 1 |
| Mandarin, canned, packed in juice | ½ cup | 46 | 0.7 | 0.0 | 12.0 | 0 | 6 |
| Oysters, raw | 1 cup | 171 | 17.5 | 6.1 | 9.7 | 136 | 278 |
| Papayas, fresh, cubed | ½ cup | 27 | 0.4 | 0.1 | 6.9 | 0 | 2 |
| Parsley, raw | 1 tablespoon | 1 | 0.1 | 0.0 | 0.3 | 0 | 1 |
| Parsnip, cooked, diced | ½ cup | 63 | 1.0 | 0.2 | 15.1 | 0 | 8 |
| Pasta, cooked | | | | | | | |
| Macaroni | ½ cup | 78 | 2.4 | 0.3 | 16.1 | 0 | 1 |
| Medium egg noodles | ½ cup | 100 | 3.2 | 1.2 | 18.6 | 25 | 2 |
| Lasagna noodles | ½ cup | 100 | 3.2 | 1.2 | 18.6 | 25 | 2 |
| Rice noodles | ½ cup | 138 | 3.1 | 1.3 | 28.6 | 0 | — |
| Spinach noodles | ½ cup | 100 | 3.8 | 1.0 | 18.9 | 0 | 22 |
| Spaghetti | ½ cup | 96 | 3.2 | 0.3 | 19.6 | 0 | 1 |
| Whole wheat pasta | ½ cup | 100 | 3.7 | 1.4 | 19.8 | 0 | 1 |
| Peaches | | | | | | | |
| Fresh | 1 medium | 54 | 0.9 | 0.1 | 13.9 | 0 | 0 |
| Canned, packed in juice | ½ cup | 56 | 0.8 | 0.0 | 14.7 | 0 | 5 |
| Peanut butter | | | | | | | |
| Regular | 1 tablespoon | 95 | 4.6 | 8.3 | 2.6 | 0 | 79 |
| No-salt-added | 1 tablespoon | 95 | 4.6 | 8.3 | 2.6 | 0 | 3 |
| Pear | | | | | | | |
| Fresh | 1 medium | 97 | 0.6 | 0.7 | 24.9 | 0 | 0 |
| Canned, packed in juice | ½ cup | 62 | 0.4 | 0.1 | 16.0 | 0 | 5 |
| Juice | ½ cup | 59 | 0.0 | 0.0 | 14.2 | — | 6 |
| Peas | | | | | | | |
| Black-eyed, cooked | ½ cup | 90 | 6.7 | 0.7 | 15.0 | 0 | 3 |
| English, cooked | ½ cup | 62 | 4.1 | 0.2 | 11.4 | 0 | 70 |
| Split, cooked | ½ cup | 116 | 8.2 | 0.4 | 20.7 | 0 | 2 |
| Peppers | | | | | | | |
| Sweet, raw, green, red or yellow | 1 medium | 23 | 0.7 | 0.5 | 4.8 | 0 | 3 |
| Sweet, chopped | ½ cup | 19 | 0.6 | 0.3 | 4.0 | 0 | 2 |
| Jalapeño, green | 1 each | 4 | 0.2 | 0.0 | 0.9 | 0 | 1 |
| Picante sauce | 1 tablespoon | 5 | 0.2 | 0.0 | 0.9 | — | 108 |
| Pickle | | | | | | | |
| Dill, sliced | ¼ cup | 4 | 0.2 | 0.1 | 0.9 | 0 | 553 |
| Relish, chopped, sour | 1 tablespoon | 3 | 0.1 | 0.1 | 0.4 | 0 | 207 |
| Sweet, sliced | ¼ cup | 57 | 0.2 | 0.2 | 14.1 | 0 | 276 |
| Pimiento, diced | 1 tablespoon | 5 | 0.2 | 0.1 | 1.1 | 0 | 5 |
| Pie, baked, 9-inch diameter, cut into 8 slices | | | | | | | |
| Apple, fresh | 1 slice | 409 | 3.3 | 15.3 | 67.7 | 12 | 229 |

| Food | Approximate Measure | Food Energy (calories) | Protein (grams) | Fat (grams) | Carbohydrates (grams) | Cholesterol (milligrams) | Sodium (milligrams) |
|---|---|---|---|---|---|---|---|
| Pie *(continued)* | | | | | | | |
| Chocolate meringue | 1 slice | 354 | 6.8 | 13.4 | 53.8 | 109 | 307 |
| Egg custard | 1 slice | 248 | 7.3 | 11.6 | 28.6 | 149 | 229 |
| Pecan | 1 slice | 478 | 5.8 | 20.3 | 71.1 | 141 | 324 |
| Pumpkin | 1 slice | 181 | 4.0 | 6.8 | 27.0 | 61 | 210 |
| Pineapple | | | | | | | |
| Fresh, diced | ½ cup | 38 | 0.3 | 0.3 | 9.6 | 0 | 1 |
| Canned, packed in light syrup | ½ cup | 82 | 0.4 | 0.1 | 21.3 | — | 1 |
| Canned, packed in juice | ½ cup | 81 | 0.6 | 0.1 | 21.0 | — | 1 |
| Juice, unsweetened | ½ cup | 70 | 0.4 | 0.1 | 17.2 | 0 | 1 |
| Plum, fresh | 1 medium | 35 | 0.5 | 0.4 | 8.3 | 0 | 0 |
| Popcorn, hot-air popped | 1 cup | 23 | 0.8 | 0.3 | 4.6 | 0 | 0 |
| Pork, cooked | | | | | | | |
| Roast | 3 ounces | 208 | 21.6 | 12.7 | 0.0 | 82 | 65 |
| Tenderloin | 3 ounces | 141 | 24.5 | 4.1 | 0.0 | 79 | 57 |
| Chop, center-loin | 3 ounces | 204 | 24.2 | 11.1 | 0.0 | 77 | 59 |
| Spareribs | 3 ounces | 338 | 24.7 | 25.7 | 0.0 | 103 | 79 |
| Sausage | 1 link | 44 | 2.4 | 3.7 | 0.1 | 10 | 155 |
| Sausage patty | 1 ounce | 105 | 5.6 | 8.8 | 0.3 | 24 | 367 |
| Potatoes | | | | | | | |
| Baked, with skin | 1 each | 218 | 4.4 | 0.2 | 50.4 | 0 | 16 |
| Boiled, diced | ½ cup | 67 | 1.3 | 0.1 | 15.6 | 0 | 4 |
| Fried | ½ cup | 228 | 3.4 | 12.0 | 27.6 | 0 | 190 |
| Potato chips | | | | | | | |
| Regular | 10 each | 105 | 1.3 | 7.1 | 10.4 | 0 | 94 |
| No-salt-added | 10 each | 105 | 1.3 | 7.1 | 10.4 | 0 | 2 |
| Pretzel sticks | 10 each | 106 | 2.1 | 0.0 | 23.3 | — | 772 |
| Prunes | | | | | | | |
| Dried, pitted | 5 large | 127 | 1.1 | 1.4 | 30.9 | — | 23 |
| Juice | ½ cup | 91 | 0.8 | 0.0 | 22.3 | 0 | 5 |
| Pumpkin, canned | ½ cup | 42 | 1.3 | 0.3 | 9.9 | 0 | 6 |
| | | | | | | | |
| Radish, fresh, sliced | ½ cup | 10 | 0.3 | 0.3 | 2.1 | 0 | 14 |
| Raisins | 1 tablespoon | 27 | 0.3 | 0.0 | 7.2 | 0 | 1 |
| Raspberries | | | | | | | |
| Black, fresh | ½ cup | 33 | 0.6 | 0.4 | 7.7 | 0 | 0 |
| Red, fresh | ½ cup | 30 | 0.6 | 0.3 | 7.1 | 0 | 0 |
| Rhubarb | | | | | | | |
| Diced, raw | ½ cup | 13 | 0.5 | 0.1 | 2.8 | 0 | 2 |
| Cooked, with sugar | ½ cup | 157 | 0.5 | 0.1 | 42.1 | 0 | 1 |
| Rice cake, plain | 1 each | 36 | 0.7 | 0.2 | 7.7 | 0 | 1 |
| Rice, cooked without salt or fat | | | | | | | |
| Brown | ½ cup | 102 | 2.0 | 0.6 | 21.9 | 0 | 2 |
| White, long-grain | ½ cup | 103 | 1.8 | 0.1 | 22.7 | 0 | 1 |
| White, enriched | ½ cup | 93 | 1.7 | 0.1 | 20.3 | 0 | 313 |

| Food | Approximate Measure | Food Energy (calories) | Protein (grams) | Fat (grams) | Carbohydrates (grams) | Cholesterol (milligrams) | Sodium (milligrams) |
|---|---|---|---|---|---|---|---|
| Rice *(continued)* | | | | | | | |
| Wild | ½ cup | 85 | 3.1 | 1.2 | 16.2 | 3 | 12 |
| Roll | | | | | | | |
| Plain, brown-and-serve | 1 each | 84 | 2.2 | 1.9 | 14.1 | 2 | 144 |
| Hard | 1 each | 156 | 4.9 | 1.6 | 29.8 | 2 | 313 |
| Rutabaga, cooked, cubed | ½ cup | 29 | 0.9 | 0.2 | 6.6 | 0 | 15 |
| Salad dressing | | | | | | | |
| Blue cheese | 1 tablespoon | 84 | 0.4 | 9.2 | 0.3 | 0 | 216 |
| Blue cheese, low calorie | 1 tablespoon | 14 | 0.7 | 1.1 | 1.0 | 3 | 307 |
| French | 1 tablespoon | 96 | 0.3 | 9.4 | 2.9 | 8 | 205 |
| French, low calorie | 1 tablespoon | 22 | 0.0 | 0.9 | 3.5 | 1 | 128 |
| Italian | 1 tablespoon | 84 | 0.1 | 9.1 | 0.6 | 0 | 172 |
| Italian, no oil, low calorie | 1 tablespoon | 8 | 0.1 | 0.0 | 1.8 | 0 | 161 |
| Thousand Island | 1 tablespoon | 59 | 0.1 | 5.6 | 2.4 | — | 109 |
| Thousand Island, low calorie | 1 tablespoon | 24 | 0.1 | 1.6 | 2.5 | 2 | 153 |
| Salt, iodized | 1 teaspoon | 0 | 0.0 | 0.0 | 0.0 | 0 | 2343 |
| Scallops, raw, large | 1 each | 13 | 2.5 | 0.1 | 0.4 | 5 | 24 |
| Sesame seed, dry, whole | 1 teaspoon | 17 | 0.5 | 1.5 | 0.7 | 0 | 0 |
| Shallot, bulb, raw, chopped | ½ cup | 58 | 2.0 | 0.1 | 13.4 | 0 | 10 |
| Sherbet, orange | ½ cup | 135 | 1.1 | 1.9 | 29.3 | 7 | 44 |
| Shortening | 1 tablespoon | 94 | 0.0 | 10.6 | 0.0 | — | — |
| Shrimp | | | | | | | |
| Fresh, peeled and deveined | ½ pound | 240 | 46.1 | 3.9 | 2.1 | 345 | 336 |
| Canned, drained | ½ cup | 77 | 14.8 | 1.3 | 0.7 | 111 | 108 |
| Soy sauce | | | | | | | |
| Regular | 1 tablespoon | 8 | 0.8 | 0.0 | 1.2 | 0 | 829 |
| Low sodium | 1 tablespoon | 8 | 0.8 | 0.0 | 1.2 | 0 | 484 |
| Soup, condensed, made with water | | | | | | | |
| Beef broth | 1 cup | 31 | 4.8 | 0.7 | 2.6 | 24 | 782 |
| Chicken noodle | 1 cup | 75 | 4.0 | 2.4 | 9.3 | 7 | 1106 |
| Cream of chicken | 1 cup | 117 | 2.9 | 7.3 | 9.0 | 10 | 986 |
| Cream of mushroom | 1 cup | 129 | 2.3 | 9.0 | 9.0 | 2 | 1032 |
| Tomato | 1 cup | 85 | 2.0 | 1.9 | 16.6 | 0 | 871 |
| Vegetable, beef | 1 cup | 82 | 3.0 | 1.9 | 13.1 | 2 | 810 |
| Spinach | | | | | | | |
| Fresh | 1 cup | 12 | 1.6 | 0.2 | 2.0 | 0 | 44 |
| Cooked | ½ cup | 21 | 2.7 | 0.2 | 3.4 | 0 | 63 |
| Canned, regular pack | ½ cup | 25 | 3.0 | 0.5 | 3.6 | 0 | 397 |
| Squash, cooked | | | | | | | |
| Acorn | ½ cup | 57 | 1.1 | 0.1 | 14.9 | 0 | 4 |
| Butternut | ½ cup | 41 | 0.8 | 0.1 | 10.7 | 0 | 4 |

| Food | Approximate Measure | Food Energy (calories) | Protein (grams) | Fat (grams) | Carbohydrates (grams) | Cholesterol (milligrams) | Sodium (milligrams) |
|---|---|---|---|---|---|---|---|
| Squash *(continued)* | | | | | | | |
| Spaghetti | ½ cup | 22 | 0.5 | 0.2 | 5.0 | 0 | 14 |
| Summer | ½ cup | 21 | 1.0 | 0.3 | 4.5 | 0 | 1 |
| Strawberries, raw | 1 cup | 45 | 0.9 | 0.6 | 10.5 | 0 | 1 |
| Sugar | | | | | | | |
| Granulated | 1 tablespoon | 48 | 0.0 | 0.0 | 12.4 | 0 | 0 |
| Brown, packed | 1 tablespoon | 51 | 0.0 | 0.0 | 13.3 | 0 | 4 |
| Powdered | 1 tablespoon | 29 | 0.0 | 0.0 | 7.5 | 0 | 0 |
| Sunflower seeds | ¼ cup | 205 | 8.2 | 17.8 | 6.8 | 0 | 1 |
| Sweet potatoes | | | | | | | |
| Whole, baked | ½ cup | 103 | 1.7 | 0.1 | 24.3 | 0 | 10 |
| Mashed | ½ cup | 172 | 2.7 | 0.5 | 39.8 | 0 | 21 |
| Syrup | | | | | | | |
| Chocolate-flavored | 1 tablespoon | 49 | 0.6 | 0.2 | 11.0 | — | 13 |
| Maple, reduced-calorie | 1 tablespoon | 6 | 0.0 | 0.0 | 2.0 | 0 | 4 |
| Pancake | 1 tablespoon | 50 | 0.0 | 0.0 | 12.8 | 0 | 2 |
| | | | | | | | |
| Taco shell | 1 each | 52 | 0.7 | 2.8 | 5.9 | — | 62 |
| Tangerine | 1 each | 38 | 0.5 | 0.1 | 9.6 | 0 | 1 |
| Tapioca, dry | 1 tablespoon | 32 | 0.1 | 0.0 | 7.8 | 0 | 0 |
| Tofu | | | | | | | |
| Firm | 4 ounces | 94 | 9.0 | 6.5 | 1.5 | — | 8 |
| Soft | 4 ounces | 65 | 6.0 | 4.0 | 2.0 | — | 2 |
| Tomato | | | | | | | |
| Fresh | 1 each | 27 | 1.2 | 0.3 | 6.1 | 0 | 11 |
| Cooked | ½ cup | 30 | 1.3 | 0.3 | 6.8 | 0 | 13 |
| Juice, regular | 1 cup | 41 | 1.8 | 0.1 | 10.3 | 0 | 881 |
| Juice, no-salt-added | 1 cup | 41 | 1.8 | 0.1 | 10.3 | 0 | 24 |
| Paste, regular | 1 tablespoon | 14 | 0.6 | 0.1 | 3.1 | 0 | 129 |
| Paste, no-salt-added | 1 tablespoon | 14 | 0.6 | 0.1 | 3.1 | 0 | 11 |
| Sauce, regular | ½ cup | 37 | 1.6 | 0.2 | 8.8 | 0 | 741 |
| Sauce, no-salt-added | ½ cup | 42 | 1.2 | 0.0 | 9.7 | — | 27 |
| Whole, canned, peeled | ½ cup | 25 | 1.2 | 0.2 | 5.1 | — | 155 |
| Whole, canned, no-salt-added | ½ cup | 22 | 0.9 | 0.0 | 5.2 | — | 15 |
| Tortilla | | | | | | | |
| Chips, plain | 10 each | 135 | 2.1 | 7.3 | 16.0 | 0 | 24 |
| Corn, 6" diameter | 1 each | 67 | 2.1 | 1.1 | 12.8 | 0 | 53 |
| Flour, 6" diameter | 1 each | 111 | 2.4 | 2.3 | 22.2 | 0 | 0 |
| Turkey, skinned, boned, and roasted | | | | | | | |
| Dark meat | 3 ounces | 159 | 24.3 | 6.1 | 0.0 | 72 | 67 |
| White meat | 3 ounces | 115 | 25.6 | 0.6 | 0.0 | 71 | 44 |
| Turnip greens, cooked | ½ cup | 14 | 0.8 | 0.2 | 3.1 | 0 | 21 |
| Turnips, cooked, cubed | ½ cup | 14 | 0.5 | 0.1 | 3.8 | 0 | 39 |

| Food | Approximate Measure | Food Energy (calories) | Protein (grams) | Fat (grams) | Carbohydrates (grams) | Cholesterol (milligrams) | Sodium (milligrams) |
|---|---|---|---|---|---|---|---|
| **Veal** | | | | | | | |
| Loin, broiled | 3 ounces | 199 | 22.4 | 11.3 | 0.0 | 86 | 68 |
| Cutlet, pan-fried | 3 ounces | 155 | 28.2 | 3.9 | 0.0 | 111 | 69 |
| Vegetable juice cocktail | 1 cup | 46 | 1.5 | 0.2 | 11.0 | 0 | 883 |
| **Venison** | | | | | | | |
| Raw | 4 ounces | 143 | 23.8 | 4.5 | 0.0 | 74 | 102 |
| **Vinegar** | | | | | | | |
| Distilled | 1 tablespoon | 2 | 0.0 | 0.0 | 0.8 | 0 | 0 |
| Red wine | 1 tablespoon | 2 | 0.0 | 0.0 | 0.0 | 0 | 1 |
| White wine | 1 tablespoon | 2 | 0.0 | 0.0 | 0.0 | 0 | 2 |
| Tarragon | 1 tablespoon | 0 | — | — | 0.2 | — | 0 |
| **Water chestnuts, canned,** | | | | | | | |
| sliced | ½ cup | 35 | 0.6 | 0.0 | 8.7 | 0 | 6 |
| Watercress, fresh | ½ cup | 2 | 0.4 | 0.0 | 0.2 | 0 | 7 |
| Watermelon, raw, diced | 1 cup | 51 | 1.0 | 0.7 | 11.5 | 0 | 3 |
| **Whipped topping,** | | | | | | | |
| non-dairy, frozen | 1 tablespoon | 15 | 0.1 | 1.2 | 1.1 | 0 | 1 |
| **Worcestershire sauce** | | | | | | | |
| Regular | 1 tablespoon | 12 | 0.3 | 0.0 | 2.7 | 0 | 147 |
| Low sodium | 1 tablespoon | 12 | 0.0 | 0.0 | 3.0 | 0 | 57 |
| **Yeast, active, dry** | 1 package | 20 | 2.6 | 0.1 | 2.7 | 0 | 4 |
| **Yogurt** | | | | | | | |
| Plain, made from whole milk | 1 cup | 138 | 7.9 | 7.4 | 10.6 | 30 | 104 |
| Plain, nonfat | 1 cup | 127 | 13.0 | 0.4 | 17.4 | 5 | 173 |
| Plain, low-fat | 1 cup | 143 | 11.9 | 3.5 | 16.0 | 14 | 159 |
| Fruit varieties, low-fat | 1 cup | 225 | 9.0 | 2.6 | 42.3 | 9 | 120 |
| Frozen | ½ cup | 124 | 3.1 | 2.1 | 23.7 | — | 51 |
| **Zucchini** | | | | | | | |
| Raw | ½ cup | 9 | 0.7 | 0.1 | 1.9 | 0 | 2 |
| Cooked | ½ cup | 9 | 0.7 | 0.1 | 1.9 | 0 | 2 |

Sources of Data:

Adams, Catherine F. *NUTRITIVE VALUE OF AMERICAN FOODS.* U. S. Government Printing Office, 1975.

Computrition, Inc., Chatsworth, California. Primarily comprised of *The Composition of Foods: Raw, Processed, Prepared.* Handbooks - 8 series. United States Department of Agriculture, Human Nutrition Information Service, 1976-1986.

# RECIPE INDEX

# SUBJECT INDEX

Grapefruit, 195
Gravy, 27, 31
Guar gum, 131

# H

Habit(s), eating, 26, 27
Ham, 27
Heart
  attack, 11
  conditioning of, 23
  rate, 23
Heart disease
  and exercise, 22
  explanation of, 11, 12
  reducing risks of, 10, 13,
    22
  risks of, 11
Heart-Healthy Substitutions
  Chart, 27
Herbs, 27
  Chart, 214
HDLs, 10
  explanation of, 12, 13
  raising level of, 13, 22
Honey, 16
Hormones, 11
Hot dogs, 30
Hydrogenated
  explanation of, 15, 16
  shortening, 29, 33
  vegetable oils, 30

# I

Ice cream, 27, 33
Ice milk, 27
Iron, 151, 195

# L

Labels
  cholesterol on, 28
  reading, 28, 30
Lard, 26, 33
Legumes, 16, 17, 60
  in guide, 24
  soluble fiber in, 13
Lemon, 27, 31, 32

Lifestyle
  changing of, 13, 25
  exercise and, 22
  sedentary, 22
Lipid profile, 12
Lipoproteins
  HDLs *vs.* LDLs, 12
  high density (HDLs), 10
  low density (LDLs), 12
Liver, 11, 12, 13
LDLs
  explanation of, 12, 13
  reducing level of, 13
  risk level, 13
Luncheon meats, 26, 27, 30
Lungs, conditioning of, 23

# M

Margarine(s), 15, 16, 26, 27,
  32, 33
Mayonnaise labels, 28, 29
Meats, 26, 30, 31. *See also*
  specific types.
  cholesterol in, 11, 16, 17
  cooking, 32
  in guide, 24
  luncheon, 26, 27, 30
  processed, 26, 30
  seasoning, 34
Microwaving, 32
Milk
  buttermilk, 27, 33
  evaporated skim, 27
  low-fat, 27
  non-fat dried, 27
  one percent, 27
  reducing fat in, 26
  skim, 27
  whole, 11, 16, 27
Minerals, 10, 24, 130
Monounsaturated fat
  explanation of, 15
  on labels, 29, 30
  sources of, 15
Muffins, English, 27, 32
Muscle(s), 22, 23
Mushroom(s), 31

# N

Neufchâtel, 33
Nonstick vegetable spray,
  27
Noodles, cooking, 18
Nutrient-dense, 17
Nutrition labels, 29
Nuts, 16, 32

# O

Oat bran, 17, 151
Oatmeal, 17
Oats, soluble fiber in, 13,
  17, 151
Obesity, 13
Oils, 33
  in guide, 24
  reducing, 26
Olive oil, 15
Omega-3(s)
  explanation of, 17, 18
  sources of, 17, 18
  supplements, 18
Organ meats, 16
Overeating, 21
Overweight, 21
Oxygen, 11, 23

# P

Palm kernel, 29
  oil, 15, 33
Pancakes, 32
Pasta, 16
  cooking, 18, 32
  in guide, 24
Peanut oil, 15
Peas, 32
  dried , 60
Pectin, 131
Physical activity, 10. *See
  also* Exercise.
  to increase HDLs, 13
  to lose weight, 21
Pie(s), 16, 21, 27, 33
Pizza(s), 33, 65